SHAW 13

SHAW

The Annual of Bernard Shaw Studies
Volume Thirteen

Fred D. Crawford, *General Editor*

SHAW
AND OTHER
PLAYWRIGHTS

Edited by
John A. Bertolini

The Pennsylvania State University Press
University Park, Pennsylvania

All quotations from the published plays and prefaces, unless otherwise identified, are from the *Bodley Head Bernard Shaw* (*Collected Plays with Their Prefaces*).
Quotations from published Bernard Shaw writings are utilized in this volume
with the permission of the Estate of Bernard Shaw. Shaw's hitherto unpublished
writings © 1993 The Trustees of the British Museum, The Governors and Guard-
ians of the National Library of Ireland, and the Royal Academy of Dramatic Art.

Library of Congress Cataloging-in-Publication Data

Shaw and other playwrights / edited by John A. Bertolini.

    p.   cm. — (Shaw, the annual of Bernard Shaw studies ; v. 13)
    Includes bibliographical references.
    ISBN 0-271-00908-X (alk. paper)   ISSN 0741-5842
    1. Shaw, Bernard, 1856–1950—Criticism and interpretation.
    2. Shaw, Bernard, 1856–1950—Knowledge—Literature. 3. Shaw,
    Bernard, 1856–1950—Influence. 4. Influence (Literary, artistic,
    etc.) 5. Drama—History and criticism.   I. Bertolini, John A.
    (John Anthony), 1947–   .   II. Series.
    PR5367.S473   1993
    822'.912—dc20   92-34784
                                                 CIP

#00119669

It is the policy of The Pennsylvania State University Press to use acid-free
paper for the first printing of all clothbound books. Publications on uncoated
stock satisfy the minimum requirements of American National Standard for
Information Sciences—Permanence of Paper for Printed Library Materials,
ANSI Z39.48–1984.

Note to contributors and subscribers. *SHAW's* perspective is Bernard Shaw and his
milieu—its personalities, works, relevance to his age and ours. As "his life, work,
and friends"—the subtitle to a biography of G.B.S.—indicates, it is impossible to
study the life, thought, and work of a major literary figure in a vacuum. Issues and
men, economics, politics, religion, theater and literature and journalism—the
entirety of the two half-centuries the life of G.B.S. spanned was his assumed
province. *SHAW*, published annually, welcomes articles that either explicitly or
implicitly add to or alter our understanding of Shaw and his milieu. Address all
communications concerning manuscript contributions (in 3 copies) to Fred D.
Crawford, General Editor, *SHAW*, 1034 Hickory Street, Lansing, MI 48912-1711.
Subscription correspondence should be addressed to *SHAW*, Penn State Press,
Suite C, Barbara Building, 820 North University Drive, University Park, PA
16802. Unsolicited manuscripts are welcomed but will be returned only if return
postage is provided. In matters of style *SHAW* recommends the *MLA Style Sheet*.

CONTENTS

John A. Bertolini

INTRODUCTION: SHAW AS MIMIC AND MODEL

However idiosyncratic Shaw's plays may appear, and however inimitable their style and dramaturgy may be, Shaw did not create them out of nothing, nor did they echo hollowly—like sounds in the Caves of Marabar—in the plays of his contemporaries or in those of his successors. The present volume is a modest but determined attempt to begin assessing synoptically Shaw's plays in relation to those of his predecessors, contemporaries, and successors. Shaw scholarship has devoted itself so assiduously to explicating the plays, the life, and the times of Shaw that it has taken too little care of Shaw as a reader and an audience of other people's plays, and of Shaw's plays as read and responded to by other playwrights.

If critics expect to understand a playwright's mind and imagination, then they must investigate what the playwright made of other plays—both the external evidence that comes in the form of letters, reviews, reported remarks, and the like, and the internal evidence that comes in the form of mirrors and ghosts of moments and patterns in other plays. What would we not give to have Shakespeare's "Quintessence of Ovidism," his review of Marlowe's *Tamburlaine*, a letter about John Marston, a diary entry about Middleton? In many cases we have Shavian equivalents, such as the three volumes of Shaw's collected theater criticism from the 1890s. Had these contained only Shaw's reviews of Wilde's plays in their first performances, they would still give us indispensable clues to the development of Shaw's ideas about the kind of plays he wanted to write. And if we do not have such sustained assessments by Shaw of other playwrights, we do not lack extraordinary Shavian remarks and comments. Of Pirandello's *Six Characters in Search of an Author*, Shaw observed that he had "never come across a play so original."[1] What did Shaw mean by this? Surely it was not merely the play's metatheatricality. Perhaps he saw in its "characters" a reflection of the half-existence he had given the inhabitants of *Heartbreak House,* who "haunt" their own dwelling. Or did he respond to the forcefulness of Pirandello's having put a primal fantasy—a fantasy of origin—on stage in the encounter between the father and the stepdaughter at Madam Pace's house of assignation? We know that Shaw went to Cambridge to see Pirandello's *Henry IV,*[2] but we do not know what he thought of it. To understand Shaw's place in modern drama, it would be helpful to know what he thought of Pirandello's greatest play.

We also need to understand more about Shaw's place in the tradition of English drama, especially of high comedy. His dismissal of Shakespeare's contemporaries as mostly Grand Guignol and his labeling of Ben Jonson as "so dull a dog" may be only an overflow of his reaction against "bardolatry," or simply a matter of temperament and taste, but the rejection and name-calling do not tell the whole story of Shaw's relation to Elizabethan and Jacobean drama. His aspersions against Restoration and eighteenth-century dramatists are well known: on Sheridan's loose syntax, full of dashes; on Congreve's misguided sense of humor, which found an old woman's concupiscence hilarious. And yet Shaw smuggled an ironic version of Sheridan's *Duenna* into the subplot of *Man and Superman* involving Mendoza with Henry and Louisa Straker, while he identified Orinthia in *The Apple Cart* with Millamant in *The Way of the World.*[3]

New items, however, are always coming to light, giving us additional avenues into that protean creativity of Shaw. For example, we have long known T. S. Eliot's several and ambivalent public pronouncements on Shaw, but until Shaw's correspondence with Lord Alfred Douglas was published, we did not know what Shaw thought of the rival who would supplant him in the estimation of the youthful literati of the 1930s—we did not even know whether Shaw had read Eliot. But Shaw did know Eliot's work, and as he reveals in two letters to Douglas written in 1943, Shaw knew *Murder in the Cathedral* well enough to have formed an opinion about it:

> T. S. Eliot made a fool of himself in his reaction against formalism, as all young reactionaries do; but his Murder in the Cathedral is dramatic poetry good enough to make it ridiculous to dismiss him as a sham poet of no account. . . . Don't be too disrespectful of Eliot. His Cathedral play not only took him out of the mob of would-be moderns whose stuff is neither prose nor verse but just twaddle: it shows he is a bit of a virtuoso in versification when he needs it to express himself. Anyhow do not treat him as a moral delinquent. That is a bit too Victorian and pre-Shavian.[4]

These pronouncements are remarkable in several ways, and not merely because they prove that Shaw had read Eliot. They imply that in order to appreciate Eliot, one has to have read Shaw first—to judge Eliot negatively is to be "pre-Shavian." Such a posture toward Eliot insures that Shaw will be counted in any assessment of Eliot and that Shaw will be granted priority: Eliot is born into a Shavian world. Shaw's tone throughout is cautious, even wary. When Shaw read the play (it seems unlikely that he saw it at Canterbury in 1935), did he hear the influence of his Epilogue to *Saint Joan* in the Knights' speeches to the audience? (Eliot confessed to being "for all" he knew "under the influence of *Saint Joan*" when he wrote the final scene for the Knights.) And if Shaw did, what did he make of the resemblance?

Shaw's remarks also seem to indicate that he had read Eliot's poetry because he notes Eliot's break with "formalism." But his opinion of Eliot is based mainly on *Murder in the Cathedral*, which Shaw does not exactly recognize as a masterpiece. He allows that its dramatic poetry is "good enough" to distinguish him from the rest of "the would-be moderns" who mostly write "twaddle." Although these observations are addressed to Lord Alfred Douglas, they seem more a form of self-censorship, a deflection of the temptation to dismiss Eliot. How much of a rival Eliot is, Shaw is not willing to assess. He acknowledges Eliot as a worthy competitor—that is all. The work of finding, gathering, and evaluating what Shaw really understood about Eliot as a dramatist still needs to be done, not only because our knowledge of these two writers would be extended, but because our understanding of modern British drama would be deepened.

Apart from the play reviews Shaw wrote in the 1890s—and Shaw's books on Ibsen and Wagner—his judgments of other dramatists come to us mainly in fragmentary form through letters or parts of articles on other subjects. This is also true of other dramatists' judgments of Shaw. Insofar as scholarship has addressed the subject of Shaw and other playwrights—and John Pfeiffer's user-friendly bibliography near the end of this volume ably outlines the story of that address—it has concerned itself mainly with Ibsen and Shakespeare. But there is much more that we need to know and explore if we are to be able to say with any authority what Shaw's plays mean and what Shaw's achievement in drama was, both in relation to the achievements of other playwrights and in comparison to those achievements, and to assess the force of his presence in the minds of succeeding playwrights.

Neil Simon has said (on a television talk show) that he learned from Shaw to treat all his characters fairly, not to tip the scales of sympathy or rightness on one side or the other but to let both sides have their best say. If we knew that other comic playwrights as well as Simon had absorbed this same lesson from Shaw (which he articulates about his own characters in the Epistle Dedicatory to *Man and Superman*—"They are all right from their several points of view"), we would know something important about Shaw's influence. From Molière Shaw learned that if a playwright creates a character who speaks for the playwright's point of view, then that character had better be presented as a fool rather than a hero, or as both. When Molière had the cowardly, hypocritical, and stupid Sganarelle defend belief in God against Don Juan's atheism, Molière knew what he was doing. The Church objected to Molière's putting the defense of atheism into the mouth of a brave and suave aristocrat while the defense of religious belief was assigned to an inarticulate buffoon. This was because the Church wanted propaganda, the seventeenth-century version of political correctness, whereas Molière (like Shaw after him) was interested in dramatic art. If an audience is going to accept a message from a character, that character can be neither an undiluted hero nor the most attractive character on stage; for the audience would not then be able to separate the message from the messenger, and the playwright would not know whether it was the messenger being embraced or the message. Hence Sganarelle makes the most incompetent and idiotic defense of what Molière himself believes, and Shaw makes Tanner a vain, imperceptive, and foolish crusader for most of the ideas to which Shaw has declared his allegiance.

The present volume addresses some aspects of what we do not know about Shaw and other playwrights. Evert Sprinchorn in the first essay argues that the 1908 meeting between Shaw and Strindberg (where Shaw witnessed a private performance of *Miss Julie*—in Swedish!) marked a turning point in the developments of both dramatists whereby they drew closer in their thinking, with Strindberg's views of capitalism and socialism coming to resemble Shaw's, and with Shaw's darkening view of humanity's potential coming to resemble Strindberg's. Professor Sprinchorn begins by collating several published versions of that strange meeting between the two re-makers of modern drama. In the course of his subsequent argument, he provides many specific parallels between the plays of Shaw and Strindberg while noting their basic differences in tone and temperament: for example, that in Strindberg sexual relations between men and women are a tragic theme, while in Shaw they are comic.

After Professor Sprinchorn's essay (which represents an example of what can be done with Shaw in the context of international drama) comes a series of essays on Shaw's relations with British dramatists, led by Stanley Weintraub's thorough and revealing account of Shaw's social and literary relations with Wilde, who surely was to Shaw what Marlowe was to Shakespeare. Professor Weintraub uses Shaw's diaries and other materials to detail the history of their social encounters and to place them in the London literary scene of the 1880s and 1890s, when they were both writing unsigned reviews for the *Pall Mall Gazette* and people assumed that reviews were written by one when they were actually written by the other. Weintraub discusses Wilde's presence in Shaw's plays and makes the strongest case yet for Wilde's influence on *You Never Can Tell* by way of *The Importance of Being Earnest* (in spite of Shaw's attempt to treat *Earnest* as an early effort by Wilde—which Shaw needed to do, so as not to be overwhelmed by Wilde's achievement). While Shaw began by imitating Ibsen in the Unpleasant Plays, *Widowers' Houses* and *Mrs Warren's Profession*, he had absorbed a good amount of Wilde's propensity for absurd humor by the time he came to write his own Pleasant Plays. Yet neither man was ever quite at ease with the other. The threat posed to each by a rival talent was perhaps too big.

In an essay that extends the volume's consideration of Shaw and British playwrights, Leon Hugo explores a little-known but very important subject: Shaw's relations with the (mostly) younger playwrights who shared the bill with him at the Court Theatre during the Vedrenne-Barker management. It is a story of generosity and encouragement from Shaw to his fellow dramatists: Barker, Gilbert Murray, St. John Hankin, Galsworthy, and Masefield. Where there was talent and achievement, Shaw recognized and delighted in it; when the critics failed to appreciate either the talent or the achievement, Shaw revealed their failure with large public gestures that left the critics looking foolish. Professor Hugo also shows how Shaw could steal effective techniques (as a "mature" playwright would—to borrow Eliot's Blakean definition of the real poet) from the Court Theatre confraternity, especially from Barker.

The case of Arnold Bennett differs greatly from Wilde's but resembles that of several playwrights who wrote for the Court Theatre. Bennett was not a playwright by trade, but he was solicited and encouraged to write plays by Shaw. Bennett was primarily a novelist who treated writing plays as a sideline and an easier task than writing novels (a view which annoyed Shaw considerably). Still, he wrote a significant number of plays, some of them quite successful. The value of T. F. Evans's comprehensive discussion of how these two playwrights—almost exact contemporaries—viewed and treated one another is that it shows us both how Shaw's plays struck a major literary figure of the period and how Shaw distinguished novel writing from playwriting. To Bennett, Shaw seemed too little solicitous of proper plotting and form and too much concerned with ideas—a view which seems very odd to us now, perhaps because Shaw's ideas were more disturbing then. Professor Evans has drawn from published and unpublished materials to illuminate Bennett's friendly rivalry with Shaw.

My own article on Rattigan deals with a successor to Shaw and argues for the strong presence of *Man and Superman* in Rattigan's first successful play, *French Without Tears*. Shaw's silhouette can be discerned in the way Rattigan makes the reversed love chase of a battling couple the center of his play, revising Shaw's image of the lovers as female predator and male prey into a sustained allusion to the myth of Diana and Actaeon.

In an essay that rounds out the volume's consideration of Shaw's relations with British dramatists, Fred D. Crawford provides a survey of Shaw's influence on his successors. Many succeeding dramatists of stature had to reckon with Shaw's achievement, and whether they began by imitating a particular Shaw play (as Noël Coward did in *The Young Idea*), reacted violently against Shaw (as John Osborne did), or remained faithful to Shaw's art and thought their whole lives (as O'Casey did), Shaw was a distinct, if Puckish, presence for them all—now here, now there, in that character, in this situation, around the corner of an idea, or haunting the tone and atmosphere of a play.

With A. M. Gibbs's essay on the presence of other texts in *Heartbreak House*, we turn to the investigation of multiple literary presences in a single Shaw play, in this case Shakespeare, Chekhov, Strindberg, and a particular motif in nineteenth-century novels: the shipshape house. The special value of such a study of a Shaw text in dialogue with other texts— plays and novels—is the insight it gives us into the workings of Shaw's omnivorous imagination: how everything his mind seizes from other works is transformed—ironized, reversed in meaning, complexified, or humorized.

Christopher Newton, the artistic director of the Shaw Festival in Niagara-on-the-Lake, Ontario (founded in 1963), where many superb productions of plays by Shaw and his contemporaries have been staged, offers a perspective on the theme of Shaw and other playwrights complementary to those of literary history and critical analysis, that of the director/actor. Mr. Newton writes about specific productions and provides fascinating views, often contrary to popular wisdom, about the acting of Shaw's plays. He contrasts, for example, the requirements of playing Chekhov, whose characters' subtexts are usually so unspecific that the actors are in danger of overcompensating, with the demands of playing Shaw, whose characters' inner lives are quite difficult to realize in spite of their superficial transparency. Shaw scholarship needs to hear much more from experienced and thoughtful Shavian actors and directors.

The last two items that complete the theme section of the volume (apart from the already mentioned bibliography by John Pfeiffer) fall into a special category: a teleplay by a Welshman, Gwyn Thomas, about the relationship between an Irish playwright, Shaw, and a Scottish playwright, J. M. Barrie; and an interview given by Shaw about Barrie after his death. The Thomas teleplay, which Richard F. Dietrich has edited from a difficult technician's script, dramatizes the encounter between Shaw and Barrie as a clash between Shaw's optimistic, outer-directed, demonic energy and Barrie's pessimistic, introverted, melancholic reverie. This, of course, is an exaggeration, but its fundamental truth is confirmed by the view of Barrie which Shaw expresses in the moving interview he gave after Barrie's death. It testifies to Shaw's genuine feeling for Barrie as a friend and fellow playwright, and also to how unsettling Shaw found Barrie's antithetical soul. The interview appears here for the first time since its original publication, at the suggestion of the patron saint of all Shaw scholars and critics, Dan H. Laurence, who has also provided Shaw's pronouncing guide to troublesome names of his stage characters.

The definitive history of Shaw's role in the dramatic literature of the twentieth century has yet to be written. The story of Shaw's digestion of preceding and contemporary playwrights also remains incomplete. The contributors to the present volume make significant gestures toward the writing of that history and the completion of that story, but the volume is less an attempt to cover the subject of Shaw and other playwrights in a comprehensive way than a sampler of what can be done and an indication of what still needs to be done.

As a final note, I wish to express my gratitude to all the contributors to this volume (including Sally Peters for her review)—they have given the collection an international flavor, working as they do in the motherland and various outposts of the Empire, in England, Canada, Australia, South Africa, and the United States; to Alfred Turco, Jr., whose guest-editorship of *SHAW 7: The Neglected Plays* provided a model of responsibility which I have tried to match; and especially to Fred Crawford, the general editor of SHAW, who fully deserves the title of co-editor of "Shaw and Other Playwrights," which he is too modest to take.

Notes

1. Michael Holroyd, *Bernard Shaw: The Lure of Fantasy, 1918–1950* (New York: Random House, 1991), p. 90.

2. Dan H. Laurence, ed., *Bernard Shaw: Collected Letters, 1911–1925* (New York: Viking, 1985), p. 879, letter of 15 June 1924.

3. Dan H. Laurence, ed., *Bernard Shaw: Collected Letters, 1926–1950* (New York: Viking, 1988), p. 129, letter of 8 February 1929.

4. *Bernard Shaw and Alfred Douglas: A Correspondence*, ed. Mary Hyde (London: John Murray, 1982), pp. 160, 165, letters of 2 December 1943 and 11 January 1944.

Evert Sprinchorn

SHAW AND STRINDBERG

George Bernard Shaw and Johan August Strindberg undoubtedly make an odd couple. If they had been horses, they would instinctively have run off in opposite directions, and it is difficult to imagine them hitched to the same wagon. Apart from the fact that both were giants of the modern drama and that both preferred their middle to their first names, Shaw and Strindberg seem to have little in common. Yet on some important issues they were brothers in arms. Temperamentally they were opposites, but politically they moved in much the same direction, and philosophically they were at the end yoked together.

The two men met once—and once only—in an encounter made memorable by Shaw's report of how things went. Accompanied by his wife, Shaw journeyed to Stockholm in the summer of 1908 to meet his Swedish translator Hugo Vallentin, who suggested that Shaw should try to meet Strindberg, not an easy thing to do. Strindberg led a Garboesque existence, receiving at his home only a few friends, mainly musicians and artists, while being publicly visible nearly every day on his strolls through the streets of Stockholm. Shaw wrote to Strindberg, saying he would "value the privilege of calling on him."

> By return mail I got a very long and keen letter written one third in French, one third in German, and the remaining third in English.
>
> He said he was living in complete seclusion; that he never went out except between three and four in the morning when no one was about; that it was impossible for him to meet anyone; that he was dying of a mortal disease, and that as we did not speak one another's languages, an interview between us would be a conversation of the dumb with the deaf. Next morning I got an urgent letter asking me to come to see him at his little Intimes Theatre.
>
> My wife came with me. . . . We found Strindberg in a mood of

extreme and difficult shyness; but his sapphire-blue eyes were
irresistible; the man of genius was unmistakable. He had lived
longer in France than in any foreign country; so I thought French
would be the best language, and I had carefully prepared a few
sentences as I am a villainous linguist. Then he declared that he
preferred German. My wife talked to him and jollied him a little;
and finally he smiled and became quite at ease. . . .

We were getting on capitally when he suddenly took out his
watch, looked at it, and announced in a solemn voice, "*Um zwei
Uhr werde ich krank sein!*" At two o'clock I shall be sick.

I could hardly believe my ears, or trust my knowledge of German. But as it was a quarter to two then, and, as he had evidently quite made up his mind to be sick, there was nothing for
us to do but leave. That was the mortal disease from which he
was suffering.[1]

When he retold the story a little later, Shaw reversed the roles of
himself and Strindberg with regard to the languages in which they attempted to communicate. It was the Swede, not the Irishman, who
worked up a few phrases in French.

The next morning there came a message asking myself and my
wife to come at once. We went. Strindberg had prepared some
conversational material in French, but took the wind out of his
own sails by addressing me in German. Things went along quite
well, and Strindberg became quite animated, then suddenly re-
lapsing into a spasm of gloom, took out his watch and said: "At a
quarter before two I shall be sick."

I looked at my watch and said we must be going. With polite
farewells we left.[2]

A good story can be told in more ways than one, and it is hard to say
which of Shaw's two recitals is the better. As for what actually was said
and done, the Swedish version of the event has to be entered into the
record also. According to August Falck, who was Strindberg's partner in
the Intimate Theatre venture, Shaw had written to ask if he might call on
Strindberg at two in the afternoon. Strindberg had replied that he would
be feeling ill at that hour. Then, regretting his rudeness, he had sent the
urgent letter to Shaw, inviting him to a special performance of *Miss Julie*
at the Intimate Theatre.[3]

This Swedish account is amplified by the observations of Gustaf
Uddgren, a journalist and friend of Strindberg. According to him,
Strindberg had been irritated by the prattling of Mrs. Shaw, who kept on

talking through the performance of the play.[4] Although he had seen parts of the play in rehearsal, this was, astonishingly, the first time in his life that Strindberg had ever seen his naturalistic masterpiece on stage. He knew it would have a deeply troubling effect on him, reviving memories of the 1880s and his first wife, so much so that prior to the performance he had asked the actress playing Julie to go easy in the part. His impatience with Mrs. Shaw together with his emotional involvement in the performance would have been enough to make the oversensitive Swede sick. In a brief essay that must have been written at about this time, Strindberg recounts occasions when he became physically ill or felt dizzy in the presence of people who were somehow not right for him.[5]

What prompted Strindberg to put on a special peformance of *Miss Julie* for Shaw? It was not an easy task and required elaborate preparations. The theater had closed for the season, and the actors had dispersed. Now they had to be called in from their summer cottages; the theater had to be swept out and redecorated; the set put in place; the pots and pans for Miss Julie's kitchen hung up; and the accordion player summoned to provide music for the dance of the peasants. Jean and Julie ran through their lines on the ship that carried them in from the Stockholm skerries, rehearsed the play on stage on 15 July, and performed it for their exclusive audience the next morning. It was not an effective performance. Strindberg himself faulted the actors for giving flat, uninflected readings of their lines; but had he not cautioned Julie against playing all out? Shaw found the emotions of the tragedy too big for the small stage, which was only eighteen feet wide and twelve deep. Falck, who played Jean, wondered why Strindberg had chosen this play of the 1880s, whose daringness and sexual boldness could hardly be appreciated by someone who did not understand the language.[6] It must be assumed that Strindberg, who was virtually unknown to English theatergoers, was hoping to impress Shaw, who had done so much to make Ibsen a household name in England. But what did Strindberg know about the man he was trying to impress? The only plays by Shaw that Strindberg might have read were those that Hugo Vallentin had translated: *Arms and the Man*, *Candida*, *The Man of Destiny*, and *You Never Can Tell*.[7] *Candida* had been produced in Stockholm only a few months before Shaw came to Sweden, but Strindberg had not seen it. Since these were scarcely avant-garde dramas in the eyes of the man who had written *To Damascus*, *A Dream Play*, and *The Ghost Sonata*, he must have thought that the best way of winning Shaw's support was to offer him something in the realistic vein, something not radically different from *Candida* or Ibsen's *Hedda Gabler*.

Upon his return to England Shaw did make an effort to introduce Strindberg to English producers, but the play he promoted as possibly having a chance for success on the London stage was *Lucky Peter's Travels*, a light-hearted satire that Strindberg had tossed off in 1882.[8] He was convinced that Strindberg's sexual tragedies *The Father* and *Miss Julie* would not go over with the English playgoer. Although he had praised Strindberg in 1900 in the preface to *Three Plays for Puritans* as "the only genuinely Shakespearean modern dramatist," he had at the same time admitted to having what he called "a technical objection to making sexual infatuation a tragic theme," saying that "experience proves that it is only effective in the comic spirit." If he had had in mind only ordinary sexual arousal or the sort of sexual rivalry he had depicted in *Candida,* he would have been right. But he clearly meant more than that. He was talking about the war of the sexes, for he remarked that Strindberg shows "that the female Yahoo, measured by romantic standards, is viler than her male slave and dupe."[9] This is a pointed reference to *The Father,* and *The Father* is not so much concerned with sexual infatuation as with the struggle for power between two eternally inimical forces.

When Shaw turned his attention from the sexual peccadillos of *Candida* and brought the full force of his intellect to bear on the question of the war of the sexes, he did indeed produce one of the comic masterpieces of the English drama: *Man and Superman.* There the battle of the sexes is revealed as a conflict between two kinds of creativity, the male kind and the female kind. "Of all human struggles there is none so treacherous and remorseless as the struggle between the artist man and the mother woman. Which shall use up the other? that is the issue between them. And it is all the deadlier because . . . they love one another."[10]

If Strindberg offended women by picturing them as voracious, cunning, and conscienceless, Shaw offended feminists by picturing women as predestined mothers, creatures with wombs as opposed to men, creatures with brains, the former intent upon bringing to life a higher type of human being, the latter intent upon bringing more knowledge to life. Shaw's version of the sexual struggle is comic and theatrically effective in the vulgar sense because he eventually puts the woman hors de combat. In *Man and Superman* the war of the sexes turns out to have been merely a chase, and Shaw skirts the issue he had raised by making woman the embodiment of love and revealing that the basic conflict after all was the war between the male devil and the male saint. Woman, he explained, "cannot, like the male devil, use love as mere sentiment and pleasure; nor can she, like the male saint, put love aside when it has once done its work as a developing and enlightening experience. Love is neither her pleasure nor her study: it is her business."[11]

In contrast to this highly romantic view of woman as nurturing mother and loving wife who indulgently watches the male devil and male saint do battle with each other, Strindberg saw woman as madonna and

FIG. 1.   The 1987 Shaw Festival Theatre production of Strindberg's *Playing
with Fire* at Niagara-on-the-Lake, directed by Frances Hyland. Photograph by
David Cooper. Reproduced by permission of The Shaw Festival Theatre.

whore, with man going mad trying to decide which he wants. In the
bitter conflict between the sexes man really defeats himself, thus putting
an end to the civilization that he as artist, philosopher, and soldier had
created. This is the story that Strindberg tells in *The Father*. Writing in the
1880s, Strindberg saw the sexual war as a Darwinist struggle for survival
with man, the weaker because the more civilized, losing out to woman
who, having had no share in the civilizing values that man created, could
therefore have neither honor nor conscience, which were of man's making. Or, as Shaw's Don Juan says, "He has created civilization without
consulting her, taking her domestic labor for granted as the foundation
of it."[12]

Both *Man and Superman* and *The Father* are unrealistic dramas, the one
a debate and the other a nightmare, because their authors were more
concerned with getting at what underlies the sexual conflict than with
depicting believable, flesh-and-blood individuals. Shaw explained that

his comedy stated "the extreme case, of course; but what is true of the great man who incarnates the philosophic consciousness of Life and the woman who incarnates its fecundity, is true in some degree of all geniuses and all women."[13] In like manner and for the same reason, Strindberg made the protagonist of his tragedy an army officer, a scientist, and an agnostic all in one so that this figure could represent the apogee and last stage of European civilization, while his wife appears as woman stripped of nearly all her attributes and reduced to little more than an unthinking mother animal possessive of its young.

As the century wore to an end, however, Strindberg's representative man was no longer a soldier, scientist, and free-thinker. In the 1890s, the decade that saw the bankruptcy of science (Brunetière's phrase) and the dissolution of the atom, Strindberg suffered through an emotional and intellectual crisis that he delineated step by step in his ground-breaking dramatic trilogy *To Damascus*. The great struggles were no longer social or sexual; they were psychological and religious. The reborn Strindberg renounced Darwinism, materialism, and positivism, and affirmed a belief in spiritual forces that he denominated the Higher Powers. Their sphere is the conscience, and they compel the autobiographical hero of the *Damascus* trilogy to examine his past life.

> You shall go up and denounce yourself from the roof tops and the chimney pots. You shall unravel the fabric of your soul thread by thread. You shall flay yourself alive on every street corner. You shall turn yourself inside out. It will take courage, yes, but he who has played with lightning will not be afraid. Oh, yes, sometimes— when night falls and those invisible beings, seen only in the dark, ride a cockhorse on your chest. You'll be afraid, even of the stars, but mostly of the mills of god that grind and grind and grind the past, the past, the past.[14]

In this new evangel the sexual war did not come to an end, since the Higher Powers expressed themselves through human emotions. Strindberg's hero laments, "I sought in woman an angel who would loan me her wings, but I fell into the arms of an earth-spirit, who suffocated me with pillows stuffed with the feathers from her wings. I sought Ariel and I found Caliban."[15] But the sexual conflict is now subsumed under a grander concept in which justice, not power or subjugation, is central.

Similarly Shaw, at about this time in *Man and Superman*, introduced into his philosophy the concept of the Life Force, a nonmaterial entity shared by man and woman. With both sexes striving for higher life, the one through the mind, the other through the flesh, the war of the sexes turns out to be merely a training exercise to improve the species. This sounds Darwinistic, and it is—up to a point. But at that point Shaw parts company with the Darwinists (strictly speaking, the Neo-Darwinists) by insisting that man's will rather than natural selection determines the path of evolution. Life seeks "not only to maintain itself, but to achieve higher and higher organization and completer self-consciousness," and that requires brains and intelligence.[16] "Things immeasurably greater than man in every respect but brain have existed and perished. . . . These things lived and wanted to live; but for lack of brains they did not know how to carry out their purpose, and so destroyed themselves."[17]

Consequently, in Shaw's cosmogony heaven is the place of intelligence, the home of the philosopher-artist, whereas Shaw's hell resembles Blake's, a place of corporeal desire where the intellect is no more. Heaven is the home of the masters of reality, who will change circumstances rather than, as in the Darwinian world, be changed by them. Strindberg's hell, in contrast, is the more conventional one, a place of torment—not the physical torments of Dante's inferno, with its frost, fire, and filth, but the torments of conscience, the remorse for deeds done in the past. To go through the excruciating ordeal of seeing oneself as one really is inwardly, to experience what Swedenborg calls vastation, is to progress through the nine circles of hell. But the venture brings a reward. To endure it is to become one of the elect. To be humbled by the Higher Powers is to be exalted.

Not so with Shaw's elect, the progenitors of the superman, as he saw them in *Man and Superman*. There nothing but brains, energy, and an aversion to the pleasures enjoyed by *l'homme moyen sensuel* marked the superior individual, and consequently the Life Force within him could all too easily appear to be no more than Nietzsche's Will to Power in its most simplistic sense. Having allowed Nietzsche to supervene upon Darwin, Shaw had in effect made power the be-all and end-all of the Life Force. But if this force strove for higher organization, what attributes defined this higher level? Not greater appetites, surely; not larger social aggregations; only something that could overcome matter and circumstances; only something spiritual. It was for that reason that he introduced into his next play, *John Bull's Other Island*, the ex-priest Peter Keegan as a counterweight to the man of enterprise, the capitalist Broadbent, who is, in Keegan's words, "efficient in the service of Mammon, mighty in mischief, skilful in ruin, heroic in destruction."[18] Keegan, who not unlike Strindberg has been humbled by the world, envisions a hell far different from Don Juan's. To him, the earth is a place of torment and penance:

> a place where the fool flourishes and the good and wise are hated and persecuted, a place where men and women torture one another in the name of love; where children are scourged and en-

slaved in the name of parental duty and education; where the
weak in body are poisoned and humiliated in the name of healing,
and the weak in character are put to the horrible torture of imprisonment, not for hours but for years, in the name of justice. . . .
There is only one place of horror and torment known to my
religion; and that place is hell. Therefore it is plain to me that this
earth of ours must be hell, and that we are all here . . . to expiate
crimes committed by us in a former existence.[19]

Although these ideas have a wide provenience, they have a peculiarly
Strindbergian ring here that is all the more noticeable because Keegan
has only a minor part in the mechanics of the plot. He functions as an
ironic chorus, emptying of meaning all the blithe optimism of the capitalist Broadbent. Keegan's vision of heaven is also different from Don
Juan's philosopher's paradise. Keegan's heaven is "the dream of a mad-
man": "It is a country where the State is the Church and the Church is
the people: three in one and one in three. . . . It is a godhead in which all
life is human and all humanity divine: three in one and one in three."[20]

This trinity was too vague to satisfy Shaw, yet he recognized the need
for something like it if the world was not to be given over to those
efficient in the service of Mammon. In his next play, *Major Barbara*, he
pitted the energetic entrepreneur against a practicing Christian: Undershaft the munitions manufacturer against his daughter Barbara, an
officer in the Salvation Army. Here is a man who was indeed "mighty in
mischief" and "heroic in destruction." Undershaft is, in his own words,
"not one of those men who keep their morals and their business in water-
tight compartments."[21] Conscience and morality have no hold on him.
His only concerns are making munitions and selling to those who can
pay. And here is a woman whose efforts to make life on earth better
consist of more than idle speech-making. Barbara learns from her father
that she has indeed been keeping her morals and her religion in separate
compartments, accepting money from the dispensers and distillers of
alcoholic beverages to help the alcoholics who find refuge in her Salvation Army shelter. Recognizing the falsity of her position, she joins forces
with the unhypocritical Undershaft, as does her fiancé Cusins, the professor of classics.

At first glance, it seems that Shaw has gone even further in identifying
power with the Life Force than he had in *Man and Superman*. When Don
Juan argues that the Life Force at the present stage of development seeks
better brains, the Devil counters him with that colossal set speech in
which he demonstrates with examples drawn from the newspapers, painting, literature, jurisprudence, science, and invention that the Life Force
as it expresses itself in human beings seeks in a thousand ways the death

and destruction of other human beings. Juan's response to this is desperately ingenious. The Life Force blunders into death and destruction because it has not yet developed brains clever enough to avoid them. "But it is not so stupid as the forces of Death and Degeneration. Besides, these are in its pay all the time. And so Life wins, after a fashion. What mere copiousness of fecundity can supply and mere greed preserve, we possess. The survival of whatever form of civilization can produce the best rifle and the best fed riflemen is assured."[22]

In *Major Barbara* Shaw elaborates the point. He would have us believe that even the merchant of death, the munitions manufacturer Undershaft, promotes the Life Force because the brains that the Life Force has been developing need weapons to protect what has been gained against those who have less brain power but as much war matériel as the Shavian elite. In this, the most paradoxical and most optimistic of all his plays, Shaw's thought advances beyond *Man and Superman,* in which the Life Force seeks to perfect itself through bigger and better brains, and also beyond *John Bull's Other Island,* in which the visionary dreams of a holy trinity comprising the people, the State, and the Church—life, society, and divinity. In *Major Barbara* a new trinity comes into being, symbolized by the corporate union of Undershaft, Barbara, and Cusins: the millionaire, the savior of souls, and the poet. The shameless credo of the armorer—"Nothing is ever done in this world until men are prepared to kill one another if it is not done"[23]—is by itself not enough to save the human race. Making war against war is not enough. Even Undershaft admits that although he can make cannons, he cannot make courage and conviction; and Cusins tells him that the cannons will not go off by themselves: "all power is spiritual."[24] Although the Christian soldier Barbara comes to recognize the merit in her father's Nietzschean ruthlessness and in his belief that poverty is the worst of crimes, her teaming up with him does not mean that she surrenders to his philosophy; it means she must work with him to temper his energy with her spiritual insight. And although Shaw brings his story to a conclusion in the munitions factory, the symbolic ending is a vision of a godhead of power, spirit, and culture.

That vision formed the capstone on the grand design that Shaw had worked out in these three plays, a synthesis of ideas that was intended to answer all the important social, political, and religious questions.[25] This is the point that Shaw had reached when he met Strindberg in 1908, but Strindberg knew nothing about these three major plays. To him, Shaw was the author of *Candida,* a West End entertainment.[26] And Shaw apparently knew nothing about Strindberg's post-*Inferno* experimental dramas. So the breakdown of communication in their brief meeting had a deeper cause than the language barrier. If Strindberg felt he was going to be sick, it was because he had had his fill of a commercial playwright and his nattering wife.

Nevertheless, their lines of thought began to converge shortly thereafter. Strindberg's career took a new tack, and what happened to him—or, rather, what he made happen—anticipated what would happen to Shaw a little later. In 1910 Strindberg, in a series of newspaper articles published gratis, launched an attack on the Swedish establishment. His interest shifted from the Higher Powers to the earthly powers. He returned to the socialism of his youth, assailed the privileged upper classes, ridiculed the Swedish Academy (which awarded the Nobel Prize for literature), and unpatriotically lampooned the hero-worship of the warrior kings of Sweden's golden age. The Beast was now a political entity, the upper class.

> The members of the upper class are the liegemen of the prince of this world, who awards them with idleness while punishing the laborers with disdain and low wages, and who countenances major crimes while prosecuting minor faults. That is why Swedenborg describes the hells as if they were exactly like life on earth, perhaps because he didn't want to say in so many words that we are actually in hell.[27]

Strindberg's particular target was the Junker, the aristocratic barbarian. To his editor he said, "Beware of the sword-rattling Junker, who offers votes to all with one hand and with the other demands a billion for the army, who makes no distinction between right and left, is ready to stand up for injustice and everything ugly and abnormal, and who points to the left while saving himself on the right."[28]

Nothing inflamed the upper class more than Strindberg's attack on the military. He saw that building warships would not lead to peace, that the glorification of Sweden's past battlefield heroes was a worship of tyranny, and that the underlying purpose of the military organization was to keep the people in line. Conscripting young men, he said, was a way of brainwashing them so that they could be made to believe any sort of nonsense. "With their physical development came the stupefying of the intellect— and, worst of all, moral cowardice."[29] (Shaw had said much the same thing earlier: "Among people who are proof against the suggestions of romantic fiction there can no longer be any question of the fact that military service produces moral imbecility, ferocity, and cowardice.")[30]

The Strindberg feud, as it was called, continued until his death in 1912 and made him the most controversial figure in Sweden, the most reviled and the most praised: an unpatriotic renegade, a half-mad mystic, and a totally confused thinker to the upper class; a clear-sighted humanitarian, a defender of Christian virtues, and a tribune of the people to the wage-earning class and university students. In retrospect he emerges as one of the more prescient observers of his time. On his deathbed he remarked, "I believe that those who bring about the next war will perish in it. And rightly so. Perhaps [another] Napoleon will arise from the bloodbath, with a whole pack of tyrant soldiers who will ride over the people. It will be a witches' Sabbat."[31] (It is worth noting that those who most prominently aligned themselves against Strindberg in this controversy and who lived on into the 1930s turned out to be Nazi sympathizers.)

In 1914 the Great War broke out, and Shaw made himself the most unpopular man in the British kingdom by publishing *Common Sense About the War*, in which he coolly assessed the causes of the conflict, showing that Junkerism and militarism were as prevalent in England as in Germany. For his pains and insight he was subjected to imprecations similar to those hurled at Strindberg. Theodore Roosevelt called him a "blue rumped ape"; his fellow playwright Henry Arthur Jones anathematized him as a "freakish homunculus, germinated outside of lawful procreation"; and H. G. Wells lamented that Shaw was "an elderly adolescent still at play."[32] (Sven Hedin, the famous explorer, had called Strindberg "a rotten character, an amazing mixture of Titan, sphinx, vampire, and parasite. Like the jackal, he prefers corpses, but will also have a go at the living, as long as they cannot bite.")[33]

All this Shaw could take in stride, knowing the quality of mind behind the insults. Less than two years later, however, as the war degenerated into the bloodiest and most senseless conflict in history, Shaw was forced to take himself to task. In the summer of 1916 he realized that his system, which he had reaffirmed only the year before, was coming apart. The Shavian trinity of power, spirit, and culture dissolved under the impact of the figures from the front: 1,700,000 English, French, and German casualties in three months in the battles of Verdun and the Somme without any significant change in the battle lines; two British casualties for every yard of the British front on 1 July when the troops went over the top to begin the Battle of the Somme. "All the great words were canceled for that generation," said D. H. Lawrence, and so too was Shaw's grand conception of progress. As the war mindlessly wore on, the bright hopes expressed in *Superman* and *Major Barbara* acquired a hellish glare. Undershaft and the munitions manufacturers had their day; the credo of the armorer and millionaire became the living gospel. With every bulletin from the front it became even clearer that the best rifle and the best-fed riflemen were no guarantees of the survival of civilization and even more obvious that the marvelous force of life was indeed a force of death.

In *Heartbreak House*, written in 1916 and 1917, Shaw reveals his own anguish—the heartbreak is manifestly his own—as he was compelled to recant much of what he had affirmed in *Major Barbara*. The root of all evil is poverty, Undershaft had told Barbara. But in *Heartbreak House,* Shotover, the munitions manufacturer grown older and wiser, cautions the disillusioned Ellie Dunn, who contemplates marrying for money, that riches will "damn her ten times deeper" than poverty.[34] Evil puts down deeper roots than does lack of money, and wars have other causes than economic ones. Shaw now attributes the outbreak of the war to the separation of power from culture and to the lack in both of soul. The inhabitants of Heartbreak House are "very charming people, most advanced, unprejudiced, frank, humane, unconventional, democratic, free-thinking, and everything that is delightful to thoughtful people";[35] but preoccupied by love and beautiful things they are incapable of running the government, whereas the barbarians in Horseback Hall can command the crews that run the ship of state but, concerned only with power, they cannot navigate. They are individualistic, athletic, rosy-cheeked, vigorous, and self-confident, hardly distinguishable from Matthew Arnold's Barbarians who, even in his eyes, needed "for ideal perfection a shade more *soul*." They lead lives as undirected as those of the neurotic inhabitants of Heartbreak House. And so the ship threatens to crash on the rocks. Learn the art of navigation, says Captain Shotover. To navigate is not to proceed by trial and error, as the Life Force does in *Man and Superman* even after it develops some brains. What is required to direct the Life Force and to steer the ship of state is a combination of mind, spirit, and conscience. And that was what was missing in Heartbreak House and Horseback Hall and in all the so-called civilized world.

In the Preface to *Heartbreak House* Shaw traced the loss of mind back to the nineteenth century and the advent of Darwinism:

> Naturalists and physicists assured the world, in the name of Science, that salvation and damnation are all nonsense, and that predestination is the central truth of religion, inasmuch as human beings are produced by their environment, their sins and good deeds being only a series of chemical and mechanical reactions over which they have no control. Such figments as mind, choice, purpose, conscience, will, and so forth, are, they taught, mere illusions, produced because they are useful in the continual struggle of the human machine to maintain its environment in a favourable condition, a process incidentally involving the ruthless destruction or subjection of its competitors for the supply (assumed to be limited) of subsistence available. We taught Prussia this religion; and Prussia bettered our instruction. . . .[36]

Great as were the triumphs of science, "there was only one result possible in the ethical sphere, and that was the banishment of conscience from human affairs, or, as Samuel Butler vehemently put it, 'of mind from the universe.' "[37]

On this most fundamental level the comic and tragic voices of Shaw and Strindberg blended in almost perfect harmony. They both recognized that the moral law and conscience are, in Shaw's words, "matters of fact more obvious than electro-magnetism."[38] They both saw that, given a Darwinian world in which only the fittest survive, "Nature must be the God of rascals," as Shaw put it.[39]

In a 1910 article Strindberg had voiced very similar thoughts, attacking Darwinism as the root of all that was evil in the modern world and, moreover, ridiculing it as fundamentally illogical:

> The disciples of Darwin "evolved" backwards and preached that Creation created itself, which is an impossibility. And with that came all those horrible theories about the right of the strong and cunning to grab whatever they can, the justification of the capitalist's methods by which he half starves the poor in order to deprive them of the strength to combat the capitalist in the struggle for existence.... All that is contrary to humanity, fellow-feeling, compassion, and fairness is the inevitable consequence of Darwinism....
>
> Darwinism is the philosophy of the upper-class. It is politically conservative, hostile to the people, and the direct opposite of socialism....
>
> For the Darwinists there is no other life than this one, and therefore they must adapt themselves to it. They must take their pleasure in this their only life, no matter what the price. There can be no pity in them, for that is weakness. There can be no union of the people (socialism) because without religion there is no honor, no faith, no self-sacrifice. They cannot trust one another because they are all faithless. All this is the triumph of science over charity.[40]

Apart from the emphasis on Christian virtues, Strindberg's views on the need for a religious revival to counteract Darwinism and science anticipate the central part of the new Shavian creed. After *Heartbreak House*, Shaw drew closer than ever to Strindberg. In a grand effort to reconstruct his philosophy after the great catastrophe, he wrote *Back to Methuselah* and *Saint Joan*. The former, to which Shaw gave the subtitle "A Metabiological Pentateuch" to emphasize its religious purpose, contains in its eighty-page Preface one of the most brilliant polemics in the English language, a sustained criticism of Darwinism with an incisive explanation of how it came to be almost universally accepted, embraced by scientists and laymen, capitalists and socialists alike, and how the acceptance of the doctrines of survival of the fittest and natural selection—circumstantial selection is Shaw's more accurate term—caused humanity to "rush down a steep place" and plunge into war. Thereupon followed *Saint Joan,* in which Shaw restored part of his broken trinity by uniting in the person of its heroine the promoter of war and the hearer of divine voices. Saint Joan is Undershaft and Barbara in one, power and spirit together. But clearly it is now spirit that dominates and that enables Joan to pilot the ship of state in its time of peril. Thus *Heartbreak House, Back to Methuselah,* and *Saint Joan* form a triad, the crowning arch of Shaw's collected works, which completes and revises the system of the earlier triad, *Man and Superman, John Bull's Other Island,* and *Major Barbara.*

Regrettably Shaw and Strindberg never got to talk about the things that most concerned them and never realized how close they were in their thinking. Strindberg died long before *Back to Methuselah* was published, and Shaw went on believing that Strindberg was the voice of pessimism and despair. In 1921 in the Preface to *Methuselah* Shaw described the "giants of the theatre of our time, Ibsen and Strindberg . . . gnashing their teeth in impotent fury in the mud, or at best finding an acid enjoyment in the irony of their predicament. . . . [They] are infernal in everything but their veracity and their repudiation of the irreligion of their time: that is, they are bitter and hopeless."[41] But in 1944, when he revised *Methuselah* for the Oxford World's Classics series, he deleted this passage. Did he find his prose too purplish? Or did he realize in the middle of the Second World War that the new religion needed its Jeremiah as well as its preacher with the glad tidings?

Notes

1. *Shaw: Interviews and Recollections,* ed. A. M. Gibbs (London: Macmillan, 1990), pp. 416–17. Originally in *Pearson's Magazine,* February 1927.

2. "Shaw Tells How He Finally Met Strindberg," *New York Times,* 25 March 1928, sec. 3, p. 8.

3. August Falck, *Fem år med Strindberg* (Stockholm: Wahlström & Widstrand, 1935), p. 170.

4. Jarl W. Donner, ". . . detta styke kommer att noteras in annalerna," *Sydsvenska Dagbladet Snällposten,* 19 February 1974.

5. *En blå bok, avdelning III*, in Strindberg, *Samlade skrifter*, ed. John Landquist, 55 vols. (Stockholm: Bonniers, 1914–23), 48:890–91.

6. Falck, *Fem år*, p. 173.

7. These were the plays in Strindberg's library. See Hans Lindström, *Strindberg och böckerna: vol. 1, Biblioteken 1883, 1892 och 1912* (Uppsala: Svenska Litteratursällskapet, 1977), p. 145.

8. Bernard Shaw, *Collected Letters, 1898–1910*, ed. Dan H. Laurence (New York: Dodd, Mead, 1972), pp. 906–9.

9. *Three Plays for Puritans* (London: Constable, 1931), pp. xviii–xix.

10. *Man and Superman* (London: Constable, 1931), p. 24.

11. Bernard Shaw, *Collected Plays with Their Prefaces* (London: Reinhardt, 1970–74), 2:802–3.

12. *Man and Superman*, p. 107.

13. Ibid., p. xx.

14. Strindberg, *Samlade skrifter*, 29:223–24.

15. Strindberg, *Samlade skrifter*, 29:277.

16. *Man and Superman*, p. 108.

17. *Man and Superman*, p. 102.

18. *John Bull's Other Island, with How He Lied to Her Husband and Major Barbara* (London: Constable, 1931), p. 172.

19. Ibid., pp. 151–52.

20. Ibid., p. 177.

21. Ibid., p. 261.

22. *Man and Superman*, p. 108. The line of argument here may derive from Ernst Haeckel, the German scientist, ardent Neo-Darwinist, and popularizer of the theory of evolution. "In human life . . . this struggle for life will ever become more and more of an intellectual struggle, not a struggle with weapons of murder. The organ which, above all others, in man becomes more perfect by the ennobling influence of natural selection is the *brain*. The man with the most perfect understanding, not the man with the best revolver, will in the long run be victorious; he will transmit to his descendants the qualities of the brain which assisted him in the victory." [*The History of Creation*, 2 vols. (New York: D. Appleton, 1889), 1:174.]

23. *Major Barbara*, p. 326.

24. Ibid.

25. " 'Major Barbara' is the third of a group of three plays of exceptional weight and magnitude on which the reputation of the author as a serious dramatist was first established, and still mainly rests"—Shaw, "Facts About Major Barbara," *Collected Plays with Their Prefaces* 3:193.

26. In 1908 Strindberg, contrasting the repertoires of the ideal state-supported theater with that of the commercial theater, assigned Goethe, Schiller, Shakespeare, Molière, and Holberg to the former and Shaw to the latter. Strindberg, *Samlade skrifter* 50:149–50.

27. *Samlade skrifter*, 53:530.

28. Letter to Höglund, 19 July 1910, quoted in Björn Meidal, *Från profet til folktribun: Strindberg och Strindbergsfejden 1910–12* (Stockholm: Tidens förlag, 1982), p. 69.

29. Ibid., p. 11.

30. *John Bull's Other Island*, p. 44.

31. Walter A. Berendsohn, *Strindbergs sista levnadsår* (Stockholm: Saxon & Lindströms förlag, 1948), p. 88.

32. Michael Holroyd, *Bernard Shaw: The Pursuit of Power, 1898–1918* (New York: Random House, 1989), pp. 354–55.

33. *Strindbergsfejden*, edited by Harry Järv (Uddevalla: Bo Cavefors, 1968), p. 228.

34. *Heartbreak House,* in *Collected Plays with Their Prefaces* 5:145.
35. Ibid., p. 173.
36. Ibid., p. 19.
37. Ibid., p. 20.
38. Preface to *Saint Joan,* in *Collected Plays with Their Prefaces* 6:29.
39. *Man and Superman,* p. 224.
40. *Samlade skrifter* 53:20–21.
41. *Back to Methuselah: A Metabiological Pentateuch* (London: Constable, 1921), p. lxxxiv.

Stanley Weintraub

"THE HIBERNIAN SCHOOL": OSCAR WILDE AND BERNARD SHAW

When Oscar Wilde in May 1893 thanked Bernard Shaw "for Op[us] 2 of the great Celtic school," he was referring to a presentation copy of Shaw's first play, *Widowers' Houses*.[1] Wilde had already opened, to acclaim, what he labeled Opus 3, *A Woman of No Importance,* at the Haymarket Theatre. He called on Shaw for the Celtic School's Opus 4.

Earlier, in sending Shaw *Lady Windermere's Fan,* his first major play, Wilde had described the comedy as "Op. 1 of the Hibernian School." The joke was more than half in earnest since the two were the first Irish playwrights in decades to make a major impact upon the London theater. However different their personalities and life-styles, their relationship was, and would continue to be, mutually useful.

Exempt from the Hibernian School, apparently, was Wilde's *Salomé,* which had been mailed to Shaw in February. Wilde had written *Salomé* in French for Sarah Bernhardt and then published an English translation of his biblical melodrama. Somehow, it seemed wrong to refer to it in Irish terms. By 28 February Shaw had not yet received it, explaining to Wilde, "Salome is still wandering in her purple raiment in search of me, and I expect her to arrive a perfect outcast, branded with inky stamps, bruised by flinging into red prison [Post Office] vans, stuffed and contaminated. . . . I hope to send you soon my play Widowers' Houses which you will find tolerably amusing."

That *Salomé* arrived soon after is obvious from the purple prose of Shaw's letter of 3 March to actress Janet Achurch, with whom he was infatuated. "I can write nothing beautiful enough for you. And I can no longer allow myself to be in love with you: nobody short of an archangel with purple and gold wings can henceforth be allowed to approach you."

By that time, Shaw had known Wilde for nearly fifteen years and had been aware of the family even longer. Oscar's father, Sir William Wilde, a Dublin ophthalmologist, had operated on Shaw's father to correct a squint, Shaw remembered, "and overdid the correction so much that my father squinted the other way all the rest of his life." To Frank Harris in 1916 Shaw recalled seeing the Wildes at a concert in Dublin. The goatish Sir William "was dressed in snuffy brown; and as he had the sort of skin that never looks clean, he produced a dramatic effect beside Lady Wilde (in full fig) of being, like Frederick the Great, Beyond Soap and Water, as his Nietzschean son was [later] beyond Good and Evil. [Sir William] was reported to have a [bastard] family in every farmhouse; and the wonder was that Lady Wilde didn't mind. . . ."[2]

"Speranza"—the name she used for her poetry—did mind, but in double-standard Victorian society she could do nothing about it. When Sir William died, however, leaving little more than his debts, Lady Wilde escaped to London, first to a too-expensive house at 116 Park Street off Grosvenor Square, then to 146 Oakley Street, Chelsea, near the Albert Bridge. At her Saturday and Wednesday afternoon salons, where the curtains were drawn early for the cosmetic effect of gloomy gaslight on Speranza's stoutness and wrinkles, Shaw came to know the family, probably through his sister Lucy, "then a very attractive girl who sang beautifully, [who] had met and made some sort of innocent conquest of both Oscar and [his brother] Willie."

Shaw's first visit to Lady Wilde's at-homes in Park Street was in November 1879, where he met Mrs. Lynn Linton, a veteran novelist. These were forlorn years for Shaw, then working briefly for the Edison Telephone Company and spending off-hours at the British Museum writing hopelessly unpublishable novels. For the good-hearted Lady Wilde, Shaw recalled to Harris, the at-homes were "desperate affairs," attempts to gain entrée into Society but failing, usually, to draw more than has-beens or young people, aspirants for whom she predicted, encouragingly, future fame. "I once dined with her in company with an ex-tragedy queen named Miss Glynn, who having no visible external ears, had a head like a turnip. Lady Wilde talked about Schopenhauer; and Miss Glynn told me that Gladstone formed his oratorical style on Charles Kean."

Shaw's first meeting with Oscar, a self-dramatizing, already mildly notorious literary man two years older than Shaw and sophisticated by Trinity College (Dublin) and Oxford, was awkward for the younger Irishman, a school dropout who had been nowhere. Wilde, Shaw remembered, "spoke to me with an evident intention of being specially kind. . . . We put each other out frightfully, and this odd difficulty persisted between us to the very last, even when we were no longer mere boyish novices and had become men of the world with plenty of skill in social intercourse. I saw him very seldom, as I avoided literary and artistic society like the plague, and refused the few invitations I received to go into society with burlesque ferocity, so as to keep out of it without offending people past their willingness to indulge me as a privileged lunatic." Shaw's diary through 1885 is marked with invitations to Lady Wilde's salons, many of which he avoided, even when it meant spending his after-five hours alone at home playing the piano.[3] The last reference to Lady Wilde's is 18 July 1885, when he met J. S. Stuart-Glennie, an historian and folklorist who would become a good friend. After that the invitations disappear, Speranza's interest in Shaw cooling as she perceived him more as socialist activist than as promising author. As a novice music critic, however, Shaw had already observed of a Bach Choir concert that the majestic *Mass in B Minor* "disappointed some people, precisely as the Atlantic Ocean disappointed Mr. Wilde" (*Dramatic Review*, 28 March 1885).

Shaw was already seeing Oscar elsewhere, although later he could recall to Frank Harris only six meetings and was certain that there were not many more. By the next year he was encountering Wilde at the homes of émigré Irish writers who were mutual friends. One was novelist Fitzgerald Molloy. At Molloy's, Shaw noted in his diary on 14 September 1886, Oscar Wilde and novelist Richard Dowling watched as a "chiromantist," Edward Heron Allen, "told my character by reading my hand very successfully." That the reading of Shaw's palm led to Wilde's story "Lord Arthur Savile's Crime," published in three parts in the *Court and Society Review* in May 1887, seems likely from Oscar's care in sending Heron Allen a copy of the numbers with a reference to "the chiromancy of the story."[4] No G.B.S., however, the demonic Sir Arthur Savile has his palm read by the fat, coarse Podgers, who finds a streak of blood in Savile's palm that embodies his sanguinary future as well as that of Podgers, who must be murdered if Sir Arthur is to purify the evil within himself. Shaw may exist in it only in the stature of the tall and attractive Savile. After the palm reading, according to Wilde, Shaw aired his idea of a new magazine that would proselytize for socialism across the breadth of Britain. Recognizing the unreality of the dream, Wilde interrupted and observed, so he recalled, "That has all been most interesting, Mr. Shaw, but there's one point you haven't mentioned, and an all-important one—you haven't told us the *title* of the magazine."

"Oh, as for that," Wilde quoted Shaw as replying, "what I would want to do would be to impress my own personality on the public—I'd call it *Shaw's Magazine:* Shaw—Shaw—Shaw!" He punctuated his enthusiasm by banging his recently read fist on the table.

"Yes," Wilde claimed, punning on *pshaw*, "and how would you spell it?"

At Molloy's on 4 October, with Oscar again present, there was more palm reading, a popular late-Victorian pastime. This time it was accomplished by MacGregor Mathers who, as an occultist, was interested in Molloy's novel *A Modern Magician,* then being written. (Shaw would review the book in the *Pall Mall Gazette* in December 1887.) Mathers, very likely a model for Molloy's hero, would become a great friend of Yeats who, upon seeing Mathers in the British Museum Reading Room "in a brown velveteen coat, with a gaunt resolute face, and an athletic body," thought this was how "might Faust have looked in his changeless aged youth."

Reviewing for the *Pall Mall Gazette* would be an occupation that Wilde and Shaw would have in common, but since Wilde was already a public personality, Shaw had the license to refer to him, as he had already done, in humorous asides in reviews. In the socialist *Our Corner* (February 1886), Shaw had done it again. Reporting a lecture by Edmund Russell, he had noted that Russell had worn "a colored silk neckcloth instead of the usual white tie," resulting in paragraphs comparing Russell with Oscar Wilde—not, Shaw noted, "the staid and responsible Oscar Wilde of to-day, but the youth whose favorite freak it was to encourage foolish people to identify him with the imaginary 'aesthete' invented [for *Punch*] by Mr. [George] du Maurier." By then, Yeats remembered, Wilde had coined an observation that even Shaw would quote, since it was impossible to forget—that "Bernard Shaw hasn't an enemy in the world; and none of his friends like him." It made Yeats feel "revenged upon a notorious hater of romance, whose generosity and courage I could not fathom."[5]

For several years, beginning in 1886, Wilde and Shaw would pass each other in the *Pall Mall Gazette* office, picking up review copies of new books or submitting copy for anonymous publication. Each reviewed three or four books a month, as did William Archer and George Moore. In a letter to *New Review* editor Tighe Hopkins, Shaw recalled their

> barbarous amusement of skinning minor poets alive . . . ; and an *auto da fe* took place once a month or so with a batch of them, the executioner being sometimes Oscar Wilde, sometimes William Archer, sometimes myself. As only our elementary vices were brought into play; and as the literary manifestations of these are much alike in all men at a couple of pounds a column, there was no saying, in the absence of signatures, which was the real torturer on these occasions; and to this day there are men who hate me for inhumanities perpetrated by Archer or Wilde. . . . The tendency of men to ascribe injuries to persons who know them led to each of us being credited, within his own circle of acquaintances, with the reviews of the whole three.

All the reviews "of a distinctly Irish quality during the 1885–1888 period," Shaw confessed to Dublin newspaperman David O'Donoghue, "may, I think, be set down to either me or to Oscar Wilde, whose reviews were sometimes credited to me. His work was exceptionally finished in style and very amusing."

One wonders how many readers of a review of W. E. Norris's novel, *My Friend Jim,* on 2 September 1886, could have guessed the identity of the critic who excoriated a "barbarism" at the end of the tale. "A whole railway train is wrecked to get rid of Lord Bracknell. This is burning down the house to roast the pig. Why should a number of innocent passengers be maimed, slain, or delayed in their travels merely to kill a man who might have been removed without any such sacrifice of life or rolling-stock?" Wilde would later appropriate the peer's surname in *The Importance of Being Earnest* for his Lady Bracknell, but the reviewer was Shaw.[6]

Certainly Fitzgerald Molloy might have wondered whether any of his Irish cronies in London had laid hands on a review copy of his novel, *A Modern Magician,* in 1887. Both Wilde and Shaw had been at his house when the talk was of occult matters. The critic in the *PMG* on 5 December 1887 characterized Molloy amusingly as "the Bobadil of fashionable mysticism." Molloy was "a pretentious bungler: his syntax is inconceivable, his dialogue impossible, his style a desperately careful expression of desperately slovenly thinking, his notions of practical affairs absurd, and his conception of science and philosophy a superstitious guess: yet he has an indescribable flourish, a dash of half-ridiculous poetry, a pathetic irresponsibility, a captivating gleam of Irish imagination. . . ." Molloy remained on speaking terms with Shaw, apparently guessing—erroneously—that his reviewer was Wilde.

By 1888 Shaw was no longer a guest at Lady Wilde's at-homes, but he owed her something. Oscar could not fairly review his mother's books, so Shaw took on the duty, writing a notice of *Ancient Legends of Ireland* that appeared on Shaw's thirty-second birthday, 26 July 1888. Had she known it was by Shaw, his invitations might have been renewed. She must have sensed a friendly mediator, someone who confessed to not affecting "impartiality" because Lady Wilde's "position, literary, social, and patriotic," was "unique and unassailable." The book could have been dull in another's hands, Shaw wrote anonymously, but "Lady Wilde can write scholarly English without pedantry and Irish-English without vulgarity or impracticable brogue phonetics. She has no difficulty in writing about leprechauns, phoukas [*sic*], and banshees, simply as an Irishwoman telling Irish stories, . . . with a nursery knowledge at first hand of all the characteristic moods of the Irish imagination. Probably no living writer could produce a better book of its kind."

Oscar could not have written those lines, but some writers reviewed in the *PMG* assumed unhappily from internal evidence that either Wilde or Shaw had done short work upon them. That concern emerges in a letter from William Michael Rossetti to Dr. Frederick James Furnivall complaining to his sympathetic friend about the amusingly adverse *Pall Mall Gazette* review of Rossetti's biography of Keats. Dismissing the book as ponderous, ill-chosen verbiage, the critic had written, after citing chapter and verse, "There is no necessity to follow Mr Rossetti further as he flounders about through the quagmire that he has made for his own feet." The entire notice was devastating. "As I understand it," the unhappy biographer confided to Furnivall, "Shaw is the writer of that critique: though I have more than once been told that notices . . . which I supposed to be by Shaw, are in fact by Oscar Wilde. Apart from seeing and hearing Shaw at the Shelley Society etc., I don't know him: but [I] shall be equally well pleased to encounter him hereafter, and hear what he has to say—which I always find clever and telling, and the reverse of commonplace."[7] The review was by Wilde.

Unkindness, as Yeats understood, was not characteristic of either Wilde or Shaw, and for Shaw what really established his friendly feelings toward a colleague accused of wielding a poisonous pen was the affair of the Chicago anarchists in 1887. The Haymarket Riots of the year before had led to death sentences for the imprisoned Radicals, whose guilt in the matter had been dubiously proved. "I tried to get some literary men in London, all heroic rebels and skeptics on paper, to sign a memorial asking for a reprieve of these unfortunate men," Shaw wrote. His diary notes on 6 November 1887 his failure to convince William Archer to sign, "which he did not care to do." Shaw tried other friends of liberal persuasion; all shied away. "The only signature I got was Wilde's. It was a completely disinterested act on his part; and it secured my distinguished consideration for him for the rest of his life."

On 17 November, Lucy Shaw was married, and although Shaw furnished the whisky and cake he did not turn up at the church in Fitzroy Square, going off instead to Willis's Rooms, where artist and critic Selwyn Image was lecturing, then returning to wedding "tea" at St. John's Church, "where," Shaw noted in his diary, "I had a talk with Wilde. . . ." Shaw thought that still another meeting with Oscar at about that time occurred in Fitzrovia, at the home of Scottish architect A. H. Mackmurdo, but the encounter, on 15 December, actually occurred at Herbert Horne's house. Horne edited the Century Guild's magazine, *The Hobby Horse*, with which Mackmurdo was associated. The talk was stimulating, and Shaw did not leave until one in the morning.

"A stream of visitors all the afternoon, mostly chatterboxes," Shaw wrote about another semi-social occasion. "Oscar Wilde was there." It

was the first of June 1888, a Sunday, and Shaw was visiting Miss Charlotte Roche, in Cadogan Gardens, to be photographed. Hobbyist portrait
photographers—"Lewis Carroll" had been one—were often very good,
and Shaw knew Miss Roche through artist and typographer Emery
Walker and musician Felix Moscheles. Although Wilde was deaf to music, he remained with Shaw while Natalie Janotha played a Chopin
scherzo, and the conversation afterward was of art and—inevitably—
how socialism would metamorphose it.

The talk when Shaw was present was often about how socialism would
alter the way that art was created as well as how and by whom it was
consumed. When illustrator Walter Crane spoke in July 1888 at the
Fabian Society's monthly meeting at Willis's Rooms, and his subject was
"The Prospects of Art under Socialism," the afternoon paper *The Star*
reported on 7 July,

> Mr. Crane believed that art would revive under these new socialis-
> tic conditions. Mr. Oscar Wilde, whose fashionable coat differed
> widely from the picturesque bottle-green garb in which he ap-
> peared in earlier days, thought that the art of the future would
> clothe itself not in works of form and colour but in literature. . . .
> Mr. Herbert Burrows contended that the masses loved good art, a
> fact which Mr. George Bernard Shaw deplored, as he said it
> proved that the lower classes were following the insincere cant of
> the middle classes. Mr. Shaw agreed with Mr. Wilde that literature
> was the form which art would take, pronounced [John] Bunyan
> the tinker a supreme genius, and voted Beethoven rather vulgar,
> saying that if a middle-class audience were told that "Pop Goes the
> Weasel" was a movement from Beethoven's Ninth Symphony they
> would go into ecstasies over it.

Wilde and Shaw continued the discussion after the meeting broke up.
"He parted from us," Shaw noted in his diary, "in St. James's Square, and
the rest of us—Carr, Webb, and Wallas—walked together as far as the
corner of Grafton St. in Tottenham Court Rd." Later Wilde told Robert
Ross, who told Shaw, that Wilde's "Soul of Man under Socialism" (*Fortnightly Review*, February 1891) had its origin that night.

Wilde was back the next week for another of the Arts and Crafts
lectures, this one, on printing, by Emery Walker, as Shaw reported in an
Art paragraph in *The World*.[8] William Morris spoke, and Joseph Pennell,
but Wilde, Shaw noted, remained only a spectator. Still, some ideas generated by the Fabian series, and by Shaw in particular, stuck, although
socialism meant something different to Wilde. Like Shaw he foresaw
with approval the end of property, family, marriage, and covetousness.

Like Shaw he clothed his concepts in aphorisms peppered with para-
doxes. But for Wilde, the best government an artist could have was no
government at all, which suggested anarchism more than socialism.

   To Wilde in "The Soul," altruism was "unhealthy." Encouraging "charity, benevolence and the like," altruism was an impulse that "degrades
and demoralizes." Charity was responsible for "a multitude of sins."⁹ It
was a paradox that Shaw understood, and that would be central to his
1905 play *Major Barbara*. Poverty, both agreed, could not be solved that
way. "The proper aim," Wilde wrote, "is to try and reconstruct society on
such a basis that poverty will be impossible." Socialism, he prophesied,
would change all that. "There will be no people living in fetid dens and
fetid rags, and bringing up unhealthy, hunger-pinched children in the
midst of impossible and absolutely repulsive surroundings." Once everyone shared "in the general prosperity and happiness of society," Wilde
continued in another paradox which he found congenial, however unrealistic to readers of the *Fortnightly Review*, socialism would "lead to
Individualism." Only under socialism could people cultivate their personalities, for without material well-being, each person was "merely the
infinitesimal atom of a force that, so far from regarding him, crushes
him."

   Like Shaw, Wilde never accepted the cliché that the impoverished
were automatically more virtuous than the rich. "There is only one class
in the community that thinks more about money than the rich, and that
is the poor. The poor can think of nothing else." Further, "what are
called criminals nowadays are not criminals at all. Starvation, and not sin,
is the parent of modern crime." The apostle of Aestheticism was sound-
ing more like Shaw in his Sunday streetcorner addresses, or "General"
William Booth of the Salvation Army, than those that knew Oscar could
have imagined, but the familiar figure reappeared in the closing paragraphs. There, Wilde predicted that under socialism—the philosophy
was William Morris's—machinery would no longer compete with man,
but would serve him. And, while Art could then be enhanced, "Art
should never try to be popular. The public should try to make itself
artistic." Art that by conventional standards was considered immoral and
unhealthy was really the opposite. "The work of art is to dominate the
spectator; the spectator is not to dominate the work of art." Individualism, Wilde concluded, would have its greatest opportunities under socialism, "whether it wills it or not."

   When Shaw relinquished regular art criticism for *The World*, he nominated his friend Lady Colin Campbell as his replacement. In the course
of her reviewing, Lady Colin began encountering Wilde. She found him
physically disgusting, his paleness accentuated by teeth blackened from
mercury doses he had taken for syphilis and often hidden while he

talked by an oversized hand clapped across the mouth. She described him to Shaw as "that great white caterpillar."[10] Shaw explained—not that it helped—that he thought Oscar's bigness was pathological. "You know," he observed to Frank Harris, and very likely earlier to Lady Colin Campbell, "that there is a disease called gigantism, caused by"—and Shaw quoted from what he had looked up in an encyclopedia—"a certain morbid process in the sphenoid bone of the skull . . . , an excessive development of the anterior lobe of the pituitary [gland]." The overproduction of the growth hormone created the condition Shaw described as acromegaly. He saw the evidence in Lady Wilde as well as in her son. "I never saw Lady Wilde's feet; but her hands were enormous. . . . And the gigantic splaying of her palm was reproduced in her lumbar region." In adult life, after cessation of normal growth, acromegaly—the overgrowth of hands, feet, and face rather than full gigantism—results from pituitary imbalance. In Wilde, Shaw thought, acromegaly led not only to coarseness and enlargement of the face, nose, and jaws, but also to an impairment of mental ability which emerged in sexually sinister fashion. It was questionable as medical diagnosis, and even more questionable as causal analysis, but, Shaw contended, "I have always maintained that Oscar was a giant in the pathological sense, and this explains a good deal of his weakness."

A later lecture by Shaw seems to have had its impact on Wilde—Shaw's 1890 talk to the Fabians, "The Quintessence of Ibsenism." The next year Shaw sent a copy of the book version to Wilde. Where Shaw accepted, in his early extreme phase of socialism, Pierre Proudhon's contention that property is theft, Wilde preferred the more amusing paradox that the possession of private property was "very often extremely demoralising. . . . In fact, property is really a nuisance." In *The Quintessence*, Shaw began with the necessity for "the repudiation of duty," a "gloomy tyranny" that impeded the progress of humankind. Apparently adopting the concept—it fit in with his predilections—Wilde in "Soul of Man" turned Adam and the apple into the paradox that disobedience was "man's original virtue. It is through disobedience that progress has been made. . . ." Another concept that seems to parallel, if not emanate directly from, *Quintessence* is Wilde's charge "that Individualism does not come to man with any sickly cant about duty, which merely means doing what other people want because they want it. . . ." However, "Selfishness is not living as one wishes to live, it is asking others to live as one wishes to live."

The opening sections on Idealists and Realists, in which Shaw used the term *Idealist* to characterize people who clung to outworn and untenable "masks" shielding them from disagreeable truths, may have had an immediate effect on Wilde as a playwright. In *Lady Windermere's Fan*, Opus

1 of the Hibernian School, the innocent Lady Windermere confides to Mrs. Erlynne, "a lady with a past"—and her mother, although Lady Windermere will never know that secret—"We all have ideals in life. At least we should have. Mine is my mother."

"Ideals are dangerous things," Mrs. Erlynne warns—but cautiously. "Realities are better. They wound, but they are better."

Shaking her pretty head, Lady Windermere rejects the notion. "If I lost my ideals, I should lose everything." What drives the play are such hazards of "Idealism."

Perhaps a later echo emerges from *The Importance of Being Earnest* when Gwendolyn tells Jack, who has just proposed to her, "We live, as I hope you know, Mr. Worthing, in an age of ideals. The fact is constantly mentioned in the more expensive monthly magazines, and has reached the provincial pulpits, I am told: and my ideal has always been to love someone of the name of Ernest." If Shaw took this as a playful poke at the *Quintessence,* it could not have seemed funny to him.

Only after Wilde's *Salomé* was banned by the Censor of Plays did he respond to Shaw about *The Quintessence of Ibsenism,* enclosing a just-published copy of the purple-bound melodrama. "You have written well and wisely and with sound wit," he noted in February 1893, "on the ridiculous institution of a stage-censorship: your little book on Ibsenism and Ibsen is such a delight to me that I constantly take it up, and always find it stimulating and refreshing: England is the land of intellectual fogs but you have done much to clear the air: we are both Celtic, and I like to think that we are friends: for these and many other reasons Salome presents herself to you in purple raiment. Pray accept her with my best wishes. . . ." Another copy went to Shaw's friend William Archer, already a drama reviewer of some influence. "I have not forgotten," Wilde explained, "that you were, with the exception of George Bernard Shaw, the only critic of note who upheld me at all against the Censorship."

Just before *Widowers' Houses* opened in December 1892, Shaw had published anonymously, as publicity for the play, an "interview" he had written himself for the afternoon newspaper *The Star* (29 November), in which the supposed reporter had asked whether audiences might "anticipate some of your unrivalled touches of humor. . . ."

"Certainly not," said Shaw (to Shaw).

> . . . Being an Irishman, I do not always see things exactly as an Englishman would: consequently some of my most serious and blunt statements sometimes . . . create an impression that I am intentionally jesting. I admit that some Irishmen do take advantage of the public in this way. Wilde, unquestionably the ablest of our dramatists, has done so in *Lady Windermere's Fan.* There are

FIG. 2. The 1987 Shaw Festival Theatre production of Wilde's *Salomé* at Niagara-on-the-Lake, directed by Sky Gilbert. Photograph by David Cooper. Reproduced by permission of The Shaw Festival Theatre.

lines in that play which were put in for no other purpose than to make the audience laugh. . . . However, I do not blame Wilde. He wrote for the stage as an artist. I am simply a propagandist.[11]

Although Wilde had written that he liked to think that he and Shaw were friends, they had seen little of each other since the *Pall Mall Gazette* days. Wilde had become famous, if not infamous, while Shaw had secured his small niche in the press with music reviews as "Corno di Bassetto" and as "G.B.S." As a playwright, Shaw in 1893 hardly counted. Of his three plays, the first, *Widowers' Houses*, had managed two unrewarding performances in December 1892, while *The Philanderer* had frightened away producers and *Mrs Warren's Profession* had been proscribed by the Censor.

At a performance of *As You Like It* opening the Shaftesbury Theatre in October 1888, Shaw had chatted with Wilde between the acts. Their "shyness of one another," Shaw recalled to Frank Harris, "made our resolutely cordial and appreciative conversation so difficult that our final laugh and shake-hands were almost a reciprocal confession." It was a confession, he did not need to add, that their worlds were moving even farther apart than ever. On 5 February 1889 Wilde had been in the audience when the Rev. Stewart Headlam's Church and Stage Guild—an effort to bring the two professions closer together—presented a talk by Shaw with the paradoxical title, "Acting, by one who does not believe in it; or the place of the Stage in the Fool's Paradise of Art." It was received, Shaw told actress Janet Achurch, the first Nora in Ibsen's *Doll's House* in England, "with inexpressible indignation by all the members of the profession who happened to be present." When Shaw edited his remarks for publication in Headlam's journal, *The Church Reformer,* he noted that he had intended to spur the audience into "fierce discussion," but, he summed up, "the discussion did not get beyond a volley of questions and fragmentary remarks from Mr. William Archer, Mr. Oscar Wilde. . . ."

On 14 February 1890, while still a music critic, Shaw noted in his diary, "Go to Military Exhibition and see whether there is any music there." Afterward he added, "Met Oscar Wilde." "It was," he recalled to Frank Harris, "some exhibition in Chelsea: a naval exhibition, where there was a replica of Nelson's Victory and a set of P. & O. cabins which made one seasick by mere association of ideas. . . . The question of what the devil we were doing in that galley tickled us both." That incongruity set into motion "Oscar's wonderful gift as a raconteur."

The cramped cabin reminded Wilde, Shaw recalled, "of a young man who invented a theatre stall which economized space by ingenious contrivances. . . . A friend of his invited twenty millionaires to meet him at dinner so that he might interest them in the invention. The young man convinced them completely by his demonstration of the saving in a theatre holding, in ordinary seats, of six hundred people, leaving them ready and eager to make his fortune." Unfortunately, in his enthusiasm the young genius, who also had a fanatical gift for calculation, went on to extrapolate "the annual saving in all the theatres in the world; then in all the churches of the world; then in all the legislatures; estimating finally the incidental and moral and religious effects of the invention until at the end of an hour he had estimated a profit of several billions." By then the worried millionaires had "folded their tents and silently stole[n] away, leaving the ruined inventor a marked man for life."

Wilde hit it off with Shaw "extraordinarily well," G.B.S. thought, because Shaw only had to listen, and with an audience of one, Wilde was not tempted into his pompous public pose. "We did not talk about Art, about which, excluding literature from the definition, [Wilde] knew only what could be picked up by reading about it. He was in a tweed suit and low hat like myself . . . instead of pontificating in his frock coat. . . . And I understood why [William] Morris, when he was dying slowly, enjoyed a visit from Wilde more than from anybody else. . . ."

Years later the claimed visits were called into question since Morris actually died during Wilde's time in prison; but Shaw remembered that Morris had long been failing, and that even in Oscar's heyday of fame, after *Lady Windermere's Fan,* Wilde would take time off to amuse the old man to whom he owed ideas about decoration that Oscar promoted in such lucrative lectures of the 1880s as "The House Beautiful."

Shaw had seen *Lady Windermere's Fan* in the company of the lady then in his life, actress Florence Farr, at a St. James's Theatre matinee on 6 April 1892. The play had opened in February and would run for 197 performances—not long enough for Shaw to metamorphose into a drama critic. He would be professionally stalking the concert halls for two more years. When Shaw did become a play reviewer, however, he tucked into a review, in a musical metaphor, his observation that Wilde had "written scenes in which there is hardly a speech which could conceivably be uttered by one real person at a real at-home; but the deflection from common sense is so subtle that it is evidently produced as a tuner tunes a piano; that is, he first tunes a fifth perfectly, then flattens it a shade." The play had succeeded despite the acting, Shaw told Janet Achurch in a letter (21 April 1892): "There is one actress supported by a crowd of people not one of whom is better than a fairly good walking gentleman or lady. . . ."

Although Shaw had endured his fill of Victorian fallen women rehabilitated by suffering and repentance or abandoned by polite society, it is possible that something of the former demimondaine Mrs. Erlynne and the daughter who does not know her echoes in *Mrs Warren's Profession,* which Shaw began on 20 August 1893 and which focuses upon a similar pair. Wilde's next play, *A Woman of No Importance,* also features a woman who yields to a wicked aristocrat and is left with a child she raises in penury and sorrow, but Shaw would have cut through the sentimentality to the fact that Mrs. Arbuthnot refuses, like Mrs. Warren, to repent.

Shaw's diary notes his plan to attend *A Woman of No Importance* on 26 April 1893, but also the cancellation of the matinee. When he did see it— it ran for 113 performances—he neglected to record the fact, but later wrote (1 March 1895) to Charles Charrington, Janet Achurch's husband, in the vein of someone who had seen the play. Commenting upon Wilde's purported facility of dashing off dramas with lazy ease, Shaw alluded to "the Wilde who makes notes on his shirtcuffs" skeptically, "as if *A Woman of No Importance* could be produced in any such silly way . . . without the solid detail of humanity underneath. . . ."

By then Shaw had produced his newest work in the Hibernian School,

Arms and the Man, set in an underdeveloped Balkan country that might just as easily, given its backwardness at the time, have been Ireland itself. He made sure that the manager of the Avenue Theatre sent first-night tickets for 21 April 1894 to two Irishmen, Oscar Wilde and George Moore. No reaction from Wilde survives, but while several critics deplored Shaw's wit as "second-hand Gilbertism," Oscar might have seen his own influence at work. In many ways it was "low-Society Wilde." Wilde-like absurdities enliven the play, culminating in the social vanity of the heroine's mother's boasting to her daughter's suitor, "The Petkoffs and the Saranoffs are known as the richest and most important families in the country. Our position is almost historical: we can go back for twenty years."

Shaw was on the aisle as a theater critic for Frank Harris's *Saturday Review* when Wilde's *Ideal Husband* opened on 3 January 1895, and his notice (12 January 1895) was only his second for Harris's paper. Sadly, Henry James's *Guy Domville* competed for attention that week, and Shaw, while giving it first place in his columns and praising its artistry, recognized that it would not survive on the commercial stage. Wilde's comedy, on the other hand, was certain to make money, although Shaw warned that Wilde was hazardous for most critics. "They laugh angrily at his epigrams. . . . They protest that the trick is obvious, and that such epigrams can be turned out by the score by anyone lightminded enough to condescend to such frivolity. As far as I can ascertain, I am the only person in London who cannot sit down and write an Oscar Wilde play at will. The fact that his plays, though apparently lucrative, remain unique under these circumstances, says much for the self-denial of our scribes."

Wilde, Shaw concluded, "was our only thorough playwright. He plays with everything: with wit, with philosophy, with drama, with actors and audience, with the whole theatre. Such a feat scandalizes the Englishman, who can no more play with wit and philosophy than he can with a football or a cricket bat." Confronting the contention that Wilde's artistry was somehow slothful or slack, Shaw added, "Mr. Wilde, an arch-artist, is so colossally lazy that he trifles even with the work by which an artist escapes work. He distils the very quintessence, and gets as [his] product plays which are so unapproachably playful that they are the delight of every playgoer with twopenn'orth of brains." But it was "useless" to sum up a play that had no point other than play. "The six worst epigrams are mere alms handed with a kind smile to the average suburban playgoer; the three best remain secrets between Mr. Wilde and a few choice spirits." Yet Shaw saw "a modern note" (perhaps out of Ibsen) in the hero's "assertion of the individuality and courage of his wrongdoing as against the mechanical idealism of his stupidly good wife, and in his bitter criticism of a love that is only the reward of merit."

Wilde's mocking curtain speech as author was condemned in the press. He had been accused of insolence before when, after the curtain came down on *Lady Windermere's Fan,* he had congratulated the audience on its good taste in applauding his play. Shaw ignored the controversial aftermath of *An Ideal Husband* in his review, but when his young friend Reginald Golding Bright, aspiring to become a critic himself, objected to it, Shaw loyally wrote (30 January 1895), "You are really too hard on Wilde. His 'I have enjoyed myself very much' was an Irishman's way of giving all the credit to the actors and effacing his own claims as author."

Oscar, however, was hell-bent toward personal disaster and, in an arrogance far more dangerous than his curtain-call remarks, was busily flaunting his relationship with Lord Alfred Douglas and less pretty boys. Six weeks later, when Wilde opened *The Importance of Being Earnest* (G.B.S. went on the fourth night, 18 February 1895), Shaw was disappointed by what he saw as its coldness and suggested in the *Saturday Review* (23 February 1895) that it must have been an earlier work, now refurbished, "because it was too clever and too decent." Two plays in two months was too much even for Shaw. One had to have been manufactured earlier, and he took the second comedy's apparent lack of surface seriousness as its core, failing to realize that it satirized the late-Victorian veneer of *earnestness.* He found amusing some remarks by other critics that Wilde's play "could never have been written but for the opening up of entirely new paths in the drama last year by Arms and the Man."

The Importance of Being Earnest "amused me," Shaw confessed, ". . . but unless comedy touches me as well as amuses me, it leaves me with a sense of having wasted my evening. I go to the theatre to be moved to laughter, not to be tickled or bustled into it. . . ." He found little beyond the "rib-tickling: for instance, the lies, the deceptions, the cross-purposes, the sham mourning, the christening of two grown-up men, the muffin-eating, and so forth. These could only have been raised from the farcical plane by making them occur to characters who had, like Don Quixote, convinced us of their reality and obtained some hold on our sympathy." Wilde's play, Shaw thought, not his own *Arms and the Man,* had lapsed into "Gilbertism." Still, although the play lacked a humanity he thought necessary to the best drama, he admitted to "the force and daintiness of its wit," which required "an exquisitely grave, natural, and unconscious execution on the part of the actors" that he found wanting.

If the play had been performed with the grave absurdity Shaw deemed necessary, he might have found more in it. Meeting Wilde soon after, he understood that Oscar had read disloyalty in the review. But at that point the question was not how long the farce could run—it looked as if it might go on forever, unaffected by Shaw's unhappiness with it— but whether homosexual scandal would close it down. The matter came up at one of the Monday lunches which Frank Harris arranged for his writers at the Café Royal. For a while Shaw had attended with some reluctance. ("These lunches wasted my time and were rather apt to degenerate into bawdy talk," he noted in his 1895 diary.) "Oscar Wilde came . . . , immediately before the Queensberry trial, with young Douglas. They left in some indignation because Harris refused to appear as a witness—a literary expert witness—to the high artistic character of Wilde's book *Dorian Gray*."

"On that occasion," Shaw told Harris in 1916, Wilde "was not too preoccupied with his [legal] danger to be disgusted with me because I, who had praised his first plays handsomely, had turned traitor over The Importance of Being Earnest. Clever as it was, it was his first really heartless play." At the Café Royal he asked Wilde "calmly" whether the guess about the play—that it had been an early work influenced by W. S. Gilbert, then modernized—had been on the mark. "He indignantly repudiated my guess, and said loftily (the only time he ever tried on me the attitude he took toward . . . his more abject disciples) that he was disappointed in me. I suppose I said, 'Then what on earth has happened to you?' but I recollect nothing more . . . except that we did not quarrel over it."

Shaw offered to leave when Wilde and Harris began discussing what moves might be made to evade Oscar's inevitable conviction. They insisted that he stay. Harris's answer to Wilde had been, Shaw recalled, something like,

> For God's sake man, put everything on that plane out of your head. You don't realize what is going to happen to you. It is not going to be a matter of clever talk about your books. [Your attorney, Sir Edward] Clarke will throw up his brief. He will carry the case to a certain point; and then, when he sees the avalanche coming, he will back out and leave you in the dock. What you have to do is to cross to France tonight. Leave a letter saying that you cannot face the squalor and horror of a law case; that you are an artist and unfitted for such things. Don't stay here clutching at straws like testimonials to Dorian Gray. *I tell you I know.* I know what is going to happen. . . . I know what evidence they have got. You must go.

Wilde made no claims of innocence, nor did he question the folly of his libel action against Douglas's father. "But he had an infatuate haughtiness as to the impossibility of his retreating. . . . Douglas sat in silence, a haughty indignant silence, copying Wilde's attitude as all Wilde's admirers did. . . . Oscar finally rose with a mixture of impatience and his grand air, and walked out with the remark that he had now found out who were his real friends; and Douglas followed him, absurdly smaller, and imitating his walk, like a curate imitating an archbishop."

Harris recalled, rather, that Douglas got up first and said, "Your telling him to run away shows that you are no friend of Oscar's." Then Oscar rose and said goodbye to Shaw, whom he had not asked to testify. A notorious socialist, Shaw could do little by expatiating to a jury on the salubrious morality of *Dorian Gray*.

"I hope you don't doubt my friendship," said Harris; "you have no reason to."

"I don't think this is friendly of you, Frank," said Wilde, walking out.

Shaw never again went to Harris's lunches, with their "brag and bawdry." They soon collapsed anyway when Wilde was arrested and went to trial. On 25 May 1895 he was sentenced to two years of hard labor. Many of Wilde's cronies fled across the Channel. Afterward Shaw thought that the "hateful" inhumanity revealed in Oscar's *Earnest* "represented a real degeneracy produced by his debaucheries," but this did not keep Shaw from trying to act in the imprisoned Wilde's interest. On a railway journey to the north, where he was to lecture, remembering the Chicago anarchists, Shaw drafted a petition to the Home Secretary for Wilde's release.

Returning to London, he discussed strategy with Oscar's brother, Willie, asking whether other efforts of the sort were in the works. Although Shaw offered the petition, he warned that although he and Stewart Headlam would sign, it would be "of no use, as we were two notorious cranks, and our names alone would make the thing ridiculous and do Oscar more harm than good."

Willie agreed, adding "with maudlin pathos and an inconceivable want of tact" as they stood talking in St. Martin's Lane, outside the Duke of York's Theatre, that "Oscar was NOT a man of bad character: you could have trusted him with a woman anywhere." Willie also thought that useful signatures would be unobtainable and dropped the idea.

All that was left for Shaw was to mention Wilde's artistry wherever he could, to keep his reputation alive. In a review of a play by Jerome K. Jerome on 26 October 1895, a few months later, he referred to "a remarkable scene" by Wilde in *An Ideal Husband* since Jerome had handled a similar one ponderously, "laboriously explaining Mr Oscar Wilde's point . . . , thereby very effectually reducing it to absurdity." A year later (17 October 1896), with Oscar still in prison, Shaw reviewed a play by Charles Hawtrey in which Charles Brookfield had a leading role. Both had procured perjured evidence against Wilde and had joined the Marquess of Queensberry for a victory dinner on the night the third and last trial had ended. Shaw wrote, intending that both playwright and player would understand, that the play "cannot be compared to the comedies of Mr Oscar Wilde, because Mr Wilde has creative imagination, philosophic humor, and original wit, besides being a master of language; whilst Mr Hawtrey observes, mimics, and derides quite thoughtlessly, . . . and otherwise keeps on the hither side of the boundary that separates the clever *flâneur* from the dramatist."

Late in 1897, with Wilde out of prison and in abject exile, Shaw entered into a correspondence in *The Academy,* which had published (6 November) a list of possible candidates for a British Academy of Letters, on the French model. In a rejoinder published on the thirteenth Shaw suggested, daringly since Wilde had become a nonperson in the English press, "The only dramatist, besides Mr Henry James, whose nomination could be justified, is Mr Oscar Wilde." (In the same issue, H. G. Wells even more bravely recommended Shaw as well as Wilde.) In March of the next year, Shaw referred to Wilde four times in a review and then, a few weeks later (2 April 1898), wrote of a minor effort by a minor playwright, "Will he ever handle a pen and play with an idea as . . . Mr Oscar Wilde can? Clearly never—not even were we to wrap him in blotting paper and boil him in ink for a week to make his literary faculty supple and tender." The remark was, in context, gratuitous, but Shaw was keeping Wilde's name before the serious reader while it was blotted off the stage and eliminated from the bookshops. Aside from any loyalty, Shaw had found in him something he did not want lost from the stage— a peculiarly Irish exasperation with English solemnity.

By then some suggestions of Wilde had begun echoing in Shaw's own plays, some of them apparently intentional. As early as 19 November 1894 Shaw had warned Golding Bright, "You must give up detesting everything appertaining to Oscar Wilde. . . . The critic's first duty is to admit, with absolute respect, the right of every man to his own style. Wilde's wit and his fine literary workmanship are points of great value. There is always a vulgar cry both for and against every man or woman of distinction, and . . . you have heard it about Whistler, Sarah Grand, Ibsen, Wagner—everybody who has a touch of genius." When Shaw began writing his comedy *You Never Can Tell* in July 1895, he gave it the working title "The Terrestrial Twins," after Mrs. Grand's feminist novel *The Heavenly Twins.*[12] It also would have something of Wilde in it, emanating from the very heartless play that Shaw had disliked and responding to Shaw's own sense of the play's chilly mechanicalness.

You Never Can Tell would have a dentist as young lover, Valentine; a Gorgon of a dowager feminist, Mrs. Lanfrey Clandon; her twins, Dolly and Philip; her elder daughter, Gloria; the children's father and estranged husband of their mother, the cranky Fergus Crampton; a serenely comic waiter, William Boon; and his omniscient lawyer-son, Walter Bohun. Comic figures seemingly drawn at a level of deliberate unreality, as were Wilde's characters, Shaw's characters were as rational and outspoken as Wilde's, and their motives, as in Wilde's play, were clear and never in doubt. Wilde's characters remained stylized from beginning to end, almost to abstraction; Shaw's were more warmly conceived, for as he wrote in a review of some farces in 1896, perhaps still remembering *The Importance of Being Earnest,* "To laugh without sympathy is a ruinous abuse of a noble function, and the degradation of any race may be measured by the degree of their addiction to it." When barren of sympathy, he insisted, farce was "at bottom . . . the deliberate indulgence of that horrible, derisive joy in humiliation and suffering which is the beastliest element in human nature."

With Wilde out of the picture in the summer of 1895 (he was in prison) Shaw had been tempted to turn to "fashionable comedies for the West End theatres"—satirical fun on the order of his *Arms and the Man* but raised some social notches for fashionable audiences. Determining to humanize the genre of "imperturbably impudent comedies," and very likely recalling his cavils about Wilde's *Earnest,* he blended Oscar Wilde with Sarah Grand. In Wilde's play, Jack Worthing must find a father if he is to capture his society bride, Gwendolen Fairfax, ward of that apostle of propriety, Lady Bracknell. By the curtain, after some accidents and coincidences, he has located a father in the Army lists—a satisfactory general, safely deceased. In *You Never Can Tell,* the Clandon children are in search of a father, and they find one, under another name (their mother lives under her pen name), as a patient in a dentist's office.

The dentist, meanwhile, requires a father so that his suit for Gloria Clandon has credibility, citing to the twins an apparent echo of Lady Bracknell's injunction to Jack Worthing that he produce at least one parent before the end of the social season. "In a seaside resort," Valentine explains, "there's one thing you must have before anybody can be seen going about with you, and that's a father, alive or dead." Valentine's beloved begins the play with the same predicament, redoubling Wilde's parental predicament. "A woman who does not know who her own father was," she informs her emancipated mother, cannot accept a respectable offer of marriage.

Even the profession of dentistry—unusual in drama then and now—is found in both comedies, Shaw turning allusion into reality. "Come, old boy," says Algernon in Wilde's farce as he tries to extract the identity of the mysterious Cecily Cardew from Jack Worthing, "you had much better have the thing out at once."

"My dear Algy," retorts Jack, trying to evade the question, "you talk exactly as if you were a dentist."

Shaw's irrepressible lover, Valentine, is a "five-shilling dentist," new to his role and struggling to earn a living. Philip Clandon thinks that "dentist" is "an ugly word," but Valentine, who has tried and failed in other occupations, has a symbolic profession as well as a farcical one in Shaw's play. (His very name may be a deliberate echo from *Earnest*—of "the 14th of February last," Valentine's Day, when Cecily claims to have accepted Algernon, posing as Jack's wayward brother Ernest, "under this dear old tree here.") Old Crampton follows young Dolly in having the throbbing thing out, but he suffers from a pain beyond dentistry, he admits, upon seeing Dolly and Phil: "A twinge of memory, Miss Clandon, not of toothache."

"Have it out," Dolly advises, quoting from *Macbeth*, " 'Pluck from the memory a rooted sorrow.' With gas, five shillings extra."

Name changes—Algernon and Jack in Wilde's play schedule baptisms, in order to become "Ernest" to satisfy their brides-to-be—are significant in both comedies. Mrs. Clandon—formerly Crampton—has changed her daughter's name from the dowdy Victorian Sophronia to the more modern Gloria, while waiter William Boon, content with the English corruption of his name, finds that his son Walter, for professional respectability, has restored the Norman original, Bohun. The suggestively named young lover Valentine, in fruitless quest for a father, aptly has no other name, and whether Valentine is surname or Christian name is left in Shavian uncertainty.

Other elements of the play suggest a close study of *Earnest*.[13] The muffin-eating scene, more serious farce than Shaw realized, becomes a full, formal luncheon in *You Never Can Tell*, and Wilde's irreverent servant Lane, who serves bread and butter in lieu of cucumber sandwiches, becomes the deferential and even more shrewd waiter Boon. The haughty Gwendolen is metamorphosed into the even more haughty Gloria; the imperious but conventional Lady Bracknell becomes the even more imperious and emancipated Mrs. Clandon.

More significantly, the play is replete with earnestness, both purported and real. Mrs. Clandon, whose earnest and "scientific" tracts for the twentieth century demonstrate a love of humanity, is unable to show warmth for the individual human being, not even for her children. Even in the play the irrepressible twin, Dolly, makes fun of her mother's tracts on modern ethics, and Mrs. Clandon retorts that although her values are a joke to the younger generation, "It is such bitter earnest to me." And *earnestness* reappears literally throughout the comedy. When Mrs. Clandon interrogates Valentine about his intentions in Act III, as Lady Bracknell had done with Jack in *Earnest*, she inverts the conventional social premises for marriage, declaring that she cares little for money and that Valentine has a right to amuse himself with women as he pleases. "Amuse myself!" Valentine protests. "Oh, Mrs Clandon!"

"On your honor," Gloria's mother asks skeptically, "Mr Valentine, are you in earnest?"

"On my honor," he claims ("*desperately,*" in Shaw's stage directions), "I am in earnest. Only," he confesses, "I have always been in earnest; and yet—! Well, here I am, you see."

The wordplay on *earnestness* is too pervasive to be coincidence. Later, Mrs. Clandon's old family friend, Finch McComas, warns the effervescent Dolly, who has interrupted him, "I insist on having earnest matters earnestly and reverently discussed." And Gloria rebukes Valentine for the levity in his personality ("lightness of heart," he labels it) that his infatuation with her cannot conceal: "If you were really in love, it would not make you foolish: it would give you dignity! earnestness!" "Ah," Valentine retorts, "you see you're not in earnest. Love can[']t give any man new gifts. It can only heighten the gifts he was born with."

In the last act, Valentine contends to Gloria that his brand of earnestness is driven by biology, the necessity to complete their mutual genetic fate. "Why was I tempted? Because Nature was in deadly earnest with me when I was in jest with her." It was not sensible, but as Bohun points out, "All matches are unwise. It's unwise to be born; it's unwise to be married; it's unwise to live; and it's wise to die." "So much the worse," says William, his father, "for wisdom!" The world of feeling, nonexistent in the heartless universe of *The Importance of Being Earnest,* is reborn in *You Never Can Tell,* where biology is destiny. While Wilde's farce remains a masterpiece of artifice, Shaw's response has become a belatedly recognized masterwork itself.

When Shaw completed *You Never Can Tell* in 1897, he began his answer to Shakespeare, *Caesar and Cleopatra,* going for his facts to Theodor Mommsen's massive *History of Rome,* which he followed closely.[14] The subject and Shaw's source seem almost to have emanated from an implicit challenge in Wilde's *Soul of Man under Socialism,* gestating through the decade as Shaw recoiled from late-Victorian interpretations of Shakespeare. "It is a question," Wilde had written, "whether we have ever seen the full expression of a personality, except on the imaginative plane of art. In action, we never have. Caesar, says Mommsen, was the complete and perfect man. But how tragically insecure was Caesar! . . . Caesar was very perfect, but his perfection travelled by too dangerous a road." It is the note on which Shaw ends his play. Caesar, warned about the knives being sharpened for him in Rome, responds with a stoic shrug and sets sail from Egypt anyway.

When Shaw turned again to drawing-room comedy for his next major stage work, *Man and Superman* (1901–2), the frame-play was Shavianized Wilde, and the epigrammatic nature of the dialogue suggested another work in the Hibernian School, complete with an Irish-American father and son among snobbish Londoners. When a character at the close offers the paradox, "There are two tragedies in life. One is to lose your heart's desire. The other is to gain it. Mine and yours, sir," Wilde, by then dead, seems resurrected. Dumby's remark in *Lady Windermere's Fan* had been, "In this world there are only two tragedies. One is not getting what one wants, and the other is getting it." And John Tanner's "Maxims for Revolutionists," an epigrammatic catalogue that Shaw's leading character has attached to his allegedly notorious handbook, reads like a political parallel to Wilde's "Phrases and Philosophies for the Use of the Young."

A second play that begins in the drawing room, written in 1905, also seems like Shavianized Wilde and echoes *The Importance of Being Earnest*. Lady Britomart, a champion of public form, again suggests Wilde's society Gorgon, Lady Bracknell, and *Major Barbara*'s outcome hinges on foundlings and fathers despite its dark philosophical dimensions. The drawing-room wit suggests that *Lady Windermere's Fan* also lingered in Shaw's memory, most vividly Lady Windermere's "*grave*" observation to Lord Darlington, chastising him, "Believe me, you are better than most other men, and I sometimes think you pretend to be worse." Lady Brit improves on this in her exasperated aspersions upon Andrew Undershaft's character, for her estranged husband goes about "saying that wrong things are true" and pretends to a wickedness that is closer to saintliness. Shaw was not paying debts but recognizing stageable devices that had passed the test of usage.

Shaw's last personal contact with Wilde had come via an inscribed copy of "The Ballad of Reading Gaol," sent from Paris in 1898. (Wilde died in 1900.) No acknowledgment survives, but Shaw, who would write an influential essay, *The Crime of Imprisonment*, could not have forgotten it. Yet Shaw told Harris that the long poem was not essential for Wilde's posthumous reputation. "Well," Shaw suggested,

> suppose Oscar . . . had . . . died the day before Queensberry had left that [accusing] card at the Club! Oscar would still have been remembered as a wit and a dandy, and would have had a niche beside Congreve in the drama. A volume of his aphorisms would have stood creditably on the library shelf with La Rochefoucauld's Maxims. We should have missed the Ballad of Reading Gaol and De Profundis; but he still would have cut a considerable figure in the Dictionary of National Biography and been read and quoted outside the British Museum reading room.

"We all dreaded to read De Profundis," Shaw observed of the posthumously published text of Wilde's long prison letter to Douglas: "Our instinct was to stop our ears, or run away from the wail of a broken, though by no means contrite, heart. But we were throwing away our pity.

De Profundis was de profundis indeed. Wilde was too good a dramatist to throw away so powerful an effect; but none the less it was de profundis in excelsis. There was more laughter between the lines of that book than in a thousand farces by men of no genius. Wilde, like Richard and Shakespear, found in himself no pity for himself." Few read Wilde that way, but Shaw knew him.

To Lord Alfred Douglas, who first ranted at Shaw and then strove to become a Shavian parasite, G.B.S. was pointed. Realizing that Douglas lived for decades on his notorious relationship with Wilde, Shaw attempted to disabuse Douglas of his feeling that the past was his bread and butter. It meant diminishing Oscar's presence, and in Shaw's letters to Douglas, most of them from the 1930s, he downplayed the post-prison Wilde as a drunkard and swindler, but excused him as a diseased and broken man.[15] Wilde, Shaw explained, had been reduced by circumstances to exile and beggary. "Let me again remind you that I am an Irishman. I know that there is no beggar on earth as shameless as an Irish beggar." He detested attempts by Wilde's former cronies to exploit their association, approving only of Frank Harris's efforts because Harris, he knew, had tried to save Oscar from himself.

Often asked for his opinions of Wilde, and even to write a screenplay of the Oscar Wilde catastrophe, Shaw resisted all pleas but Harris's, and his long letter to Harris (7 August 1916) remained his most extended recollection, reprinted with amendments in Harris's biography of Wilde. In life, Shaw had concluded for Harris, Wilde "was no doubt sluggish and weak because of his gigantism." Shaw could not reproach him for that. And for the "Ballad," Wilde's only post-prison work, Wilde received Shaw's blessing, despite the obvious borrowings from "The Ancient Mariner," because he showed "that he could pity others when he could not seriously pity himself." It was a gesture Shaw did not forget despite his feeling that Wilde would survive in the wit of his plays.

"When Oscar heard the child crying in prison," he recalled again to Harris (7 May 1918),

> his pity was certainly not for himself. There is a story that Jesus Christ once began to notice that some very shady people were getting into Heaven. At last he could stand it no longer, and went to the gate and accused Peter of neglecting his duties. Peter immediately became very sulky, and would neither deny nor explain. Jesus would not be put off; and at last Peter took him round outside the wall to one of the bastions, where they peeped round the corner and saw the Virgin Mary letting down her girdle from the parapet and helping up the poor devils whom Peter had turned away. Wilde might have half a chance there because he not

only felt for the children but stuck to it and wrote about it when he got out.

Much of Shaw's respect for Wilde was due to Oscar's artistry, and some, it seems, to that belated humanity. Some, too, may acknowledge their early days in London as aspiring writers and the Haymarket petition. But Wilde paid Shaw the compliment of ranking their works together in the "great Celtic School" while Shaw was still a nobody in the theater with only two forgettable performances of a single play to his credit, which was encouragement above and beyond the sense of Hibernian duty. Few people who counted had taken Shaw seriously then. Wilde had.

Notes

1. Wilde's letters are quoted from the Rupert Hart-Davis edition of *The Letters of Oscar Wilde* (Oxford: Oxford University Press, 1962); Shaw's letters, except where noted otherwise, are quoted from Dan H. Laurence, *Bernard Shaw: Collected Letters, 1874–1897, 1898–1910*, and *1911–1925*, rev. eds. (New York: Viking, 1985).
2. Shaw's letters to Frank Harris, including the one later published, somewhat altered, by Harris as "My Memories of Oscar Wilde," are quoted from the originals as they appear in *The Playwright and the Pirate: Bernard Shaw and Frank Harris: A Correspondence*, ed. Stanley Weintraub (University Park: Penn State University Press, 1982).
3. Shaw's diary entries are quoted from *Bernard Shaw: The Diaries 1885–1897*, ed. Stanley Weintraub, 2 vols. (University Park: Penn State University Press, 1986).
4. *Court and Society Review*, 11, 18, and 25 May 1887. Wilde's letter to Heron Allen is postmarked 17 October 1887.
5. W. B. Yeats, *Autobiographies* (London: Macmillan, 1955), p. 283.
6. Shaw's complete *Pall Mall Gazette* reviews, most of them anonymously published, appear in *Bernard Shaw's Book Reviews Originally Published in the* Pall Mall Gazette *from 1885 to 1888*, ed. Brian Tyson (University Park: Penn State University Press, 1991).
7. Rossetti to Furnivall, 30 September 1887, letter 426 in *Selected Letters of William Michael Rossetti*, ed. Roger W. Peattie (University Park: Penn State University Press, 1990), pp. 510–11.
8. *The World*, 21 November 1888, unsigned, in *Bernard Shaw on the London Art Scene*, ed. Stanley Weintraub (University Park: Penn State University Press, 1989), pp. 249–50.
9. Quotations from "The Soul of Man under Socialism" (*Fortnightly Review*, February 1891) are from *The Artist as Critic: Critical Writings of Oscar Wilde*, ed. Richard Ellmann (New York: Random House, 1969).
10. Shaw's recollections of his conversation with Lady Colin Campbell are recounted to Harris in the letter Harris published as "My Memories of Oscar Wilde."
11. *The Star* self-interview is reprinted in *Collected Plays with Their Prefaces*, ed. Dan H. Laurence (London: Reinhardt, 1970), 1:122–32, as "The Playwright on His First Play."
12. British Library Add. Ms. 50605A (December 1895).

13. Some of the parallels in artifice between the two plays are noted in Thomas R. Whitaker's "Playing in Earnest," *Omnium Gatherum*, ed. Susan Dick, Declan Kiberd, Dougald McMillan, and Joseph Ronsley (Gerrards Cross: Colin Smythe, 1989), pp. 416–17.

14. Stanley Weintraub, "Shaw's Mommsenite Caesar," in *The Unexpected Shaw* (New York: Ungar, 1982), pp. 111–23.

15. Shaw's letters to Douglas, which refer often to Wilde, are collected in *Bernard Shaw and Lord Alfred Douglas: A Correspondence,* ed. Mary Hyde (New York: Ticknor & Fields, 1982).

Leon H. Hugo

SHAW AND THE
TWENTY-NINE PERCENTERS

The call for a new drama to replace the shopworn dramaturgy of the
nineteenth century first went out in 1891, when J. T. Grein established
the Independent Theatre Society in London for the production of plays
"free from the shackles of the censor, free from the fetters of convention, unhampered by financial considerations."[1] Aspirant English playwrights, although full of promises, were short on delivery—until, of
course, Shaw made his entry. *Widowers' Houses* may be thought to have
been sufficient reward for Grein's endeavors; he was very proud of it
himself (not so overcome as to want either *The Philanderer* or *Mrs Warren's
Profession* anywhere near him), but he may well have wondered whither
English talent had fled and whether the solitary and rather unusual
Shavian swallow he had hatched was all the summer the country could
manage. The Independent Theatre languished, and it was only when a
group of enthusiasts founded the Incorporated Stage Society in 1899,
with substantially the same aims as Grein's, that a permanent base for the
new drama was established.

Shaw, now with a drawerful of plays on offer, was the local standby, but
gradually a few other would-be playwrights who knew they had scant
chance of acceptance in the commercial theater began to gather in the
wings and managed once or twice to get onto the stage itself. An interesting young actor, Harley Granville Barker—interesting because he was
plainly more than an actor—essayed a play with a collaborator, *The
Weather-hen* (1899), then another on his own, *The Marrying of Ann Leete*
(1901), both of which were produced in London, the second by the Stage
Society. There was also the brilliant young Australian-born classicist Gilbert Murray, who had the satisfaction of having his first play, *Carlyon
Sahib* (1899), condemned for its anti-imperialism. And there was St. John

Hankin, whose first effort on his own, *The Two Mr Wetherbys* (1903), was also mounted by the Stage Society.

At this time and in ensuing years, Shaw approached several established writers (mainly novelists) for plays, including Conrad, Hewlett, Wells, Chesterton, and Kipling. He does not seem to have made any approaches to Henry James although he may well have. At all events, James remained drawn to the stage in spite of the humiliation he had suffered in the commercial theater with *Guy Domville*, and he offered the Stage Society a play, *Saloon*, rather late in the day, in 1909. It was rejected. Shaw told him this in a letter that surprises by its unfunny brashness.[2] James defended his play vigorously and felt confirmed in his dislike of Shaw's work.

Joseph Conrad also tried his hand. His first meeting with Shaw, amusingly recounted by Wells, ended with Conrad hugely affronted by Shaw's manner and Wells, reluctantly abandoning the idea of arranging a duel, having to explain to him that this was Shaw's "humour."[3] The dour Pole would not be mollified, and thenceforth, whenever he mentioned Shaw in his letters, he was at pains to do so sarcastically. Still, he did give the Stage Society a one-act play, an adaptation of his short story "Tomorrow" produced in 1905 as *One Day More,* and he did unbend fractionally to remark of the production that "the celebrated 'man of the hour' G.B. Shaw was exstatic [*sic*] and enthusiastic. 'Dramatist!' says he. With three plays of his own running simultaneously at the height of the season, he's entitled to speak. Of course I don't think I'm a dramatist." Shaw urged him to write more plays, "practically guaranteeing acceptance somewhere," said Conrad. But no more came from his pen.[4]

Maurice Hewlett succumbed to Shaw's blandishments to offer Vedrenne and Barker two plays which, presented at the Royal Court Theatre as a double bill, sank unlamented after six performances, Hewlett's playwriting ambitions going down with them. Wells, also encouraged by Shaw, tried his hand but without success, while Chesterton, badgered, bullied, and insulted by Shaw to bring forth the plays that resided in his capacious bosom, eventually obliged with the successful *Magic*, but this was in 1913, when the Edwardian "revolution" in drama had run its course. Other writers were also approached. Barker sounded out Laurence Housman, who stipulated that he would only consider a stage work if Barker collaborated.[5] The result was *Prunella*, initially a failure, then a favorite at the Court Theatre and elsewhere, and the first of a long line of plays by Housman. Kipling was one of the few to resist the temptation to write for the theater.

Therefore, when Vedrenne and Barker launched their seasons at the Court Theatre, they could scarcely boast of a queue of neophytes behind them, clutching brand-new playscripts in their hands and clamoring to be staged. There was Shaw, of course. His tally of plays was now increased by the formidable *Man and Superman,* while he was working at white-hot speed to add to this his dramatized thought on the Irish question. Two more new plays, *Major Barbara* and *The Doctor's Dilemma,* followed in 1905 and 1906. The statistics, cited so often, testify to the way he came to dominate the seasons. Of the total of 988 performances of separate plays presented at the Court in 1904–1907, 701 were of plays by Shaw—71 percent, which would certainly have been more had Vedrenne and Barker—with Shaw's concurrence—not stuck to their policy of short runs. Inevitably the seasons became associated with Shaw to the virtual exclusion of anyone else: to the public the Court was "Shaw's Theatre," and to Vedrenne and Barker he was the goose that laid all the golden eggs—or nearly all.

This admitted, one cannot consign the balance of 29 percent to oblivion like incidental, expendable players. That 29 percent was not incidental and was as much a part of the seasons and as little expendable at the time as Shaw's 71 percent. Vedrenne and Barker were committed to launching not Shaw, but the new drama, and those lesser English lights, and the occasional major Continental lights, that found their names on the billboards—the unknowns as much as the knowns, the failures as much as the successes—added significantly to the excitement and momentousness of the seasons, to the sense that, in Galsworthy's phrase, a "renascent drama" was being launched at the Court. This 29 percent comprises sixteen playwrights, many of whose names read like a roll-call of the "new" and "revolutionary" at the turn of the century: from the Continent, Ibsen, Hauptmann, Schnitzler, Maeterlinck; from England, among others, Galsworthy, Murray (in his translations of Euripides), Masefield, Hankin, and Barker himself; from Ireland, Yeats. The playwrights from the Continent were already well established, individually and collectively a force to be reckoned with. The English playwrights were all comparative tyros, indication in itself of the way Vedrenne and Barker took their courage into their hands when producing them. Yet if one allows a longer view, their judgment was remarkably acute at times. Those young men—and Shaw—went on from the Court to illustrious careers. They helped mold the first half of the twentieth century, gathering as they did so three Nobel Prizes for Literature (Yeats, Shaw, and Galsworthy), three Orders of Merit (Masefield, Galsworthy, and Murray), one O.M. refused (Shaw), one poet laureateship (Masefield), and dozens of other distinctions, not the least of these being Barker's legendary reputation as a director of plays. The recognition all this reflects did not necessarily derive from drama, still less from the Court Theatre. All the same, it indicates the quality of mind and talent packed into not only Shaw's eleven plays but also many of the other twenty-one. The contributions of at least a few of these twenty-nine percenters, and the critical but friendly watch Shaw kept over them, seem worthy of review.

Gilbert Murray (1866–1957) should come first because his translation of Euripides' *Hippolytus* was the first production Vedrenne and Barker put on, starting 18 October 1904, for five afternoon matinees. Purists might object that Murray should not come anywhere at all: he was, after all, merely the translator. To see his contributions in this light—three of his translations were mounted during the seasons—is to miss an important point about the venture. The *Hippolytus* asserted a mood; it established a tone, reasserted by its Euripidean successors, that characterized the seasons throughout. The message was clear: dramatic excellence was to be the criterion. What was more, Murray's translations were so effective that Shaw, for one, saw each of them as coming into English dramatic literature "with all the impulsive power of an original work."[6]

Archer started Murray off. He heard him read some excerpts from his translation of the *Hippolytus* and decided then and there that Murray had "found a satisfying solution to the problem of reproducing in English the very life and movement of Greek tragedy."[7] Encouragement soon came from another source. Shaw attended one of Murray's readings and, when proposing the vote of thanks, said that "he had felt, while the reading was in progress, that the Professor was reading one of his own original compositions, and being so generous as to give Euripides the credit for it."[8] Hearing that Murray had completed translations of the *Hippolytus*, the *Bacchae*, and Aristophanes' *Frogs* but was holding them back, he told him to stop behaving like a university professor (that is to say, like an ass) and to send Euripides to the printer by the next post. "Mind, by the next post. I am *durchaus* serious."[9] Murray pleaded timidity and admitted laziness[10] but did as he was bidden, and the plays were published in November 1902.

Then was Archer's turn again. The New Century Theatre, of which he was a founder-member, mounted a production of the *Hippolytus* in May 1904 at the Lyric Theatre. Murray recalled the occasion during his ninetieth birthday broadcast on the BBC: "the first day there were about fifty people in the house. The second day perhaps a hundred. On the third day the house was full. On the fourth day I found a crowd stretching down Shaftesbury Avenue and thought I must have come to the wrong theatre."[11] Such a success could not be overlooked, and it made good sense to Vedrenne and Barker to include the *Hippolytus* in the Court repertoire later that year.

It is difficult to determine the "newness" of Murray's translations eighty years after the event. They have a period ring to them, and T. S. Eliot, speaking as the guru of the new poetry in his 1920 essay "Euripides and Professor Murray," had good cause to condemn them for their prolixity compared to the economy of the originals. Yet Murray's declared intention at the time, "to turn the written signs in which old poetry and philosophy is now enshrined back into living thought and feeling,"[12] led to translations that made a dramatist hitherto thought unplayable, playable. As Barker wrote, and he would have known better than anyone, "He has made the plays live again as plays, that is the capital achievement."[13] Actors and actresses of the first half of the century, most notably Sybil Thorndike and Lewis Casson, confirmed the theatrical quality of the translations in memorable performances.

So did Barker in this first production at the Court. Working with Murray, he tackled the problems posed by the play as a practical man of the theater: "No principles can be invoked. There must be compromise and on a practical basis."[14] There were some thorny issues, one of these being the music. Florence Farr composed the music and led the Chorus; Barker intensely disliked the effects she produced and said as much to Murray in several letters. It was "torture to a musical ear (so I'm told)"—no doubt by Shaw—and he wondered if it would be possible to drop a little sound musical advice on her head.[15] Shaw, rather more directly and brutally, told his former mistress that her rambling up and down staircases of minor thirds was "deplorable" and created a "modern, cheap & mechanical" effect.[16] But both Barker and Shaw let their opinions be known after the rather depressing failure of the Chorus in the *Hippolytus*.

Since the production was essentially the same as the one mounted at the Lyric in May, the critics did not treat it as new, but they responded warmly. Archer, as befitted the man who had been promoting Murray for all he was worth, extolled the virtues of the text, making bold to aver (his phrase) that it was a classic of translation; he also mentioned that this production was the "first of a very interesting series of matinee performances" at the Court.[17] Others were in a lofty mood, none more so than Grein, now a full-time theater critic: "the magnificent stateliness of professor Gilbert Murray's monumental translation . . ." was how he put it.[18] Shaw, writing to Murray, was critical of some aspects of the casting— Aphrodite had "the qualifications of a horse for a quiet family—no vices"—but added, "those Greek plays of yours . . . are to me so fine that every single stroke in their production ought to be an inspiration."[19]

It was apparent that Vedrenne and Barker had gotten off to a promising start. The *Hippolytus* had stamped their venture with the kind of prestige they wanted. Another Euripides-Murray production would be mounted soon.

This was *The Trojan Women*, staged five months later. By now the critics, and the public to a certain extent, had become used to the unusual matinees at the Court; novelty in itself could not be counted on as a drawing card any longer. A run of Continental playwrights—Maeter-linck, Hauptmann, and Schnitzler—was beginning to confirm certain critical prejudices, one of which was a strongly voiced antipathy to any-thing "gloomy" and "morbid." These plays from Europe had been criti-cal and box-office failures, and the management would probably have gone under had it not been for the success of *John Bull's Other Island*. This play was scheduled to return for a three-week run of evening perfor-mances. Because of this, Vedrenne and Barker felt reasonably secure in adhering to their program, even if it meant, as *The Trojan Women* cer-tainly did mean, further doses of "gloom" and "morbidity."

Archer had advised Murray not to let Barker produce the play. It was not a "complete and independent work like the *Hippolytus*, but an epi-logue to an epic," he said.[20] But Barker wanted to do it and had his way. Shaw kept an eye on the production from a distance, and it was when the play was going into rehearsal that he told Florence Farr (in a letter of 5 March 1905, already cited) about her musical arrangements: "be very discreet about using modern fashionable discords. . . . Stick to the com-mon chord, major and minor, and avoid regular sequences & figura-tions. . . . The moment you begin to figure diminished sevenths & the like, Euripides gives way to Liszt, and the harmony becomes *instrumental* in its suggestion." In the event, at least one critic—A. B. Walkley—found the music painful and the words of the lyrics lost in the chanting and ululation.

The production had a mixed reception. Shaw was not impressed with the acting, telling Gertrude Kingston, who played Helen, that *she* was "magnificent" but that nothing else in the whole affair was really classi-cal.[21] Barker himself seems to have had mixed feelings, writing to Lady Mary Murray, Murray's wife, that they had tried their present best but "the truth is we're not big enough people for it. . . . Oh it is a big thing . . . we'll have a classic drama in our time."[22] He also hoped the play would pay its "rather costly way," and Purdom suggests that it did. In fact, as Wilson says, "The production was poor and resulted in a considerable loss of money."[23] So Archer seems to have been right after all. Wilson comments that *The Trojan Women* later came to be considered one of Murray's most powerful antiwar pieces, but in 1905, so soon after the Anglo-Boer War, this very quality may have kept audiences away.[24]

The critics were respectful on the whole except for Walkley, who com-plained at length. The play, he said, "wallows in the sufferings of captive women . . . we have one prolonged wail . . . and to be plain, we do not like it."[25] Shaw would have noted this. He would by this time have made a fair collection of critical antipathies and prejudices—all grist for his anti-the-critics mill. The time would come when he would fling it back in the critics' faces.

The impact on Shaw of Murray's translations of Euripides is well known. *Major Barbara,* which followed later that year, on 28 November 1905, was the product of considerable discussion between him and Murray. Apart from the more superficial "borrowings" that resulted— Murray as the model for Cusins, his wife as Barbara at least in part, and Murray's fabled mother-in-law, the Countess of Carlisle, as Lady Britomart—the play is so suffused with Euripides that it can be argued that *Major Barbara* is an updated version of Murray's *Bacchae.*

It was probably no accident that when *Major Barbara* went into evening performance early in 1906, its afternoon companion piece for part of its run was Murray's third Euripidean contribution to the Court, the *Electra,* which opened on 16 January for six matinees. It did not have the same impact as the earlier works, even though Florence Farr had finally been relieved of her post. The critics were respectful, however, as they felt themselves bound to be. The play was a classic after all, and this one, although tragic, did not wring critical withers quite as wrenchingly as its predecessor had done. Shaw told Murray, "The play is immense! I feel we must do that sort of thing again and now. But there are parts of it that go beyond acting: acting is only possible half-way up the mountain: at the top they should efface themselves and utter the lines."[26]

Euripides and Shaw were the high points of the Court seasons. The connection did not go entirely unnoticed. One critic, Norman Bentwich, commented shrewdly on the one hand, with extreme prejudice on the other:

> It is remarkable that at the same theatre there should be played during one fortnight a tragedy by Euripides, and during the next a play by Bernard Shaw. For they represent the extreme species of the dramatic genus, and the pleasures they afford are radically different. Euripides exhibits drama in its more elemental form, and it is as true now, after the lapse of two thousand years, as it was when Aristotle said it—that he is the most tragic of all the poets. Bernard Shaw, on the other hand, presents drama in its most disintegrated condition, converted, not to say perverted, to an intellectual entertainment, become a peg on which to hang epigrams and startling half-truths, proclaimed openly as a discussion on social philosophy and political follies.[27]

Bentwich might have considered his comment more carefully had he realized the extent to which Shaw had absorbed Euripides-Murray by this time.

The ending of the seasons at the Court did not end Murray's involvement with the theater or his association with Shaw. Shaw does not seem to have involved himself in the Vedrenne-Barker production of the *Medea* at the Savoy in October. At this time, following the banning of Barker's new play *Waste,* a strong anticensorship campaign was launched. Shaw's role in this has been fully and frequently described; Murray's role, an important one since his name carried considerable weight as a scholar and man of letters, was not as spectacular, but it deserves recognition, not least because it extended to his strenuously defending *The Shewing-up of Blanco Posnet,* when plans to perform this play in the Abbey Theatre, Dublin, brought threats of official sanction against the theater. Murray wrote to the wrong person, the Colonial Secretary, under the impression that he had something to do with Irish affairs, but Shaw was grateful all the same, assuring him that he had been a great help.[28]

Shaw's "contribution" to Murray's translation of Sophocles' *Oedipus Tyrannus* will be found in *Collected Letters 1911–1925.* Dan H. Laurence quotes a few lines from Murray's reply: "Many thanks for your advice and your sketch of the plot of Oedipus. We all found it difficult to read without tears, and we admired the accuracy of your memory."[29] Shaw's letter not only is extremely amusing but also testifies to the bond between him and Murray, founded in congeniality of spirit and strengthened during those years at the Court.

St. John Hankin (1869–1909) was the first of the up-and-coming English playwrights to be presented at the Court. His *Two Mr Wetherbys* was put on by the Stage Society in 1903, but *The Return of the Prodigal* made it apparent that the new indigenous drama might not have only Shaw to depend on.

The play was presented on the afternoon of 16 September 1905, and almost with one voice the critics cried out, "Shaw!" One critic exclaimed, "Pshaw!" Grein enthused, "At last there is another Richmond in the field. Mr St John Hankin has established his claim to rank in intellectual force with George Bernard Shaw."[30] Walkley mildly suggested that Hankin's prodigal, Eustace Jackson, had read the works of Mr Bernard Shaw,[31] and Beerbohm said, "Mr Hankin has been much likened by the critics to Mr Bernard Shaw. It is quite true that Mr Hankin has come—what young playwright, nowadays, would fail to come—somewhat under Mr Shaw's influence. But the likeness of Mr Hankin's play to what Mr Shaw would have made of it is a merely technical and superficial likeness."[32]

Apart from the Shaw likenesses, the critics saw a good deal to commend. Archer said, "I am delighted at the warm reception of the comedy by the critics in general. Ten, or even five, years ago such a piece would have been received with bewilderment, and probably with contumely. Clearly we are advancing in intelligence."[33]

Hankin himself—he was a moody, difficult man, prone to acute depression, and he committed suicide in 1909—had no such sanguinary notions. Reviewing Shaw's *Dramatic Opinions and Essays* in 1907, he offered a gloomy diagnosis and prognosis of English drama. Unlike the other arts, it was not moving forward; "At times, of course, some movement seems to be taking place. There is supposed to be one going on at Sloane Square [the Court Theatre] just now. But that is a mere ripple on the surface of contemporary drama. . . . It will soon die away, and the English theatre, which seemed to be stirring for a moment uneasily in its sleep, will turn over and doze off again."[34] He had scant faith in his ability and in that of his fellow dramatists at the Court, and yet at least two of the eight plays he wrote, *The Cassilis Engagement* and *The Last of the De Mullins*, are accomplished works. Vedrenne and Barker's decision not to produce *The Cassilis Engagement* at the Court but instead to revive *The Return of the Prodigal* in 1907 aroused a protest from Shaw (in a letter to Vedrenne) that indicates how essentially un-Shavian Hankin was:

> I am greatly depressed by this Prodigal business, because it shows that you neither of you understand [*sic*] what has made the Court possible. I have given you a series of first-rate music hall entertainments, thinly disguised as plays, but really offering the public a unique string of turns by comics and serio-comics of every popular type. . . . Make no error, VD; that is the jam that has carried the propaganda-pill down. . . . Now consider the Prodigal from this point of view. It has an idea in it, no doubt. But it has only one part in it, and that not a very entertaining one. No heroine, a father who is only a butt, nobody except Matthews whom one remembers. Compare Cassilis. It also has an idea; but it has lots of turns to back the idea up. . . . Here is value for everyone's money, and the play Hankin's best so far.[35]

Shaw was right. *The Return of the Prodigal*, when brought back on 29 April 1907, was a complete failure. It limped through a little over one of its allotted four weeks, losing money all the way, and was then taken off.

Six months before, on 23 October 1906, Hankin's second play, *The Charity that Began at Home*, was put on. The critics thought it very decidedly Hankin's best play to date (Archer),[36] rather a loose go-as-you-please play but bearable (Walkley),[37] and "pretentious drivel" (*The Observer*).[38] The public decided to withhold its support, and the production lost heavily. Shaw does not seem to have involved himself with this production, but its failure would have fueled his attack on Vedrenne and Barker for reviving *The Return of the Prodigal*.

Barker did not use Hankin again although his two later plays, *The Cassilis Engagement* and *The Last of the De Mullins*, were available when the management moved to the Savoy. It seems that Barker did not get along with Hankin. Shaw appears to have liked him; he certainly thought very highly of *Cassilis* and *De Mullins*. It was of these rather than their forerunners that he was thinking when he issued his statement to the press following Hankin's death:

> Hankin's death is a public calamity. He was a most gifted writer of high comedy of the kind that is a stirring and important criticism of life. . . . He suffered a good deal, as we all have to suffer, from stupid and ignorant criticism; but even the critics who were not stupid quarrelled with his style, which was thought thin, because it was not their style. As a matter of fact, the thinness was a quality, not a defect.
>
> In his recent letters to me there was nothing that prepared me in the very least for the shock of his death. . . . I very deeply regret it, not only on personal grounds but on public ones.[39]

The years have not endorsed this view, which is not to say that Hankin's last two plays would fail if any endowed theater were to produce them today. Shaw was right: Hankin was not "thin"; his anti-establishment views and his sardonic depiction of Victorian-Edwardian middle-class attitudes, conveyed in dialogue that was always elegant and poised, were pointed and effective. His contribution to the new drama may have been limited, but it was real for all that.

He may have influenced Shaw in one or two respects. One that comes to mind is his depiction in *The Return of the Prodigal* of the unmarried daughter fated to spend her days in the parental home that becomes her prison. This situation became something of a cliché in the dramatic literature of the time. Barker introduced it into *The Madras House*, Shaw into *Misalliance*. Hankin's version is the first and among the best.

The third of the more important of the twenty-nine percenters was Harley Granville Barker (1877–1946), whose association with Shaw began in 1900 when Barker played Marchbanks in the Stage Society's production of *Candida*. Shaw discovered Barker, and Barker discovered Shaw. "We clicked so well together," Shaw was sadly to remember forty-six years later when Barker died.[40] More than "clicking," each found in the other the will to serve the new drama and the determination to make it succeed.

Shaw, old enough to be Barker's father and already the author of ten plays, took the lead. If Archer gave Barker his goal, the formation of a national theater, Shaw in the early years directed and shaped this mission. It is doubtful whether Barker's genius would have crystallized as it did had Shaw not done his Shavian thing by him, which is to say exhorted, chided, and bullied him, adding large dollops of affection and other tokens of regard. "By the way," Shaw said to Ellen Terry, "that young man is a genius—a cold-hearted Italian devil, but a noble soul all the same."[41]

Guided as he was by Shaw, Barker remained very much his own man as a playwright. This emerges in *The Marrying of Ann Leete*, which is so unShavian as almost to be seen, technically, if not in its "modernity" of outlook, as an exercise in anti-Shavian dramaturgy. Where Shaw goes for vigor, directness, and vivid definition, Barker goes for nuance, ellipsis, and impression. Despite these differences, Shaw recognized a fine talent and described *Ann Leete* as "really an exquisite play,"[42] but other critics did not agree. As Walkley said, "It must be difficult to write a play in four acts . . . and throughout them all to keep your audience blankly ignorant of the meaning of it."[43] Even if Shaw was encouraging, he may well have told Barker that clarity was a prerequisite of effective theater. Twenty years later he did say as much when Barker sent him the text of *The Secret Life*. Barker's response points to what was innate in him as a playwright: "What you say about clarity . . . is of course the soundest sense. . . . I *may* yet arrive at clarity but I must work through my Ann Leete vein to do it, for that prevails in me."[44]

Barker's next play, *The Voysey Inheritance*, was the fifth production of the second season at the Court, opening for the usual series of matinees on 7 November 1905. Archer withdrew his previous criticism of Barker's efforts and years later was able to look back on that Tuesday afternoon and claim that it represented a red-letter day for him, and a most noteworthy date for modern drama. Beerbohm admitted that he had often inveighed against the plays written by "mimes," but that *Voysey* obliged him to bow, corrected. "May [Barker's] very bright intellect never grow dim. I may have to suggest anon that he is too purely intellectual to be perfect. For the present, though, let there be nothing but praise."[45] Walkley grumbled. Since he invariably grumbled after going to the Court one may be inclined to dismiss him, but the basis of his complaint on this occasion is worth citing:

> Yes, decidedly the Court is our "Shavian" theatre. Mr Shaw's own plays are shown there nightly, and in the afternoons they give new plays by the younger men, all different in essentials, but alike in the one particular that there clings to them a faint aroma—observe that we resist the temptations of saying the taint—of Mr Shaw. . . . Mr St John Hankin's *Return of the Prodigal* had been delicately scented with a Shaw *sachet*, and now *The Voysey Inheritance* of Mr Granville Barker gratifies your nostrils with *triple ex-*

trait de Shaw. You recognise the subtle perfume whenever the personages fall to giving solemnly nonsensical or nonsensically solemn explanations of life, morality, and one another. Mr Barker has a story to tell, an interesting story in itself. . . . But at periodical intervals, overcome by the atmosphere of the Court Theatre, he feels compelled to offer a gloss, a Shavian gloss, on the facts. Then all is confusion, "new" morality, Nietzschean "transvaluation," and goodness knows what.[46]

How Shavian is *The Voysey Inheritance?* Barker would have liked at least three of his associates to comment on the play: Archer, Murray, and Shaw. Archer refused because he had come to despair of getting Barker away from the "Shawesque" in his writing.[47] Murray's response (he appears to have attended a rehearsal) was positive: "the root situation . . . is very good indeed . . . the main characters and construction good. . . . I see what you mean about a lack of driving power. . . . But I think that came from uncertainty . . . about the main problem. If you get that clear—to speak roughly, that the old man is wrong and a failure and Edward right—I think you will find that the driving power is mostly achieved."[48] We do not know what Shaw said or wrote,[49] but his letter to Vedrenne already cited (26 February 1907) about Hankin's *Return of the Prodigal* indicates what he approved of in *Voysey:* its series of "turns": the "Booth turn, the Clarence turn, the wicked solicitor and the comic old deaf woman that consoled the house for the super drama." He may have advised Barker about the importance of such "turns," or Barker may have taken his cue from *John Bull's Other Island, Man and Superman, You Never Can Tell,* and other "series of music hall entertainments" already staged at the Court. In addition, Shaw would have satisfied himself that Barker had worked through his *Ann Leete* vein to achieve a sufficiency of explicitness, which went with the "driving power" that Murray mentioned. But he would not have tried to get Barker to rewrite the play in any Shavian way. This was not how he worked. He once remarked that literature was one of those things in which no man could help another,[50] by which he meant that no second party could interfere in the intensely personal act of literary creation. Generous as he could be with his opinions and advice, he would not have tried to undermine the governing concepts of Barker's play.

Barker's play actually influenced Shaw, first by way of a technical innovation. The dining room table that dominates the set of Acts II, III, and V of *The Voysey Inheritance* impressed Shaw as a fine stroke of naturalism. "I defy you"—he wrote to Archer—"to deny that the staging of The Voysey Inheritance produced much more illusion than the staging of The Second Mrs Tanqueray." After this he was easily persuaded to bring

Fig. 3.   The 1988 Shaw Festival Theatre production of Harley Granville
Barker's 1905 play *The Voysey Inheritance* at Niagara-on-the-Lake, directed by
Neil Munro. Photograph by David Cooper. Reproduced by permission of The
Shaw Festival Theatre.

a "huge motor car" onto the set of Act II of *Man and Superman* when the
play was brought back to the Court in 1907.[51] Not long afterward he
copied Barker shamelessly in having a large table on the set of *Getting
Married.* And twenty years later similar Barkeresque tables (two of them)
would serve as the battlefield across which Prime Minister Proteus and
his Cabinet would pitch their ultimatums against King Magnus. As for
another, more dynamic influence, we have Lillah McCarthy's word for
the way Shaw listened to Barker reading *The Madras House,* grinning all
the time, and then went away to write *Misalliance.*[52]

As for the "aroma" the play exuded at the time, certain Shavian influences could be identified, most conspicuously that it is a "discussion
drama" in which the issues are, as Beerbohm observed, intellectualized
rather than lived through in the emotions. Shaw had already given the
Court several stiff doses of discussion and intellectual acrobatics, and the
heftiest work in these respects, *Major Barbara,* was in rehearsal when

Voysey opened. It would have been difficult, perhaps impossible, for any young playwright trying to break into the new drama to avoid a touch of Shaw. This admitted, one has to see *The Voysey Inheritance* as the work of an independent and original mind. Its resonances—autobiographical, Victorian-domestic, social, and allegorical, the idealistic "new age" confronting and repudiating the corrupt legacy of the old—achieve Barker's ideal of a "symphonic effect" most satisfyingly. Barker would come to prefer *The Madras House,* and it is indeed a richly orchestrated work, but the past eighty years have tended not to support this view. As Archer said, *Voysey* is one of the most important plays of the time, and Shaw would have been the first to agree.

It was a success at the Court and was brought into the evening bill for four weeks in February 1906, the first play by someone other than Shaw to be elevated in this way. It has been revived regularly since then, most recently by the British National Theatre in 1989, when it played to intently appreciative audiences.

The banning of Barker's next play, *Waste,* in 1907 saw Shaw leaping to the defense of the play and enlarging on the issue to attack stage censorship and the untenable principles on which it was based. One statement, which appeared in *The Nation,* points to the high regard in which he held Barker. Censorship, he argued, was based on the preservation of certain taboos, and the three great taboos on the question of sex were that one must never mention an illegal obstetric operation, or incest, or venereal disease. He turned to *Waste* and asked his readers to consider the position in which Barker found himself as a result of the ban. The censor was licensing plays that were so abominable that editors would not allow Shaw to describe them in their papers. "The inevitable conclusion drawn by the man in the street is that if Mr Barker has gone beyond the tolerance that licensed these indescribable and unmentionable plays, he must have produced something quite hideously filthy." Shaw then tells the story of *Waste,* "a play about the disestablishment of the Church." He praises Barker for the "amusing and suggestive political situation" he has devised and his "real political insight and first-hand knowledge of our political personnel." But the protagonist's scheme fails because, succumbing to "a private indiscretion," he becomes the father of an unborn child of a married woman who secures an abortion and dies as a consequence. The protagonist's career collapses in ruins. Shaw points out that the censor's objection is not to the sexual indiscretion, or the adultery, or the illegitimate child, since many licensed plays have such incidents:

> It is the illegal operation that is taboo. Take Waste, and degrade its fastidiously fine style into the basest bar-loafer's slang; smudge out its high intellectual interest into the most sickeningly lascivi-

ous sentimentality; introduce incidents which could not be described in these columns; but suppress the illegal operation. Mr Redford will then license it like a lamb. That is how taboo works.[53]

Although Shaw is propagandizing as only he knew how, one may still see how well he thought of the play and the playwright. To the waste that the play depicts—the waste of a great scheme and the waste of a splendid political career—one is implicitly required to add the waste of one of the finest political plays of the century.

The banning of the play was a severe blow to Barker. He followed it with *The Madras House* in 1909 and two other plays in the 1920s, but one may wonder whether he ever recovered fully from the setback. The creativity that had gone into *The Voysey Inheritance* and *Waste,* fueled by what he and Vedrenne were achieving and fired by Shaw's encouragement and example, gradually dwindled. When the break with Shaw came, his playwriting career effectually ended. The loss to the theater of Barker's genius as a director has often been lamented; the loss to drama of his potential as a playwright may be even greater.

It was Edward Garnett who suggested to Galsworthy (1867–1933) that he write a play for Barker and Vedrenne, but Galsworthy, having just completed *The Man of Property,* the novel which was to make him famous, was not drawn to the idea. He saw himself as a novelist. There may have been another reason: the Court management was nothing if not pro-Shaw, and he disliked Shaw's plays intensely. He wrote to Garnett when the Shaw boom was at its height that he had had a letter from Conrad. "Shaw seems to have endorsed his [Conrad's] play; but that little play has more *drama* in it than any or all of Shaw's own—*he* is not a *dramatist.*"[54] The dislike was not personal. He and his wife lunched with the Shaws. "G.B.S. very garrulous and affable. As a man I greatly prefer him to the author of his works and speeches, he has a good face."[55]

If the prejudice was there, he overcame it to begin writing *The Cigarette Box,* later changed to *The Silver Box,* in January 1906. He completed it in six weeks and sent it to Barker, who received it on a Saturday. He and Shaw read it on Sunday. On Monday, Barker let Galsworthy know that they had accepted the play for production. Vedrenne, for his part, would always remember with awe the young man who confessed to him that he had tried to write a play once before but, finding it unsatisfactory, had destroyed it.[56] In Vedrenne's world playwrights did not find their plays unsatisfactory, much less destroy them.

Garnett was at hand with suggestions. He commented on the presence of a thesis in the play. Galsworthy responded, "As to the thesis—this I must keep, or start a fresh play which I'm not inclined to do. Aesthetically you're right, but I want to be played."[57] One should not infer from this that Galsworthy was subordinating aesthetic principles in order to "be played." His reputation as an author has shrunk since his death, but not his reputation for artistic integrity. He was true to the credo throughout his life that "the writer who steadily goes his own way, and never writes to fulfil the demands of public, publisher, or editor, is the writer who comes off best in the end."[58] He developed this idea in an article in *The Fortnightly Review,* asserting, " 'THE MORAL' is the keynote of all drama. That is to say, a drama must be shaped so as to have a spine of meaning." The average modern play had no such moral, but rather a distorted moral that had "infected its creators, actors, audience, critics; too often turned it from a picture into a caricature."[59] He was perhaps more Shavian in outlook, particularly in his detestation of popular drama, than he would have cared to admit, and as far as *The Silver Box* was concerned, the "thesis" (or "moral") would certainly have attracted Shaw and Barker, the "spine of meaning" of the play being a critique of class privilege.

He involved himself closely with the production, writing to Barker about the staging, the casting, and sundry "keynote" aspects of characterization. He told Garnett, "I've been at rehearsals all day. . . . On the whole, not quite so bad as I expected, but bad enough. None of one's personal conceptions quite realised—naturally. I met Shaw, who told me he'd read the play and thought it 'very fine.' Hm!"[60]

The Silver Box opened for a run of eight matinees on 25 September 1906 and was an immediate success. Galsworthy's reaction was modest. "The play seems to have struck a good many people . . . the odd thing is I can't tell in the least what it's like."[61] The critics were impressed. They spoke at length about the "stern realism" of the piece. Grein saw Galsworthy as a kinsman of Barker; Archer saw him as like Hauptmann; Walkley heaved a lengthy sigh of relief that Galsworthy was not another would-be Shaw. Generally there was readiness to acknowledge the arrival of a major new talent.

The play came into the evening bill for a three-week run in April 1907, and Shaw criticized Barker and Vedrenne at length for the quality of the production (for poor casting, mainly), which was "disgraceful in the highest degree to the theatre."[62] One may infer from this that Barker was not, in Shaw's opinion, putting into the play what the play deserved. Not long afterward, he publicly complimented Galsworthy, saying that *The Silver Box* brought onto the stage penetrating social criticism and "that charm of wonderfully fastidious and restrained art that makes me blush for the comparative blatancy of my own plays."[63]

Galsworthy soon fulfilled his promise. *Joy,* his next play, presented at the Savoy under Vedrenne and Barker, was a failure, as it deserved to be, but *Strife*, directed by Barker, soon followed. Shaw commented that the men's meeting was handled "unskilfully and without knowledge of mob oratory (give me Brutus and Mark Antony) but Galsworthy earns the right to err to that extent. The play came out very solid and absorbing, and was an important event in stage history. . . ."[64] *Justice*, a year later, also directed by Barker, was presented in repertory with Shaw's *Misalliance* and Barker's *Madras House*. Galsworthy stole the thunder, Barker had a mixed reception, and Shaw got the boos and hisses. As far as Edwardian England was concerned, there was another star in the firmament of the renascent drama, and there were times when it shone more brightly than Shaw's.

John Masefield (1878–1967) came to the Court via *Captain Brassbound's Conversion*. Barker decided to introduce some sea chanties into the second act, and quite by chance Masefield, then a young seaman, came to Barker's office at the theater and mentioned that he had been making a hobby of composing sea-songs. In due course Masefield's chanties enlivened the production of *Captain Brassbound's Conversion*. Within a few months he had written and submitted his first play, *The Campden Wonder*, which Barker and Shaw promptly accepted.

It was presented on January 1907 for eight matinees in a double bill,[65] and the critics condemned it out of hand. "Horror for horror's sake" was Beerbohm's judgment (he also wrote a cruel parody of Masefield's style);[66] "gratuitous distress of mind and nerves," said Walkley in his usual magisterial way;[67] "Mr Masefield's very horrible little interlude," said *The Evening Standard*.[68] It was the gloom and morbidity theme all over again, with interest.

Shaw attributed the failure to the pairing of two incompatible plays. A week after the opening he wrote to Vedrenne,

> The Camden [*sic*] Wonder is an ideal Guignol item, and will be safe if it is rightly placed. It should never have been put on after The Reformer: that bill, believe me, was a mistake all through. The Reformer has no business at the Court at all . . . and it killed the Wonder, which is a magnificent play, and only needs . . . a proper position in a Guignol program to bowl out the critics and be the talk of the town.
>
> Meanwhile, talk as big as you can on every occasion about the Camden Wonder. We must have no failures especially with our big things. That play has magnificent artistic qualities and its lines haunt one symphonically.[69]

Barker felt the same way and rebuked Archer for his adverse review:

> Archer, I blush for you! . . . for the man who can jump on the
> Campden Wonder which has in it the beginnings & more than the
> beginnings of good English drama of the soil, & can blame it & me
> (God help him) for its tautology, which is quite the most character-
> istic thing of West Country speech . . . and not know he is in the
> presence of the real thing, for that man—well I have just sent my
> dresser for three penny-worth of nitro-glycerine![70]

The pounding the critics meted out might well have put an end to
Masefield's career as a playwright (which became a considerable one)
had it not been for the support he received from Barker and Shaw.
Barker's support extended to producing Masefield's next play, *The Tragedy of Nan,* in 1909, the success of which more than justified the faith he
had shown in Masefield at the Court. Shaw's support was more immediate. It came out in the course of a trenchant attack on the critics, delivered on 7 July 1907 at the complimentary dinner for Vedrenne and
Barker that marked the end of the seasons at the Court. He invited his
audience to consider first-night notices of new productions:

> There you will find a chronicle of failure, a sulky protest against
> this new and troublesome sort of entertainment that calls for
> knowledge and thought instead of for the usual *clichés.* Take for
> example the fate of Mr Masefield. Mr Masefield's *Campden Wonder*
> is the greatest work of its kind that has been produced in an
> English theatre within the recollection . . . of any living critic. It
> has that great English literary magic of a ceaseless music of
> speech—of haunting repetitions that play upon the tragic themes
> and burn themselves into the imagination. Its subject is one of
> those perfect simplicities that only a master of drama thinks of.
> Greater hate hath no man than this, that he lay down his life to
> kill his enemy: that is the theme of the *Campden Wonder;* and a
> wonder it is—of literary and dramatic art. And what had the
> press to say?

Shaw then told his audience what the press had had to say, and he did
not mince his words.[71]

There was a sequel to this, a letter to Shaw from Masefield, in which he
explained that he had had to leave the dinner early and so had missed
Shaw's speech, but that he had read and heard about it:

> I will not thank you, because the praise of a great writer is beyond
> thanks: but I should like to tell you how very deeply I have felt

your sympathy. My play did not succeed, and I have felt its failure keenly, not on my account but because of Barker. It was bitter to me to think that my work should have brought him all that abuse as well as a heavy money loss. You will know how very greatly you helped me in the weeks of bitterness, by something you said to Yeats about me. Now that the bitterness is forgotten you give me encouragement to begin again. I am proud that the head of my art should have liked any of my work; but what I feel most deeply is that you, who now stand where the critics cannot hurt you, should yet think of a beginner's feelings, and go out of your way to give him confidence & a hearing.[72]

The foregoing reflects Shaw in all his dealings with his younger contemporaries. The presiding genius of the Court was Barker, but Shaw was a constant and inspirational presence. He labored mightily and disinterestedly to see the talent of others acknowledged, their work produced on stage, their merit publicly recognized. The triumph of the Court was mainly his; the legend of the Court is his and that of the handful of aspirant English playwrights who comprise the kernel of the forgotten twenty-nine percent.

Notes

1. Michael Orme, *J. T. Grein: The Story of a Pioneer, 1862–1936* (London: Murray, 1936), p. 76.

2. *Bernard Shaw: Collected Letters, 1898–1910*, ed. Dan H. Laurence (London: Reinhardt, 1972), pp. 827–28.

3. H. G. Wells, *Experiment in Autobiography* (London: Gollancz & Cresset, 1966), pp. 621–22.

4. See *The Collected Letters of Joseph Conrad*, ed. Frederick R. Karl and Laurence Davis (Cambridge: Cambridge University Press, 1988), 16 February to 6 October 1905.

5. Laurence Housman, *The Unexpected Years* (London: Cape, 1937), p. 219.

6. Shaw, prefatory note to *Major Barbara*. He is referring specifically to the *Bacchae* here, but the tenor of his remarks about the other translations makes it quite clear that he thought highly of them all.

7. Quoted by Sybil Thorndike (in collaboration with Lewis Casson), "The Theatre and Gilbert Murray," in Gilbert Murray, *An Unfinished Autobiography*, ed. Jean Smith and Arnold Toynbee (London: Allen & Unwin, 1960), p. 15.

8. Duncan Wilson, *Gilbert Murray O.M., 1866–1957* (Oxford: Clarendon, 1987), p. 94.

9. 23 March 1902. Quoted by Isobel Henderson, "The Teacher of Greek," in *An Unfinished Autobiography*, p. 135.

10. Wilson, *Gilbert Murray O.M.*, p. 94.

11. Ibid., p. 105.

12. From Murray's first presidential address to the Classical Association. Quoted by E. R. Dodds in *An Unfinished Autobiography*, p. 15.

13. "On Translating Greek Tragedy," in *Essays in Honour of Gilbert Murray*, ed. J.A.K. Thomson and A. J. Toynbee (London: Allen & Unwin, 1936), p. 245.

14. Ibid., p. 243.

15. Monday, January 1905. *Granville Barker and His Correspondents*, ed. Eric Salmon (Detroit: Wayne State University Press, 1986), p. 209.

16. *Collected Letters, 1898–1910*, p. 519.

17. *The World* (London), 25 October 1904.

18. *The Sunday Times* (London), 23 October 1904.

19. Wilson, *Gilbert Murray O.M.*, p. 105.

20. Quoted by C. B. Purdom, *Harley Granville Barker* (London: Rockliff, 1955), p. 35.

21. Ibid.

22. Ibid.

23. Wilson, *Gilbert Murray, O.M.*, pp. 106, 422.

24. Ibid.

25. *The Times Literary Supplement* (London), 14 April 1905.

26. Quoted by Sybil Thorndike and Lewis Casson, "The Theatre and Gilbert Murray," in *An Unfinished Autobiography*, p. 154n.

27. "Euripides in London," *The Nineteenth Century and After* (London) 56 (January–June 1906): p. 969.

28. Wilson, *Gilbert Murray O.M.*, p. 174.

29. 14 March 1911. *Bernard Shaw: Collected Letters, 1911–1925*, ed. Dan H. Laurence (London: Reinhardt, 1985), pp. 13–19.

30. *The Sunday Times* (London), 1 October 1905.

31. *The Times Literary Supplement* (London), 29 September 1905.

32. *The Saturday Review* (London), 7 October 1905.

33. *The World* (London), 3 October 1905.

34. *The Fortnightly Review* (London) 81 (January–June 1907): 1061.

35. 26 February 1907. Enthoven Collection, Victoria and Albert Museum, London.

36. *The Tribune* (London), 24 October 1906.

37. *The Times Literary Supplement* (London), 26 October 1906.

38. *The Observer*, 28 October 1906.

39. *Collected Letters, 1898–1910*, pp. 847–48.

40. *The Times Literary Supplement* (London), 7 September 1946.

41. 25 November 1905. *Ellen Terry and Bernard Shaw: A Correspondence*, ed. Christopher St. John (London: Reinhardt & Evans, 1949), p. 389.

42. Purdom, *Harley Granville Barker*, p. 15.

43. *The Times* (London), 23 January 1902.

44. 8 April 1922. *Granville Barker and His Correspondents*, p. 158.

45. *The Saturday Review* (London), 11 November 1905.

46. *The Times Literary Supplement* (London), 12 November 1905.

47. *The World* (London), 14 November 1905. Archer's perception of the "Shawesque" in Barker's early plays is puzzling, to say the least.

48. 11 August 1905. *Granville Barker and His Correspondents*, p. 223.

49. Shaw's letters to Barker about Barker's plays—it is inconceivable that he would not have written to him about them—do not appear to have survived. One is therefore obliged to infer rather than adduce the extent and kind of encouragement that Shaw gave Barker.

50. To McNulty, 29 June 1908. *Collected Letters, 1898–1910*, p. 790.

51. C. 20–24 May 1907. *Collected Letters, 1898–1910*, p. 686.

52. Purdom, *Harley Granville Barker*, pp. 102–3.

53. *The Nation* (London), 16 November 1907.

54. 13 July 1905. *Letters from John Galsworthy 1900–1932*, ed. Edward Garnett (London: Cape, 1934), p. 96.

55. 25 January 1907. Ibid., p. 131.

56. *The Daily Telegraph*, 14 February 1930.

57. 10 March 1906. *Letters from John Galsworthy*, p. 116.

58. Quoted in H. V. Marrott, *The Life and Letters of John Galsworthy* (London: Heinemann, 1936), p. 137.

59. "Some Platitudes Concerning Drama," *The Fortnightly Review* (London), December 1909.

60. Thursday, September 1906. *Letters from John Galsworthy*, p. 121.

61. Marrott, *Life and Letters*, p. 196.

62. 21 April 1907. *Bernard Shaw's Letters to Granville Barker*, ed. C. B. Purdom (London: Phoenix House, 1956), p. 81.

63. 7 July 1907, at the complimentary dinner for Vedrenne and Barker in replying to the toast, "The Authors of the Court Theatre." Desmond MacCarthy, *The Court Theatre 1904–1907*, ed. Stanley Weintraub (Coral Gables, Fla.: University of Miami Press, 1966), p. 171.

64. 9 March 1909. *Shaw's Letters to Barker*, p. 150.

65. Its companion piece was Cyril Harcourt's *The Reformer*, an utterly frivolous, forgettable play and a reminder that not all Vedrenne and Barker's twenty-nine percenters were well chosen.

66. *The Saturday Review* (London), 12 January 1907.

67. *The Times Literary Supplement* (London), 11 January 1907.

68. 9 January 1907.

69. 22 January 1907. Enthoven Collection, Victoria and Albert Museum, London.

70. *Granville Barker and His Correspondents*, p. 52.

71. MacCarthy, *The Court Theatre*, p. 172.

72. 10 July 1907. The Bernard Shaw Papers, British Museum.

T. F. Evans

ARNOLD BENNETT AND SHAW: "YOU WILL NOT TAKE THE THEATRE SERIOUSLY ENOUGH"

For more than thirty years at the beginning of the century, Arnold Bennett was one of the most prolific, successful, and prominent writers in England. He was born in 1867, and after a false start preparing to become a solicitor, he drifted into journalism; regular writing followed. His first published book, the novel *A Man from the North,* appeared in 1898. By his death in 1931, he had written more than fifty novels, many other books including essays and literary criticism, and masses of articles and other journalism. He kept journals that give a detailed account of his life, he wrote letters, and he composed at least twenty plays.

Bennett's place as a novelist is an honorable one. As one chronicler of the English novel, Walter Allen, has put it, "though Bennett, in three or four books, is a master, he is a minor master."[1] His greatest claim to fame may be his achievement in creating, in his best novels, the Five Towns, the fictional representation of the six pottery towns in Staffordshire—in one of which, Hanley, he was born. Although he left his birthplace at the age of twenty-one and never returned to live there, he kept it with him, as Joyce did Dublin, and it inspired him as a novelist.

As a dramatist, he reached no such distinction. A close friend, Frank Swinnerton, says in the *Dictionary of National Biography* that some of Bennett's work for the stage "brought him for a time almost unlimited theatrical popularity."[2] That time was very short. In fact, Bennett's plays do not entitle him to much more than an interesting short paragraph in any history of the English stage. By an odd coincidence, his position in this respect is very similar to that of a greater novelist, Henry James. Leon Edel remarked that "an awareness of the large incomes of playwrights such as Arthur Pinero, Henry Arthur Jones and later Oscar Wilde, made

Henry James acutely aware of the smallness of his literary income." This was when James was already a well-known writer, but Bennett was still at the beginning of his literary career when he told the actor-manager Cyril Maude that "a novelist never makes much money compared with you folks."[3] In 1921, Bennett wrote that "someone of realistic temperament ought to have advised James that to write plays with the object of making money was a hopeless enterprise. I tried it myself for several years, at the end of which I abandoned the stage for ever."[4] He explained the circumstances in which he did return for a special purpose, after which he said that he wrote plays only for his own "artistic satisfaction."

It was in a Jamesian situation that Bennett was first in the company of Bernard Shaw although it is not clear that they actually met on that occasion. The two were among the critics on the first night of James's play *Guy Domville* at the St. James's Theatre, 5 January 1895.[5] On this evening, to which James referred as "one of the most detestable incidents" of his life, Shaw was present to write a review which appeared as the second of his articles as the regular dramatic critic for the *Saturday Review,* and Bennett later reviewed the play for the magazine *Woman,* of which he was deputy editor and for which he wrote under the pen name Cecile. To complete a surprising trinity, H. G. Wells was also present, writing a dramatic criticism for the first time, for the *Pall Mall Gazette.* Unlike the other two, Wells did not become a regular dramatic critic. Bennett wrote dramatic criticism for a number of different journals for about five years, but his articles have not been collected. On this occasion, all three agreed that, despite the grace and delicacy of his dialogue at its best, James had no gift for the theater. Bennett emphasized what he thought were serious defects in the motivation of the plot, and this special concern with plot was to be a marked feature of his approach to the theater, whether in relation to his own plays or to those of other writers.

There are odd comments on Shaw and his plays to be found in Bennett's *Journal* and in his letters, but his most sustained consideration of Shaw was in an article in the *Academy* in 1902, an essay on *Three Plays for Puritans,* which had just been published in book form.[6] The main defects which he found in Shaw were the absence of the "slightest trace of emotion," and a concern with social justice that sprang merely from "an intellectual perception of it." In Bennett's view, Shaw wrote prefaces because he could not say what he wanted to say in the plays themselves and showed no hint of creative power.

> His dialogue is a continual feast. . . . But to cut it up into lengths and call it a play is simple effrontery. The dialogue is the mere exterior of a play, the part one does last, when the hard creative work is accomplished. Mr Shaw's stage-pieces may be genius; care-

ful critics have said so; but they are decidedly not drama. They might more correctly be called the Joseph's coat of a non-existent Joseph; fine raiment resembling a man until you poke it where the ribs ought to be.

It was the theoretical concern with plot or form generally that set Bennett against Shaw's plays. He did not accept that a play should be a presentation of, or treatment of, ideas, even if those ideas were shown with examination and development of character. This was not because he objected to Shaw's ideas themselves. He referred to himself as a "Socialist" frequently in the earlier part of his career, and even when his success as a writer led him to familiarity with the moneyed sections of society and when he appeared to find excessive pleasure in the satisfactions of the wealthy, he never lost entirely the traces of a Wesleyan Methodist upbringing, the memories of the humble streets of Hanley, and a contempt for many of the social values that he heard expressed in London clubs and luxury hotels.[7] From time to time, he saw Shaw plays and admired them more than the *Academy* article might suggest would be likely. Thus, on 14 February 1908 he noted in his journal that he had seen two plays by Shaw. He was "impressed by the moral power of both of them."[8] The plays were *Arms and the Man* and *Captain Brassbound's Conversion*, of which he said, "The latter is frequently dull, but GOOD, except in its melodramatic situation, which is unblushingly absurd. On the whole my opinion of Shaw is going up. The most surprising thing about his plays is that they should find a public at all. They must have immensely educated the public."

In 1911, he thought *Fanny's First Play* "poor,"[9] but in 1920 he said, "*Arms and the Man* seemed better than it did twenty-five years ago. Very fine. Shaw's title to be the modern Moliere not so rocky as I had thought. On the other hand, *Pygmalion* is on the whole poor, most of the characterisation is quite rotten, and wilfully made so for the sake of art and eloquence. The last act is foozled."[10] A little later on, things changed. In 1921, he wrote to his nephew, "Last night I had to go to Shaw's play *Heartbreak House*. 3 hours 50 minutes of the most intense tedium. I went to sleep twice, fortunately."[11]

Shaw slumped even further in Bennett's estimation during the next few years. In February 1924 he went with his partner, the actress Dorothy Cheston, to the first night of *Back to Methuselah* at the Royal Court. This was Part 1 of the play, and Bennett recorded in his journal the next day,

"House full" boards outside before the performance. I had asked for and offered to pay for seats, in order to please D., but I received an apologetic letter from the manager to say that they were really all gone. Afterwards a box was returned and Barry Jackson himself gave it to me; which, I thought, was rather graceful. The affair was a *Solemnite*. But not quite the usual form of first night. Walls of box dead black and of stone. We could see the empty orchestra, and the nakedness of Adam and Eve. Curtain going up announced by a sort of clash of a cymbal. I was very bored by the play, I could see nothing in it; neither action nor character nor a sermon nor wit. The game of finding new words played by the characters seemed silly. It was too far round to go to smoke in the interval, so we stayed in our tomb. In the second act I went to sleep and had to be wakened for fear a snore might be heard on the stage. Audience indifferent but polite. Many calls. Play began at 8.37 pm and ended at 10.15 pm. Barry Jackson said author in house but wouldn't appear till the last night. Shaw had box over us. His programme fell down at the end and was wafted into our box. D. took it away as being historical. A most depressing night.[12]

Bennett commented more briefly when he wrote to his nephew about a fortnight later. He simply said that he had gone to sleep and that "it was terrible. I think this is the general opinion." He added that he would not go to any more, by which he meant, presumably, to the other four plays in the cycle. For good measure, he said as well, "And I doubt if I shall go to *Joan of Arc;* but perhaps I shall."[13] It is not clear whether he did see *Saint Joan,* which is what he must have meant, but he noted in his journal that Beaverbrook, the wealthy newspaper proprietor, had said that it was "the greatest play I ever saw."[14] Beaverbrook is not generally regarded as a discriminating critic of the arts.

In the following year Bennett spoke most warmly of Shaw the dramatist, although he was impressed by a work that is not generally considered one of Shaw's masterpieces. This was Shaw's version of *Frau Gitta's Sühne,* the play by his German translator, Siegfried Trebitsch, to which Shaw gave the title *Jitta's Atonement.*[15] In a 1910 article Shaw had felt it necessary to defend Trebitsch against critics of the German versions of Shaw's plays. Shaw said, "It is clear to me that if his translations are not translations at all, but audacious forgeries made by a man ignorant of my language, then he must be a highly talented dramatist to achieve such success in the theatre."[16]

The words may have proved apt in reverse when, in 1921, Shaw decided to repay Trebitsch by translating a play by the German author. He chose *Frau Gitta's Sühne* and essayed an English version despite, as he alleged, not knowing a word of German. The result, *Jitta's Atonement,* was presented in New York in 1923 and at the Grand Theatre, Fulham, in the west of London on 26 January 1925. It was the latter production that Arnold Bennett saw and of which he wrote in his journal on 31 January,

> This play made a very deep impression upon me. Shaw has taken an obviously conventional and machine-made play of Trebitsch's, left the first act in all its conventional competence, "situation," and dullness, and then in the 2nd and 3rd Acts treated the development of the theme realistically and wittily. The effect is simply electrical. . . . The mere idea of starting on a purely conventional 1st Act and then guying it with realism and fun, shows genius. In the absence of a copy of the original German text of the play, it is impossible to make extensive comment on Shaw's treatment.[17]

What was said, however, by both Shaw and Trebitsch does give some indication of Shaw's approach. Shaw maintained that he had "rescued Gitta from the hopeless gloom and despair in which you plunged her deeper and deeper all through the play. . . . life is not like that here, whatever it may be in Austria."[18] There is a note of surprise in Trebitsch's letter of reply, but he acknowledged, "Your version is as much better than mine as you are the greater poet of us two. . . . The III Akt is in your version almost a comedy! . . . If this play, where I miss your name as the adapter[']s one[,] will reach the English-American footlights I shall owe it to your genious [sic]."[19]

Dorothy Cheston Bennett was very impressed with the play and saw herself in the role of Gitta. Various difficulties conspired to frustrate plans for a further production. Among them was the report given to Shaw by an informant (not named) that Dorothy Cheston Bennett could not act. The theater required was not available, and there were casting difficulties. The result was that *Jitta's Atonement* sank, if not entirely without trace, then with no great record of actual production. It was done at the small Arts Theatre in London in 1930 and in one or two repertory theaters, but, while it is included in the collected editions of Shaw's plays, it has rarely been treated entirely seriously as his.

It is hard to see why Bennett was so impressed with the play. Shaw himself told his French translator Augustin Hamon in a letter of 13 June 1922 that "there is hardly a speech in my version which corresponds word for word with the original text,"[20] and, while working on the translation, he had told Trebitsch in 1921, "I have not done justice to your poetry and your love of intense unhappiness, which convinces me that you have never been really unhappy in your life."[21] Bennett found genius in the construction of the play: "Some of the most brilliant work, some tender, some brutal, and lots of the most side-splitting fun that Shaw ever did—and he is now approaching seventy, I suppose." He ended his note by saying, "At this moment Shaw is packing the big Regent Theatre with *Saint Joan.* And a repertory theatre begins a series of twelve of his plays at the Chelsea Palace next week. At this rate Shaw will soon be nearly as popular in London as he is in Berlin and Vienna."[22] It could be that what appealed to Bennett especially was the comparative absence of the lengthy discussion of ideas characteristic of the majority of Shaw's plays. Bennett placed far more weight on a plot than Shaw ever did, and the development of the story in *Jitta's Atonement* by gradual disclosure may have retained his attention as a more customary Shavian development of characters and argument and the conflict of ideas would not have.

Shaw and Bennett knew each other and were on good terms without ever becoming intimate friends. It is strange that they do not seem to have come into closer contact in the early years of the century. One of the features of the famous Court Theatre seasons from 1904 to 1907 was the attempt made to interest writers who had established themselves in other forms to turn to drama. Thus, Galsworthy and Masefield had plays presented, and it would not have been surprising if Bennett, too, had become a playwright at this time. In fact, the first substantial contact between Shaw and Bennett was not in the strictly literary field. At the beginning of the war in 1914, Shaw was unable to take the conventional British view that all evil was on the German side. He wrote the pamphlet *Common Sense About the War,* in which, with his customary blend of a superficial lightheartedness and a fundamental seriousness, he declared that the Junkerism of the British rulers (Sir Edward Grey, the Foreign Secretary, in particular) was wholly as evil and as responsible for the war as was the German variety.[23] This caused him to lose friends and to be expelled from the Dramatists' Club. Bennett was among those who, in difficult circumstances, managed to keep some kind of balance. Shaw knew that Bennett was far from being the wildest type of jingo, and he wrote to Hall Caine, "You and I and Arnold Bennett will have to save this war."[24] Bennett, however, could not ally himself with Shaw, and he explained his position to his literary agent, J. B. Pinker, on 15 November 1914:

> I shall be sending you tomorrow a copy of an article dealing drastically with the bad parts of Shaw's manifesto on the war, published yesterday. About two-thirds of Shaw's statement is strictly first-class, and indeed quite unequalled. Most of the rest is absurd, and may do some harm. I should therefore particularly like my article to appear in some newspapers in the United States, preferably New York, whether I am paid for it or not. It will appear in the *Daily News* on Thursday.[25]

The fact that Shaw's *Common Sense* is referred to very briefly in Bennett's *Journals* and his *Letters* may mean that either he or his editors felt it would be too disturbing to dwell on the subject, or the comparative silence could be a consequence of Bennett's becoming very quickly involved in various kinds of war work.[26] Thus, it is not recorded what result, if any, came from a suggestion endorsed by Shaw that Bennett should prepare a shorter version of *Common Sense About the War.* At the end of one of their disagreements, Shaw teased Bennett by inviting him to "reserve his fine old Staffordshire loathing for my intellectual nimbleness until the war is over,"[27] and Bennett, after further differences of opinion, noted in his journal that "the fundamental decency and kindliness of Shaw was evident throughout."[28]

Shaw and Bennett came into contact again to a limited extent because both were connected with the *New Statesman.* Shaw had helped found the journal and continued to contribute, sometimes to the embarrassment of the editor and fellow directors. Bennett became a director in early 1915. However, it was not in a political controversy but in a more peaceful literary one that Shaw and Bennett found themselves once more on opposite sides. The story is told by Shaw in an article reprinted in his *Pen Portraits and Reviews.*[29] As is so often the case, it is hard to tell where exactly in his cheek he has lodged his tongue, but, as in his political writing, the flippancy on the surface does not conceal the underlying seriousness. He had been sent a book to review for the *Nation.* The book was *The Author's Craft* by Arnold Bennett.[30] Shaw reflected that "Mr Bennett talks shop and debits harmless tosh about technique for the entertainment of literary amateurs in a very agreeable and suggestive manner, as he has every right to do, being so distinguished a master of the craft." Nevertheless, contended Shaw, he could not understand why he had been asked to review the book when the payment for it would have been most welcome to a young and unestablished writer. Then he saw the reason. Bennett contended that "a play is easier to write than a novel."[31]

This set Shaw going. He did not allude to Bennett's previous writings on the subject. He could have mentioned the passages on the writing of plays in *How to Become an Author,* which Bennett had published in 1903. In that book, subtitled "A Practical Guide," Bennett was not so forthright in his references to the work of the dramatist as he was in the later book, but he laid about him fairly vigorously. Thus, he declared that no living playwright, had he had a talent for fiction, would have reached beyond the second or third rank. "Our best plays" he said, "as works of art, are strikingly inferior to our best novels." The dramatist was always limited in the full and free exercise of his art by crippling restrictions, such as those of the "hours of dinner and of suburban trains." (In this phrase,

Bennett, consciously or otherwise, echoes the aesthete Gabriel Nash, who is the alter ego of his creator Henry James in the 1890 novel about the theater, *The Tragic Muse*.) Among the things needed for a successful play were, Bennett contended, "at least one character of great wealth, and a few titled characters if possible," and finally, "a happy ending."[32]

Bennett may not have been entirely serious here, but what Shaw was pleased to call his "novelist's bluff" on the subject of the comparative length of novels and plays does seem to have been a serious comment. Shaw did not go into Bennett's detail or bother about the theoretical contention that "other things being equal, a short work of art presents fewer difficulties than a longer one." He destroyed the argument by adding that the Bible is shorter than the London Directory and then said, "Now, I am not going to argue. I never do. I will simply take one of the shortest, most intense, and most famous scenes in English literature, and rewrite it as a chapter in a novel in the style of my friends Bennett and Galsworthy when they are too lazy to write plays." Shaw then reprints the scene of thirty-four lines from *Macbeth* in which Macbeth is killed and follows this with more than six close pages of Bennettian-Galsworthian prose. He ends by saying how easy it was to write thus and that "when my faculties decay a little further, I shall go back to novel writing. And Arnold Bennett can fall back on writing plays."[33] The sting in "go back" may have passed unnoticed, but the implication was clear that, as a literary beginner, Shaw had written novels and grown out of them. Bennett, at this time deeply absorbed in the war, did not allow Shaw's mockery to worry him.

The two writers remained on good terms and visited each other during the postwar years. Of one dinner party at the home of H. G. Wells, Bennett noted that "Shaw talked practically the whole time, which is the same thing as saying that he talked a damn sight too much,"[34] but on another occasion, when Shaw came to lunch with Bennett and Dorothy, and told her that if she was to go in for theatrical management and acting there would have to be a divorce, "he was very quiet, chatty, sensible and agreeable."[35] Apart from this brief reference, the question of work in the theater did not appear to be raised between them very often. Bennett had kept up his quite amazing production rate as a novelist and, in addition to regular journalism, continued to write plays. Only rarely did Shaw have anything to say about them.

The editor of Bennett's letters, James Hepburn, has given a valuable list of Bennett's plays in the introduction to *Arnold Bennett: The Critical Heritage*. He begins with a somewhat sweeping statement: "For a few years early in the century Bennett was the very model of a successful playwright. From 1908 to 1913 he had five plays on the London stage." This introduction ends with the information that Bennett "could write to

Lord Beaverbrook in 1925 that even in a bad year he could expect 400 performances of his plays."[36] All this argues a degree of success, of course, but the weight of the initial contention depends on the force given to the words "model" and "successful." Compared with his lasting success as a novelist, Bennett's achievement as a dramatist was limited in both time and artistic value.

The play that reached the Shaftesbury Theater in the West End in 1907 was a stage version of Bennett's novel *Anna of the Five Towns,* which had been published in 1902. In it he had drawn from memories of his own youth in the grim industrial surroundings of the Potteries where he had grown up and which yielded in time his greatest work, the long novels *The Old Wives' Tale* and *Clayhanger.* The novel itself tells the story of Anna Tellwright, frustrated in her development both by the physical surroundings of her life and by the emotional pressures exerted on her by her miserly father. There is a strain of sadness in the novel, but Bennett in his stage version provided a "happy ending"[37] and, abandoning the original title, called it the deplorable *Cupid and Commonsense.* This change of title, Bennett explained, was "merely *Ad Captandum,*" which may be roughly translated as intended to appeal to popular taste. Bennett was very pleased with the play when he had finished it, calling it "one of the best things I have ever done; quite as good as most of my novels." On another occasion, he said that he thought the changes he had made in the story were an improvement. The popular taste was not so easy to catch, however, and the play did not succeed in the theater.

When it was published in book form in 1908, Bennett wrote a preface with the title "The Crisis in the Theatre."[38] This makes sad reading today, and it is full of heavy but unintentional irony.

Bennett directed his most serious criticism at theater managers, in whom he found a "quite remarkable ignorance of life and letters," adding that "as a rule they read nothing but press notices." He thought that there were signs of "a tremendous revival of interest in the drama" in England, but that this was being hindered by a reactionary press and the rapacity of ground landlords, which was crushing managers to death. He asked why "the intelligent imaginative writer" did not turn his attention to the theater and found three answers to the question. First, he thought that the dramatist felt remote from his public—as contrasted to the novelist, who was separated from his readers by the printer and binder only. Second, while the financial rewards of the dramatist could be immense (what Henry James had in mind), they were usually spasmodic, whereas the royalties of the novelist arrived in a regular flow. Third, there was greater public demand for novels than for plays. He added that "since Goldsmith and Sheridan, the literary genius of the English has turned away from the theatre."

In light of other developments, his next contentions were surprising. He said that the first manifestation of the slow-moving new spirit in the theater occurred with the first performance of Shaw's *Widowers' Houses* in 1892. He supported this by saying,

> It is remarkable that a man cannot write an essay even on the modern stage without bringing in the name of Mr Bernard Shaw. But he cannot. It so happens that Mr Shaw is the symbol of the whole shindy. He is a writer of genius, and before him, during the entire course of the nineteenth century, no British writer of genius ever devoted his creative power principally to the stage.

A little later, he added that many managers

> never connected the lack of regular vitality in box-offices with Mr Shaw and the something behind him. They never surmised—and I doubt if they even now surmise—that he is the chief outward sign of the secret force which is gradually worrying them to death; that he stands for a racial impulse towards fresh artistic expression by means of the drama, and that this impulse, having produced authors and actors, is little by little melting and remoulding taste as a strong creative impulse always does. In one more comment from the preface, he looked to the future with hope: Against the blind nescience of managers and against the Press the newly returning spirit will have a struggle. Its difficulties with even the more enlightened Press may be judged from the fact that Mr A B Walkley, a critic of quite exceptional gifts, who has grown morose while waiting for a messiah, much prefers *His House in Order* to *The Voysey Inheritance*! But the newly returning spirit is certain to win, the newly returning spirit always does. When the curtain fell on the last performance of *Arms and the Man* at the Savoy, a large portion of the Press went through the ceremony of burying the newly returning spirit. How it must have laughed![39]

It did not occur to Bennett that he had done some burying in his time. Thus, while nobody will blame the critic who changes his mind in the light of fresh experience or deeper thought, it is hard to be certain about one who does not seem to notice the change. In his *Academy* article in 1902, Bennett was certain that Shaw, obsessed with ideas and ignoring plot or form, was on the wrong track. Now, six years later, he saw in Shaw the embodiment of the new spirit but did not ask himself whether Shaw's use of the discussion of ideas, or even the music of ideas, may have contributed to that new spirit which Bennett now found so important.

Perhaps a fraction of the truth may be found in the circumstances of Bennett's own life during the first decade of the century. At a time when Shaw was contributing so greatly to the changes in the English theater, Bennett was not in England at all. He spent the greater part of his time in Paris. From this he derived great benefit and the powerful effect of such writers as Zola and, to a lesser extent, Flaubert and Balzac, as is seen in the best of his novels. It did mean, however, that in the years when, had things gone differently, he might have been working in the theater alongside Shaw, Granville Barker, and even Galsworthy at the great Court Theatre, Bennett was seeing plays in Paris where there were no writers to compare with those in the English theater. Thus, to take an example, a play to which Bennett gave great praise in Paris was *La Parisienne* by Henri Becque, first played in 1885 and seen by Bennett in December 1903 (when Shaw had just published *Man and Superman*). In his journal he said that it was "a play perfectly simple, but exquisitely constructed," and he gave his view that it was "certainly one of the great plays of the period."[40] *La Parisienne* has a fairly ordinary plot involving marital relations with neat and surprising turns in the development. The language is witty, and the play is superior to the "well-made play" of the period. Yet it is far from a masterpiece when compared with the greatest of modern drama, and while it holds a place in the repertory of the Comédie Française, it is revived as a museum piece.

Among other French plays Bennett saw were some by Brieux, of whom Shaw spoke most highly but who failed to please Bennett. He was certain that Brieux was "not a good playwright" although "his plays are very interesting as rough-and-ready presentments of urgent social problems."[41] The opinion of critics and theatergoers in the twentieth century has tended to side with Bennett on this rather than with Shaw. On the other hand, Bennett failed to appreciate the true greatness of Ibsen. He saw *Ghosts* in November 1903 and concluded that it was "not after all a good play." The symbolism did not work. The play was "stagey," "not quite sincere," and "too clever."[42] When he saw *The Wild Duck* in 1906, he thought that it was clever but not beautiful. The symbolism was "simply deplorable," and he was pretty well convinced that Ibsen was "not a writer of masterpieces." The next day, he wondered whether he had perhaps been "too hard on Ibsen last night." On reflection, he thought that "Ibsen had made one of those steps towards realism which alone constitute the progress of art."[43] In this, Bennett raised more questions than he was able to answer, and, as the progress of his own career as a dramatist was to show, the development of realism (as he used the term here) would not take him very far.

However, he could tell the value of Ibsen compared with lesser writers. Thus, the day before he saw *The Wild Duck* at Antoine's in Paris, he had been to the St. James's in London. There he had seen Pinero's new play, *His House in Order*. Bennett began his journal entry with some comparisons between the organization of the theater in the two capitals. In London at the St. James's he found "a theatre organised and worked with the perfection of a battleship. An air of solidity, richness, cleanliness, decorum; punctuality, short entr'actes; general care for the public." In all these particulars, he found the London theater immensely superior to that of Paris. Yet—and here came the thrust—"The only things that were bad at the St James's were the play and the acting. The play, which is a great success, and has been seen three times and written about three times by Wm. Archer, and praised by Walkley and Jo Knight is most certainly a thoroughly pretentious, sentimental, and dull play. It never convinces." Out of fairness to both Pinero and Bennett, an earlier opinion on Pinero may be remembered. In 1895, Bennett had seen Pinero's *Benefit of the Doubt*, which he had thought "really fine. . . . Even Shaw bent his knee before it."[44]

Bennett continued to write on the failings of the English stage. In an essay, "What Is Wrong With the Theatre?" included in the first of his collections of *Things That Have Interested Me*, published in 1921, he said that there were fallacies to which were attributed the shortcomings of the English theater. One fallacy was the often repeated assertion that there were too many American plays; another was the assertion that there were many good plays that could not obtain a hearing in the English theater because managers were too "commercially-minded." The truth, Bennett declared firmly, was "the extreme and notorious paucity of interesting plays."[45] He continued in something of the same vein, and in 1927 he wrote an introduction to a volume of collected dramatic criticism by James Agate titled *The Contemporary Theatre, 1926*. He began by discussing "the plight of the London stage." He found the principal faults to be the inaudibility or imperfect audibility of the performers, bad acting, bad producing, the deterioration of the performances during a long run, mealymouthed dramatic criticism, and the defects of management. He gave examples or explanations of these defects, and one of the most interesting is his passage on critics. He thought that, on the whole, the London critics compared very unfavorably with those in Paris and New York, being far too ready to handle the stage with great delicacy. He mentioned some exceptions, among them, perhaps not surprisingly, James Agate, but maintained that critics contributed too much good-natured or sentimental tolerance "which must count among the influences which hamper the progress of the London stage."[46]

It may have been for the obvious reason that he was writing an introduction to a collection of dramatic criticism that he did not go into detail on the quality of the plays to be seen in the London theaters at the time.

He may have felt inhibited to some extent by the fact that he was still trying to become a significant dramatist, although with decreasing success. Yet he could be firmly outspoken on the subject of plays when he felt strongly, and it is very much to his credit that he saw the greatness of one dramatist when conventional critics were unable to do so. Thus, in 1925 he wrote to Lord Beaverbrook about an article by the dramatic critic of the *Daily Express*, Basil McDonald Hastings:

> Hastings in the morning's *Express* calls Chekhov's *Cherry Orchard* "fatuous drivel." Anybody is entitled so to describe a play which after twenty years is accepted by the instructed in every European country and in America as a masterpiece. But I doubt whether anybody holding such an opinion, especially after seeing the play three times, is entitled to be a dramatic critic. And even if he is entitled to be a dramatic critic, he ought certainly to express his idiosyncrasy with some regard for the consideration due to the immense artistic prestige of a writer like Chekhov.[47]

Bennett's own career as a dramatist reached its highest point in the years immediately before and at the beginning of World War I. After *Cupid and Commonsense* he wrote *What the Public Wants*, a play about a wealthy newspaper proprietor based to some extent on a High Court case in which a celebrated newspaper owner, Lord Northcliffe, had been put in the public eye. The leading character in Bennett's play is a man from the Five Towns, Sir Charles Worgan, who has succeeded in the London newspaper world and whose policy is to give the public what it wants. He is not regarded in his native Bursley with the same veneration that he enjoys in London. The play's texture is thickened when the newspaper proprietor becomes involved with a young widow who is concerned with a theater company that has artistic objectives a little too advanced for the general public. Sir Charles is caught between his populist policies as a newspaper owner and his wish, spurred by his newfound love, to assist an unpopular theatrical enterprise. The play, which contains some modest but amusing satire on both the newspaper and theater worlds, ends on a note of ironic sadness for the great man; he loses the lady but decides to go ahead with a political campaign for the release of suffragettes, not because he knows that the public wants it but because he has become convinced that it is the right thing to do.

Max Beerbohm had admired *The Old Wives' Tale* but had been disappointed when he read Bennett's other novels and thought that a writer of some distinction had demeaned himself by writing "pot boilers." When he heard that the Stage Society was going to produce a play by Bennett, he trembled. He was happily surprised and found that *What the*

Public Wants "was one of the best comedies of our time."[48] Beerbohm remains in a small minority. The play is certainly not without solid virtues but did not hold the public, and while it has been played with success in big cities outside London, it has never been retrieved for London revival, as have plays by Bennett's contemporaries such as Granville Barker, Galsworthy, Barrie, and Maugham.

A modest comedy, *The Honeymoon,* followed, but the next two plays were the most successful of Bennett's career as a dramatist. The first was *Milestones,* written in collaboration with Edward Knoblock. Briefly, as Knoblock explained it, he put to Bennett an idea about a play in three generations. Bennett's response was that he ought to have thought of it himself since that was, to a great extent, the theme of *The Old Wives' Tale.* Generally, Knoblock said, he wrote the first scenario, and Bennett would then write a scene. The collaboration seems to have been very harmonious. According to Knoblock, Bennett tended now and again to depart from the scenario and to become more the novelist than the dramatist. When this was pointed out to him, he always took the criticism in good part. The play dealt with one of Bennett's favorite themes, the passage of time, seen in the successive generations of a family concerned with the construction of ships. A little staid by late twentieth-century standards and lacking the language to give full effect to the situations, both in characterization and in the industrial theme, the play has nevertheless both strength and dignity. It was a success in London, where it ran for 609 performances and has been revived.

Milestones was followed by *The Great Adventure,* produced in London in 1913 by Granville Barker. This was a stage version by Bennett of his successful comic novel *Buried Alive.* An unnamed reviewer had said of *Buried Alive* in 1908 that "the story is frankly impossible and extravagant, but as an ingenious vehicle for satirising the social life of the twentieth century it must be very highly praised."[49] *The Great Adventure* was very successful in the London theater just before the war, and, with a successful production in New York at the same time, more than half of Bennett's considerable income in 1913 came from his plays. He might well have looked back with satisfaction at poor Henry James and his envy of the wealth of the fashionable playwright compared with the meager returns for the craftsman of the novel.

The Great Adventure told its story in a lively and diverting way. A celebrated painter finds that, through a mix-up, the death of his valet was thought to be his own death. He allows the mistake to stand, attends his own funeral service in Westminster Abbey, and retires to seclusion and domestic bliss in a relatively obscure London suburb. Of course, circumstances change and he begins to paint again, with the inevitable result that his true identity comes to light. The play fit the public taste and has hardly lost its charm through the years, serving as the basis for two films (*His Double Life*, 1933, and *Holy Matrimony*, 1943) and being revived by the occasional repertory theater. Successful as it was, *The Great Adventure* was not much more than an elegant trifle.

The Title in 1918, joking quite pleasantly about newspapers and journalists and the award of titles for alleged public services, had a run of 285 nights in London, compared with the 673 of the first production of *The Great Adventure*. For the war-weary West End, there were some good laughs. Bennett did his best to reach the standard of Wilde and Shaw with such aphorisms as, "Journalists say a thing that isn't true, in the hope that if they keep on saying it long enough, it will be true." Bennett next wrote the play *Judith* for his friend the actress Lillah McCarthy, based on the story from the Apocrypha. Bennett was no poet, and his attempt at semi-biblical language was not a success.

In the last decade of his life Bennett continued to write novels that, while not generally thought to be up to the standard of the best of his work in the past, were still highly praised by the critics and well received by the reading public. The same cannot be said of the plays that he wrote during the postwar years. *Judith* was followed by *Sacred and Profane Love*, more successful in the United States than in England, and then by *The Love Match* and *Body and Soul*, neither of which ran for very long. Another ambitious collaboration with Knoblock, *London Life*, presented at Drury Lane in 1924, failed completely. James Agate, a personal friend of Bennett, felt obliged to say that while he thought that *London Life* would have made a capital novel, on the stage it could not come anywhere near success. Further, and worse, it was "silly on a small scale." Niceties of conduct, thought Agate, were "useless matter for Drury Lane," which is a very large theater.[50]

London Life effectively marked the end of Bennett the dramatist. On 15 February 1925 the Stage Society produced *The Bright Island*, which Bennett had written four years previously and revised for the actual presentation.[51] It was a work out of his normal style, being something of a satirical allegory on a political theme.

Despite his close friendship with people such as Beaverbrook, who were active in the world of politics, Bennett never had the knowledge and experience of politics that always fascinated Shaw, whether he was politically active or not. Moreover, Bennett's virtues as a writer were essentially down-to-earth and straightforward. He lacked anything approaching a poetic gift, and fantasy and metaphor were outside his range. Some years after *The Bright Island*, Shaw satirized the political process with a mixture of shrewdness and hilarity in *The Apple Cart*. (Unfortunately, there is no published record of Bennett's having seen this play, although he might have done so.) After Bennett's death, Shaw wrote *The Simpleton of the Unexpected Isles*, a strange and haunting mixture of farce and fantasy, absurdity and apocalyptic vision. Michael Holroyd has found many influences in the play and has compared it with other works such as *The Tempest*.[52] Different strains may be found in *The Bright Island*. Bennett took some of his characters from the *Commedia dell'Arte*, but these fit uneasily with his rather pedestrian and prosaic comments on political and social themes of the British 1920s. Bennett himself thought well of the play, and while a production at the Lyric Theatre, Hammersmith, was a possibility, he noted that the those concerned at the Lyric were "very pleased indeed" with the play, which rather reassured him.[53] A long run of *The Beggar's Opera* at the Lyric prevented the production, and when it was given by the Stage Society for two performances in 1925, the critic Hubert Griffith called it "the worst play written by a celebrated man for a long time past."[54] Bennett himself said that the reception was the worst that any play of his had ever had. It is very surprising that James Hepburn, in a footnote in his edition of the *Letters*, called *The Bright Island* "one of Bennett's best plays."[55]

Bennett had written to Bernard Shaw, who gave him advice that he was willing to receive but would not act upon. Shaw told Bennett "that the play was not really a play but a libretto. It needed music." Humanity, he said, could not stand "one hundred and fifty minutes unrelieved scoffing, no matter how witty it is." He said that there must be refuges for other qualities on the part of the audience, such as affection, admiration, or detestation or, to go in another direction, "refuges for its concupiscence and ferocity." Leaving aside the thought, obvious if ungenerous, that similar criticisms could well be made, and indeed were often made, of Shaw's own plays, Bennett replied civilly that there was probably a great deal in what Shaw said but that he had definitely arranged with the Stage Society for *The Bright Island* to be performed, and that was that. He added that he had thought the play was very good when he had written it, "and God knows what I shall think of it when I see it performed." (Dorothy Cheston Bennett confessed, but not to Bennett himself, that she lacked faith in the play.)

Shaw wrote again. He had relented to some extent:

> When I saw the Right Little Bright Little Island on the stage, I found that I was only half right about it. I said it had the makings of an Offenbachian *opera bouffe* in it; and I was right. What I did not see was that it had the makings of a powerful serious political play in it. It fell between the low stool and the high one; and you might do worse than try the high one. There are gleams and drivings in that play which seem to indicate a destiny.

After giving this much, he took away:

> But like all inveterate novelists you will not take the theatre seriously enough. And you will study the wrong models. You have nothing to learn from Scribe & Co., and everything to learn from Beethoven. A play should go like a symphony; its themes should be introduced emphatically at the beginning, and then hit on the head again and again until they are red hot, the pace and intensity increasing to the end with every possible device of unexpected modulations and changes, and suddenly pianissimos, as in the Preislied and the finale of Mozart's Figaro. You never think of this, you depend on your confounded invention, and keep ladling in primitive matter right up to the end without ever working it up, so that the last fifteen minutes of your play are exactly like the first, and there is no reason why they should be the last rather than the first, or why you should not, like George Moore, go on for ever. A play must have a destination, even if it be the bottom of the abyss, in which case the further it falls the faster it goes. Here endeth the first lesson.[56]

In fact, it was the last lesson in this particular course of instruction. There seems to be no record of any reply by Bennett. The main force of Shaw's criticism was, however, in the deadly shaft, "you will not take the theatre seriously enough." Certainly, Bennett never thought of the theater as "a factory of thought, a prompter of conscience, an elucidator of social conduct," to quote some of Shaw's ringing phrases.[57] An obvious criticism is that Bennett wrote the majority of his plays in about three weeks or a month; but he was always a quick writer, and the merit of his best novels is not lessened by the fact that he took very little time over them, compared with some other eminent novelists. Yet there can be detected in much of Bennett's writing about, as distinct from for, the theater an element that can only be described as condescension. He thought that writing for the theater was easy. In *How to Become an Author* (1903) he wrote, "In playwriting the plot is everything—or nearly so. . . . A play is a story. A play should only contain matter which helps to tell the story, and when the aspirant ceases to tell the story in order to be funny, or to draw tears, or to convey a moral or immoral lesson, he is sinning against the canons of playwriting, whether commercial or artistic."[58] In *The Author's Craft* (1914), the book which drove Shaw to his sardonic reply, Bennett laid himself open by referring to the playwright as "a sub-novelist" and by saying that, in the words already quoted, "other things being equal, a short work of art presents fewer difficulties than a longer one." A play, he maintained, could not afford the sustained subtlety of the novel. The dramatist did not have to cope with problems of "scenic and physiognomic description," and the portrayal of character could be left to the actors.

In differing ways, these contentions of Bennett supported Shaw's criticism that, as "an inveterate novelist," Bennett was unable to turn himself into a dramatist. For all his disappointments and frustrations, however, Bennett went on. He retained a deep interest in the theater and has an honorable record in his collaboration with others in the management of the Lyric Theatre, Hammersmith, when that theater made a great contribution to raising London standards. Several of Bennett's novels have shrewd and penetrating observations, scenes, and incidents set in the theater, from which some of his ambivalent thoughts about the stage may be deduced. He never resembled James in turning his back on the theater and calling it "a most unholy trade" or in retreating with relief to novels. Unfortunately, unlike James, he did not feel in the long run that he had drawn an important lesson from experience in playwriting, the lesson that, in the novel as in the drama, it was essential to dramatize and that his novels would be stronger as a result.

Nothing is easier than to set up one writer and then to knock down another by facile comparison. This approach has to be resisted when Shaw and Bennett are set side by side. In his letter about *The Bright Island,* Shaw had cited Scribe and Beethoven as examples of the antithetical styles of approach to playwriting. In some ways, this is not quite fair. Bennett was never exactly of the school of Scribe or of Sardou, the great exponents of the "well-made play." For all his insistence on plot, he did not build his plays by the type of mechanical contrivance analyzed so scathingly by C. E. Montague in *Dramatic Values.*[59] Nor, despite his considerable and sensitive interest in music, did he conceive of the playwright as a composer such as Beethoven or Mozart. There was always an element of the honest workman about Bennett. One of his biographers, Dudley Barker, gave his life of Bennett the title *Writer by Trade,*[60] and it is not to denigrate his work to say that there was always something about him of the tradesman selling his wares. In the theater, rather than in his novels, Bennett tried to give the public what it wanted. He did not descend to the lowest depths, of course, nor did he feel himself writing at full stretch. As a novelist, even writing as a tradesman, he was capable of his best work. One of his best and more sympathetic biographers, Margaret Drabble, has said that "Bennett is one of the greatest writers of the passage of time in the English language."[61] Without the wit and sparkle of Shaw, and lacking Shaw's artistic command of language and exposition and his deep social commitment, Bennett could not transfer his greatest gifts to the theater. He never crossed the divide which James found between theatre-stuff and drama-stuff, and it is sadly ironic that, as with James, other hands have made successful plays from some of his novels.

Notes

1. Walter Allen, *The English Novel* (London: Phoenix House, 1954), p. 104.

2. L. G. Wickham Legg, ed., *Dictionary of National Biography, 1931–1940* (London: Oxford University Press, 1949), p. 66.

3. *The Journals of Arnold Bennett*, ed. Newman Flower, 3 vols. (London: Cassell, 1932), 1:99.

4. Arnold Bennett, *Things That Have Interested Me* (London: Chatto & Windus, 1921), p. 315.

5. Henry James, *Guy Domville* (London: Hart-Davis, 1961), p. 214.

6. *Academy*, February 1901, reprinted in *Shaw: The Critical Heritage*, ed. T. F. Evans (London: Routledge, 1976), p. 92.

7. See Kingsley Martin, *Father Figures* (London: Hutchinson, 1966), pp. 189–90.

8. *Journals*, 1:278.

9. *Journals*, 2:6.

10. *Journals*, 3:261. See also letter to Bernard Shaw, 12 December 1919, in *Letters of Arnold Bennett*, ed. James Hepburn (London: Oxford University Press, 1970), 3:115–16, and letter to Hugh Walpole, 12 December 1919, ibid., p. 116. In the letter to Shaw, Bennett ends with the words, "there are only three dramatists worth a damn in this country." Hepburn surmises that the third "was probably Barrie—though with considerable reservation."

11. *Arnold Bennett's Letters to His Nephew* (London: Heinemann, 1936), p. 65.

12. *Journals*, 3:33.

13. *Letters to Nephew*, p. 117.

14. *Journals*, 2:42.

15. Bernard Shaw, *Jitta's Atonement*, in *Collected Plays with Their Prefaces* 5:179.

16. Bernard Shaw, "What I Owe to German Culture," *Adam International Review*, nos. 337–39 (Rochester, N.Y.: University of Rochester, 1970), p. 5.

17. *Journals*, 3:72.

18. *Bernard Shaw's Letters to Siegfried Trebitsch*, ed. Samuel A. Weiss (Stanford, Calif.: Stanford University Press, 1986), p. 225.

19. Ibid., pp. 228–29.

20. *Collected Letters, 1911–1925*, ed. Dan H. Laurence (London: Reinhardt, 1985), p. 773.

21. *Letters to Trebitsch*, p. 224.

22. *Journals*, 3:72.

23. Bernard Shaw, *What I Really Wrote About the War* (London: Constable, 1931), p. 22.

24. *Collected Letters, 1911–1925*, p. 267.

25. *Letters of Arnold Bennett*, 1:215.

26. For a full account of Shaw's controversial views and Bennett's reactions, see Kinley E. Roby, *A Writer at War: Arnold Bennett, 1914–1918* (Baton Rouge: Louisiana State University Press, 1972), pp. 52–54, 181–86.

27. Bernard Shaw, "Shaw in Rebuttal to Arnold Bennett," *New York Times* (19 November 1914), p. 3.

28. Roby, *A Writer at War*, p. 53.

29. Bernard Shaw, "Mr. Arnold Bennett Thinks Play-Writing Easier than Novel Writing," *Pen Portraits and Reviews* (London: Constable, 1932), pp. 43–52.

30. Arnold Bennett, *The Author's Craft* (London: Hodder & Stoughton, 1914).

31. "Mr. Arnold Bennett Thinks Play-Writing Easier than Novel Writing," pp. 43–44.

32. Arnold Bennett, *How to Become an Author* (London: C. Arthur Pearson, 1903), p. 209.

33. "Mr. Arnold Bennet Thinks Play-Writing Easier than Novel Writing," p. 52.

34. *Journals*, 3:169.

35. Ibid., pp. 255–256.

36. *Arnold Bennett: The Critical Heritage* (London: Routledge, 1981), pp. 119–36.

37. See Bennett's slightly admonitory reference to James, who had given a play a happy ending, in *Letters of Arnold Bennett*, 3:326n., 359.

38. *Cupid and Commonsense* (London: Hodder & Stoughton, 1908).

39. Ibid., pp. 29–33.

40. *Journals*, 1:136.

41. Ibid., p. 141.

42. Ibid., p. 133.

43. Ibid., pp. 131–32.

44. *Letters of Arnold Bennett*, 2:24.

45. *Things That Have Interested Me*, p. 111.

46. James Agate, *The Contemporary Theatre, 1926* (London: Chapman & Hall, 1927), p. v.

47. *Letters of Arnold Bennett*, 2:242.

48. Max Beerbohm, *Last Theatres* (London: Hart-Davis, 1970), pp. 455–59.

49. See *Arnold Bennett: The Critical Heritage*, p. 201, from *Spectator*, 4 July 1908.

50. James Agate, *The Contemporary Theatre, 1924* (London: Chapman & Hall, 1925), p. 241.

51. Arnold Bennett, *The Bright Island*, in *Three Plays* (London: Chatto & Windus, 1926), pp. 1–117.

52. Michael Holroyd, *Bernard Shaw: The Lure of Fantasy, 1918–1950* (London: Chatto & Windus, 1991), p. 350.

53. *Letters of Arnold Bennett*, 1:285.

54. *Arnold Bennett: The Critical Heritage*, p. 131.

55. *Letters of Arnold Bennett*, 1:285, n. 277.

56. See Letters from Shaw to Bennett, 6 November 1924 and 27 February 1925 (Humanities Research Center, Austin, Texas). See Reginald Pound, *Arnold Bennett* (London: Heinemann, 1952), pp. 284–85. See also "Arnold Bennett: Shaw's Ten O'Clock Scholar," *The Shaw Review* 13.3 (September 1970): 96.

57. Bernard Shaw, *Our Theatres in the Nineties* (London: Constable, 1932), p. vii.

58. *How to Become an Author*, p. 218.

59. C. E. Montague, *Dramatic Values* (New York: Macmillan, 1911), pp. 63–74.

60. Dudley Barker, *Writer by Trade: A View of Arnold Bennett* (London: Allen & Unwin, 1966).

61. Margaret Drabble, *Arnold Bennett* (London: Weidenfeld & Nicholson, 1974), p. 17.

John A. Bertolini

FINDING SOMETHING NEW TO SAY: RATTIGAN ELUDES SHAW

Terence Rattigan responded to Shaw the playwright in such highly ambivalent ways that it would be difficult to epitomize or even to summarize
their relationship. When Rattigan was a beginning playwright, for him
Shaw loomed as one of the immortals, especially after the impact of *Saint
Joan* and the Nobel Prize. Still, Rattigan blamed Shaw for leading drama
down the wrong path, the road of ideas instead of the road of character
and situation. One has only to compare Rattigan's published remarks
about his most successful theatrical contemporary, Noël Coward, to see
that everything Rattigan says about Shaw until the year of Shaw's death is
guarded, at a respectful distance, although admiring, while with Coward, Rattigan is unstinting and easy in his admiration and affection for
his near rival.[1]

Such a contrast should not surprise, not only because Rattigan declared himself so often to be a playwright of character and situation as
opposed to a playwright of ideas, but also because Rattigan and Shaw
professed such radically different views about the role of subtext in their
respective plays. For example, Shaw advised Ralph Richardson while he
was rehearsing Bluntschli at the Old Vic, "You've got to go from line to
line, quickly and swiftly, never stop the flow of the lines, never stop. It's
one joke after another, it's a firecracker. Always reserve the acting for
underneath the spoken word."[2] In addition to warning his actors not to
pause for implication, Shaw pointed to his endowment of his characters
with a more powerful self-awareness and a corresponding ability to articulate that awareness than verisimilitude would allow, as when he explained in the Preface to *Saint Joan* that in the play Warwick, the Inquisi-
tor, and Cauchon are able to say "the things they actually would have said
if they had known what they were really doing."[3]

For Rattigan such extreme self-consciousness and articulateness were contrary to his dramatic purposes, which were to cultivate the art of implication and subtext. Indeed, Rattigan regards these arts as essential to a "sense of theatre": "Has not the sense of theatre then something to do with the ability to thrill an audience by the mere power of suggestion, to move it by words unspoken rather than spoken . . . ?" Rattigan goes on to say that he regards "the instinct for the use of dramatic implication" as "the most important part" of the playwright's art. He then produces his most acute articulation of what is uniquely his achievement in dramatic literature, namely his identification of "those most vital problems of the whole craft of playwriting—what *not* to have your actors say, and how best to have them *not* say it."[4] Given such an aesthetic strategy, whereby an audience shall understand a character and a situation through what a character does not say, it is easier to understand Rattigan's ambivalence to Shaw—the creator of super-articulate characters—as a predecessor.

When Rattigan adapted his 1946 play, *The Winslow Boy,* for the screen in 1950 (the year of Shaw's death), he changed one line specifically in the interest of audience understanding. The line belongs to Arthur Winslow (played by Cedric Hardwicke, a leading Shavian actor), and he delivers it in the sequence in which Desmond Curry proposes to congratulate Catherine Winslow upon her engagement. He falters in his search for adequate words and ascribes his faltering to his "looking for something new to say," of which Arthur Winslow observes (in the play), "No one—with the possible exception of Voltaire—could find anything new to say about an engaged couple." In the film, "Bernard Shaw" is substituted for "Voltaire," no doubt partly because Rattigan and the film's director, Anthony Asquith, knew that far more members of the film-going public would know Shaw than would recognize Voltaire. But in another way, Rattigan was acknowledging the relationship between his play *French Without Tears* and one of its nearest forebears, *Man and Superman,* for in that play Shaw had managed to find "something new to say about an engaged couple," that they were in the grip of the Life Force, aiding the human race's evolutionary struggle toward deeper self-consciousness. The problem for Rattigan was to take two people engaged in the courting dance and say something about that couple different from what Shaw had said. Rattigan also needed to confront his own relationship to the most highly regarded British playwright of his time, especially since Rattigan knew he wanted *not* to write plays of ideas.

French Without Tears opened in London in 1936. It was not actually Rattigan's first produced play, but it was his first success, a major play, and when his plays were collected in 1953 ("at last" as Rattigan says in the Preface to the first volume), Rattigan classified himself unapologetically, even defensively, as a popular playwright. He also gave his plays a pedigree of sorts when he listed the public's preference for certain plays over others throughout English theatrical history: *The Merchant of Venice* over *Measure for Measure* and *Timon of Athens, The School for Scandal* over *The Rivals,* and *The Importance of Being Earnest* over all Wilde's other plays. But then Rattigan comes to Shaw, and he names six plays as audience favorites—*Candida, Arms and the Man, Man and Superman, Pygmalion, The Devil's Disciple,* and *Saint Joan*—in contradistinction to *Heartbreak House* and *Back to Methuselah,* which he describes respectively as a "near-masterpiece" and "a great work of philosophical literature."[5]

If we put aside Rattigan's formal obeisance to Shaw's literary reputation in his listing of the last two works, there remain two entries in Rattigan's catalogue of audience favorites which should be noted in connection with *French Without Tears: Candida* and *Man and Superman.* Elsewhere Rattigan had named *Candida* as a play of character and situation, which he preferred to Shaw's more obvious plays of ideas such as *The Millionairess,* explaining why *Candida* should head the list.[6] *Candida* is also Shaw's most Rattiganesque play in that its subplot deals with sexual shyness, pain, and shame. Rattigan's Jacqueline Maingot, the French woman who desperately loves Kit Neilan and suffers because she cannot speak her love, is cut from the same cloth as Eugene Marchbanks.

However, it is my contention that *Man and Superman,* rather than *Candida,* and the tradition of the battling couple lie behind *French Without Tears,* and that Rattigan means his play to be part of that tradition. More specifically, I want to argue that the reversed love chase in *Man and Superman,* during which Ann Whitefield sets her cap for John Tanner and pursues him (literally as well as figuratively) until he surrenders, becomes the central action of *French Without Tears,* wherein Diana Lake pursues Alan Howard until he surrenders. Both plays lead to a crisis in which the man discovers that he actually does love the woman who has pursued him and against whom he has actively and sometimes bitterly struggled. The defining elements of the reversed love chase are the woman's keen intention, made obvious to the audience but hidden from some of the other characters, and the man's obliviousness or resistance to her romantic intentions. Harold Brighouse's 1915 comedy *Hobson's Choice,* in which Maggie Hobson determines to wed and make a man of her father's "old boot hand," Will Mossop, is the chief exemplar of the reversed love chase genre between *Man and Superman* and *French Without Tears.*

Rattigan establishes almost from the beginning of the play that *French Without Tears* belongs to the tradition of the battling witty couple, the family tree of which goes back as far as *Much Ado About Nothing* (Holly Hill characterizes "Alan's description of his ideal wife" as "a little monument of Benedickian smugness")[7] and includes both *The Way of the World* and *Pri-*

vate Lives. Rattigan does so by way of two motifs that are germane to the tradition. One is the motif of gambling. Kenneth Lake and Brian Curtis discuss the odds against Alan's finishing his course of studies at the French "crammer" school that the three are attending on the west coast of France. Kenneth and Brian conduct their conversation in terms of a sustained metaphor of a horse race which they call "the diplomatic stakes." Alan joins them and continues the metaphor when he surmises his own possible "scratching" from the race. The figuration of himself as a racehorse trying to win is neither idle nor an automatic use of dead metaphor in conversation. It accomplishes two allusions: one is to the motif of love as a gamble, always the biggest gamble of one's life (hence Millamant's extreme hesitancy to unite herself to a "cold gamester" like Mirabell, and Ann Whitefield's fright that she has dared too much); the other is to the image of Alan as an animal on the run, like Jack Tanner, the quarry, the marked-down prey, as Henry Straker identifies his employer.[8]

One of Rattigan's earliest titles for his play, *Gone Away* (a fox-hunter's cry signifying that the hounds are loose and the hunt under way), indicates how central to his conception of the play was the idea of love as a chase.[9] The automobile on stage in Act II of *Man and Superman,* placed there by Shaw so that it may take Tanner away dramatically as soon as his chauffeur informs him that Ann is after no one else but him, has several expressive and symbolic purposes, but chiefly Shaw means it as a visual dramatization of Tanner's attempt to elude Ann's pursuit. Shaw had already taken the trouble to associate Tanner's automobile with races early in the second act, when Tanner concealed from his chauffeur the information that they were racing the younger Hector Malone to London. In short, what Rattigan found in *Man and Superman* ready-made was an intertwined set of metaphors for the courting of males and females: love as a race, as a chase, and as a hunt. By naming his heroine Diana, after the goddess of the hunt, Rattigan accentuated the predatory aspect of the love-chase which, although certainly present in Shaw (Tanner calls Ann a "boa-constrictor"), does not have the same edge as it does in Rattigan, where the hostility Alan feels toward Diana has in it much more of the animal at bay.

Rattigan highlights the connection between Diana Lake and her mythological forebear by means of two explicit allusions in the play to the story of Diana and Actaeon. Soon after the discussion of racehorses, odds, and betting, the conversation among Alan, Brian, and Commander Rogers turns to Kenneth's sister, Diana. Alan opines that Diana's presence has raised the odds against Kit Neilan's finishing his cram-course in French, preparatory to his entering the diplomatic corps. Just as Tanner convinces himself that Ann is after Tavy, Alan proclaims his suspicions that Diana is after nearly everyone but himself. In a continuation of the horse-race metaphor, Brian asks Alan about Kit's chances for scholastic success: "You don't think there's a chance of a well-fancied colt being withdrawn before the big contest?" After further suggestive remarks by Alan about Diana's way of affecting men, Rogers understands him to be implying that Diana is "rather fast." Alan retreats only to the extent of calling her "the fastest worker you're ever likely to see." Within the context of noting Diana's "speed" in the sexual chase, she makes her first appearance, which Rattigan describes thus in the stage directions: "DIANA LAKE *comes in from the garden. She is in a bathing wrap which she wears open, disclosing a bathing dress underneath.*" Rattigan thereby associates her with Diana bathing in her pool. Also, as the naked goddess, subjected to the gaze of Actaeon, seeks to be protected from view by the interposed bodies of her attendant nymphs, Diana Lake *"decorously pulls her wrap more closely about her."*

Even if the goddess Diana, spied upon while bathing in her pool, seems connected to Diana Lake's appearance in swimming costume only in a casual or a comical way, as if the allusion were only half meant as a bathetic comparison, the allusion is still there. Distinctly less casual and not bathetic at all, however, is Alan's comparison of himself with a stag at bay (Act II). In a discussion of Diana with Kit, Alan admits that "it is quite possible I shall end by marrying her myself.... But that'll only be—to take another sporting metaphor—like the stag who turns at bay through sheer exhaustion at being hunted." The classically educated Rattigan, author of *The Browning Version,* a play about an instructor of Latin and Greek, points here to his deliberate use of the myth of Diana and Actaeon, not only in the image of Alan turned into a stag (like Actaeon) but also in the self-conscious use of language's figurative capabilities: "to take another sporting metaphor." Alan seems to have a metatheatrical consciousness of his own role in the play, which is to enact the story of Diana and Actaeon. In this awareness he is like John Tanner, who has read the very author, Schopenhauer, who explains the symbolic nature of male capitulation to female pursuit. In the film version of *French Without Tears* (1939), directed by Anthony Asquith but scripted by Rattigan himself, the connection between Alan and the Actaeon whom Diana turned into a stag and caused to be chased and devoured by his own hounds is made even more explicit. The French school has a dog which Alan instructs to bite him if it ever catches him falling in love with Diana. At the end of the film, as Alan holds Diana in his arms, the dog carries out its instructions.

Alan, like Tanner, is an author, and the novel he is writing transmutes his own experiences into fiction just as Rattigan himself rewrites his own experiences at a "crammer" school in France. Alan's novel concerns two conscientious objectors who flee from England to South Africa. One makes love to the other's wife, and consequently the men have a fight. As their principles are overcome by feeling and reason is defeated by passion, they become animals instead of men. Similarly, Alan views Diana's seductions as reducing men to the level of animals. In a conversation with Kit, Alan compares her ensnarement of Rogers with the hooking of a salmon, and shortly thereafter he refers to her as a scalphunter (Actaeon again). Continually in *Man and Superman,* Tanner refers to Ann as a devourer of men. It seems much more of a joke in Shaw because of Tanner's blindness to his own identity as Ann's real prey, but the figure of woman as huntress with man as her prey enters *French Without Tears* by way of *Man and Superman.*

Another parallel between the two plays indicates Shaw's influence. Alan spends much of the play trying to convince his male companions of Diana's hypocrisy, deceptiveness, and predatory intentions. When he sees evidence of this, Alan whistles as a way of communicating to them his conviction that he is right about her. When he hears Diana promise Kit that she will not look at anyone else but him, Alan leans *"back in his chair"* and *"whistles a tune, softly."* Subsequently, he sings or hums the *Lorelei* on two occasions when Diana flirts with Rogers, with the ironic implication that she is luring Rogers to his doom. The obvious parallel here is Henry Straker, who whistles a popular air whenever the subject of Ann's romantic interests arises in conversation, especially when Tanner confidently refers to Ann's predilection for Octavius. Like Tanner with Ann, Alan is afraid to be left alone with Diana.

To argue for Shaw's influence on the play is not to argue that Rattigan merely copies Shaw. Rattigan transforms everything he borrows from Shaw, making his play Rattiganesque instead of Shavian. The climax of *French Without Tears* occurs when Diana shows herself to be like the goddess of chastity and that of the chase simultaneously. First she refuses to have sex with Alan, whereupon he decides to take the next day's train back to London. Diana prepares herself to flirt with a new arrival at the school, one Lord Heybrook, who turns out to be a young boy, whereupon Diana runs off to pack, crying, "I'm going to catch that London train or die." The assembled company (like the one at the end of *Man and Superman*) laughs at both lovers, at Diana's determination and at Alan's despairing curtain line, "Stop laughing you idiots. It isn't funny. It's a bloody tragedy." He says this even as he is pursuing her in order to stop her from pursuing him. Rattigan ends on a more nervous note than Shaw. At least by the end of *Man and Superman* Ann has caught Tanner, and he her, with some definitiveness. Rattigan leaves the lovers in full pursuit and flight; they are simultaneously fleeing from and pursuing one another in a relationship that seems incapable of resolution, for only the sexual attraction between them is definitive. Rattigan ends his play where Shaw ended his second act, with Jack Tanner in full flight from Ann. He thereby evades all the philosophical freight that Shaw loaded onto his play in the Don Juan in Hell interlude to make his play Shavian. There is no Life Force or father's heart in Rattigan's play, only the cold but comic pastoral of eternal flight and pursuit.

One of Rattigan's ways of making his play Rattiganesque is the inclusion of its homosexual subtext. Kit and Rogers first fight over Diana when each thinks the other should bow out of the love game. During their fight, Kit is dressed in the *"frilly skirt of a Greek Evzone"* (a well-girt infantryman). As they continue to argue, fight, and become drunk, they realize that Diana has been leading them both on and has even used the same line to each of them. Their discovery of her "double-crossing us" leads them to patch up their differences and conclude that "Diana's a bitch." They then invite Alan to come with them "to the Ball" at the casino. Alan accepts the invitation and leaves a message for Diana from all three: "Just tell her to go to hell." The idea of males finding consolation in camaraderie as a refuge from female deceptiveness and sexual withholding seems to suggest homosexuality as an alternative. In Rattigan's first version of the play Lord Heybrook, the character through whom Diana would get even with the men, turned out to be a flamboyant homosexual leading a dalmatian named Alcibiades on stage, and therefore immune to Diana's charms.[10] Only during rehearsals did Rattigan change the character to a boy of fifteen. The change only made Rattigan's point less obvious.

As in the case with Noël Coward, whose early play *The Young Idea* showed strong influence from Shaw's *You Never Can Tell,* Rattigan only needed to imitate Shaw directly once to show his inheritance from Shaw. After *French Without Tears,* Shaw's presence in Rattigan's plays is explicit; Shaw is named, not Shaw the playwright but Shaw the public figure, the reputation, the commenter on societal mores and morals. In addition to his substitution of Shaw for Voltaire in the screenplay of *The Winslow Boy,* Rattigan uses Shaw's name in two other plays (both written after Shaw's death) respectfully and even with affection. Unlike Somerset Maugham, who has a pretentious and unattractive character in *The Letter* (1927) boast that he has educated himself by reading "Nietzsche, Shaw and Herbert George Wells," Rattigan does not mention Shaw's name in order to undercut it with ironic ridicule.

In *The Sleeping Prince* (1953), which is set in 1911, a Carpathian Grand Duke sets out to seduce a musical comedy actress named Mary Morgan. In the course of warding off his attempts, she becomes embroiled in a political struggle between the Grand Duke and his son, Nicholas, who will become the ruling King of Carpathia as soon as his father stops serving as Prince Regent. Rattigan has the actress intervene to prevent a permanent rift between father and son, and part of her intervention consists of her admonishing the son, "It's wrong for boys of sixteen to plot dirty tricks on their fathers, and try to shove them off into limbo, and then justify themselves by talking as if they were George Bernard Shaw." By "Shaw" talk Mary Morgan—an American—means such pronouncements by Nicholas as, "It bears out so much of what I have heard concerning your nation's strongly emotional tendencies toward parent worship. . . . The idea that the old are wise simply because they are not young, and that the young are children until they are twenty-one." Nicholas is an engaging character whose Shavian-style aphorisms lend him added charm in the play. Also, Mary Morgan can discern the difference between an adolescent trying to play the grown-up by mimicking Shaw and the real Shaw.

In *Ross* (1960), a dramatization of T. E. Lawrence's military exploits in Arabia and his subsequent attempt to lead a more private life as Aircraftman Ross, Rattigan begins the play with the failure of that attempt. "Ross" has been away from barracks on a pass and has returned late. He is interrogated by his superior, a flight lieutenant, who demands to know with whom Lawrence ate dinner. "Ross" replies, "Lord and Lady Astor, Mr and Mrs George Bernard Shaw, the Archbishop of Canterbury—." The officer cuts him off and charges "Ross" with insubordination in the belief that "Ross" is mocking him by giving him obviously false names. Although Rattigan may have based this scene on a real incident, he again uses Shaw as a name, a metonymy for famous person, a national public figure—in short, the public persona rather than the personal friend which Shaw was to Lawrence in real life.

These references to Shaw in Rattigan's plays and in the film of *The Winslow Boy*, as well as Rattigan's references to Shaw in the preface to the first volume of his *Collected Plays*, postdate Rattigan's debate about the Play of Ideas with Shaw and others in the *New Statesman and Nation* and therefore may be said to be influenced by Rattigan's first direct encounter with Shaw.[11] The climax of that debate, which Rattigan had begun, came with the final entries by Shaw himself and then Rattigan. Shaw is both kind to and respectful toward Rattigan in allowing that his ideas, "reasonable or not, are all entertaining, and often penetrating and true," and that "his practice is pleasing."[12] Rattigan, although not so well pleased with the responses of Peter Ustinov, Sean O'Casey, and the other participants in the two-month newspaper debate who variously charged Rattigan with philistinism or worse, was rather pleased by Shaw's response. Rattigan develops a charming (if in some ways alarming) analogy between his treatment at the hands of the other dramatists and corporal punishment at an English public school:

My behind, if red, is so no more from the harsh treatment it has received than from blushful pride at the high distinction of the canes that have belaboured it. While not only my behind but the whole of my anatomy is still positively quivering with the shock and delight of having been considered worthy of the high honour of a birching from the head boy himself, who, with characteristic and Olympian generosity, dealt far more leniently with the cheeky fourth former than with the school prefects who had been bullying him.[13]

The tone and style (if not the imagery) of Rattigan's reference to Shaw show that Rattigan well understood the way in which Shaw employed humor in dealing with criticism. The content of the reference shows Rattigan recognizing the distinction of Shaw's dealings with younger rivals—the characteristic generosity—and the angle of Shaw's relationship to them—that of an immortal. The year of the debate was also the year of Shaw's death. From that point on, Rattigan's references to Shaw are easy, relaxed. In a 1963 interview with John Simon, Rattigan even called himself an "Ibsenite" playwright and listed Shaw first among the playwrights who "influenced" him when he was at school.[14] By the time of that interview, Shaw had been himself for a good long while, and so had Rattigan. The playwright whose characters articulated their own subtexts could be acknowledged as an influence by the playwright who defined the art of playwriting as knowing "what *not* to have your actors say, and how best to have them *not* say it."[15]

Notes

1. See Terence Rattigan, "Noël Coward: An Appreciation of His Work in the Theatre," in Raymond Mander and Joe Mitchinson, *Theatrical Companion to Coward* (London: Rockliff, 1957), pp. 1–6.

2. Quoted in Vincent Wall, *Bernard Shaw, Pygmalion to Many Players* (Ann Arbor: University of Michigan Press, 1973), p. 149.

3. Bernard Shaw, *Collected Plays with Their Prefaces,* ed. Dan H. Laurence (London: Reinhardt, 1970–74), 6:74.

4. Terence Rattigan, *Collected Plays* (London: Hamish Hamilton, 1953), 1:xx–xxi. All quotations from Rattigan's plays are from this four-volume edition.

5. Ibid., pp. vii, ix.

6. Rattigan, "The Play of Ideas," *New Statesman and Nation,* 13 May 1950, p. 546.

7. "A Critical Analysis of the Plays of Terence Rattigan" (Ph.D. dissertation, City University of New York, 1977), p. 31.

8. Susan Rusinko is the only critic I know who explicitly links *French Without Tears* to *Man and Superman*. She states that "certain overtones of Shaw are clearly there, particularly in the crisp, adroitly handled dialogue," and then she compares Alan to Tanner in the way both protest loudly when they discover they are the intended love victims of Diana and Ann, respectively. See *Terence Rattigan* (Boston: G. K. Hall, 1983), pp. 40–41.

9. For a full account of the evolution of *French Without Tears*, see Michael Darlow and Gillian Hodson, *Terence Rattigan: The Man and His Work* (London, Melbourne, and New York: Quartet Books, 1979), pp. 69–87.

10. Ibid., pp. 78–79.

11. The debate has been summarized in Susan Rusinko's "Rattigan Versus Shaw: The 'Drama of Ideas' Debate," *SHAW 2* (1982): 171–78.

12. *Shaw on Theatre*, ed. E. J. West (New York: Hill & Wang, 1958), p. 290.

13. *New Statesman and Nation*, 13 May 1950, p. 546.

14. "Rattigan Talks to John Simon," *Theatre Arts* 46 (April 1963): 24, 74.

15. *Collected Plays*, 1:xx–xxi.

Fred D. Crawford

SHAW'S BRITISH INHERITORS*

Although Bernard Shaw left no "school" of dramatists as such, his general influence on twentieth-century drama has been remarkable. Today we recognize Shaw as second only to Shakespeare in the British theatrical tradition, the chief modern dramatist, the innovator of "serious farce," the infuser of moral purpose into the drama, the proponent of the theater of ideas, the striker of the deathblow to nineteenth-century melodrama, and a precursor of avant-garde theater. His iconoclasm, as Frederick Lumley has remarked, roused audiences "from their nineteenth-century slumber."[1] Thanks to Shaw's breakdown of class barriers on stage, his leveling of heroes and villains, his use of literate conversation in discussion plays, and his undermining of outworn theatrical convention, Shaw has done much to make drama fit for an intelligent adult audience.

Dan H. Laurence, writing on the subject of Shaw's inheritors, had this to say:

> The key thing is that Shaw attacked 19th-century romanticism and claptrap; demanded intelligent theatre; insisted that the audience *think* but also *empathize*—no villain . . . to enable the audience to evade its own sense of responsibility. In other words, he revitalized the stage and opened the doors for a flood of new breeds of playwrights, from Galsworthy's *Justice* to Pinter's *Birthday Party*. Would there, without Shaw, have been an opening wedge for all the social and political themes of the modern theatre—or would we still be suffering with fallen women like Paula T [anqueray] and laughing at the class distinctions of *Trelawney?*[2]

*An earlier version of this paper was part of "The Once and Future Shaw" symposium sponsored by Long Island Stage (Thomas M. Madden, managing director) at the Grand Royal Hotel, Rockville Centre, New York, 20–22 April 1990.

While it would be going too far to say that, without Shaw, the theater would have remained forever in the doldrums of nineteenth-century romantic convention and general mindlessness, there is no question that Shaw opened the way for striking and lasting changes in dramatic art.

A survey such as this can hardly pretend to be exhaustive, but I would like to provide at least some sense of Shaw's influence on his dramatic successors and point to some of the more obvious inheritors of Shaw. One readily available indication of his pervasive influence is the frequency with which his name comes up in discussions of other playwrights in various reference works, such as the *Dictionary of Literary Biography* volumes devoted to British dramatists since 1900, R. F. Dietrich's *British Drama 1890–1950,* and Susan Rusinko's *British Drama 1950 to the Present.* After thumbing through these works, one cannot help regarding their "subtexts" as "The Age of Shaw."

Shaw's earlier inheritors were much more directly, and demonstrably, under Shaw's influence than those who emerged after his death. One case in point is Noël Coward. Filled with misgivings that the twins in *The Young Idea* were too close to those in Shaw's *You Never Can Tell,* Coward sent the manuscript to Shaw for his reaction and criticism. As Enoch Brater records,

> Shaw returned the script to the producer with constructive suggestions for rewriting the last act. On the margins of the typescript (which has since been lost) he wrote such admonitions as, "Oh no you don't, young author!" To Coward, however, he wrote a separate, highly supportive letter, but urged him "never to see or read my plays. Unless you can get clean away from me you will begin as a back number, and be hopelessly out of it when you are forty."[3]

Coward, of course, hardly became a back number. He found his own voice, developed comedies that depended as much on situation as on dialogue, and produced work quite distinguishable from Shaw's. However, when *The Young Idea* was produced in 1922 Coward's "bratty" characters seemed to have been "lifted" almost bodily from *You Never Can Tell,* and in later plays he also drew from Shaw's work.[4] The zany, eccentric characters of *Hay Fever* in 1925 recall those of *Heartbreak House,* while *Design for Living* (1933), about a successful ménage à trois, owes a good deal to *Getting Married.* As late as 1956, Coward's *Nude with Violin,* in its satire of the avant garde, recalls *The Philanderer,* Shaw's early satire of avant-garde Ibsenites of the 1890s.

Private Lives (1930) reveals that Coward did not follow Shaw's advice to "never see or read my plays," for it owes a considerable debt to Shaw's 1912 playlet *Overruled,* in which two married couples, the Junos and the

Lunns, have taken separate round-the-world cruises and discover on their return to England that they have become romantically involved with each other's spouses. After some discussion, the four decide to remain as they are but to continue the shipboard flirtations, which will simultaneously enliven and validate their marriages. In Coward's play a divorced couple, Elyot and Amanda, acquire new mates and go on honeymoon, only to find themselves in adjacent hotel suites. Elyot and Amanda soon abandon Sibyl and Victor to run away together. They have reached a point of renewed enmity by the time Sibyl and Victor catch up with them a few days later. Ironically enough, when Sibyl and Victor try to repossess Elyot and Amanda and bicker with each other in the process, their behavior points to the rightness of the earlier marriage, and Elyot and Amanda again flee together.

Coward's dialogue in *Private Lives* echoes many of Shaw's themes in *Overruled:* that it was "the fact of being married, and clamped together publicly, that wrecked us before"; that few people can abide by the conventions associated with "proper" marital conduct; that the "gentlemanly" expedient of knocking down interlopers simply will not work; that although Elyot and Amanda "ought to be absolutely tortured with conscience," neither is. Some lines have a distinctly Shavian ring, as when Elyot asks Victor, "Has it ever struck you that flippancy might cover a very real embarrassment?" and when Amanda tells Victor, "Don't be angry, it's all much too serious to be angry about." At one point Coward includes what might be a backhanded acknowledgment of *Overruled.* Asked whether she ever had a sister, Amanda responds, "I believe there was a stillborn one in 1912," the year that *Overruled* appeared.[5]

Sean O'Casey is another of Shaw's more obvious inheritors. Unlike Granville Barker and others, he did not later repudiate Shaw's influence. In an early attempt to interest the Abbey Theatre in his work in 1921, O'Casey submitted *The Crimson in the Tri-Colour*. Lady Gregory found it "extremely interesting" but "disagreeable," and Yeats disliked it so much that the letter rejecting the play did not invite O'Casey to submit a revision. O'Casey later described the play as "really 'a play of ideas' moulded on Shaw's style."[6]

Shavian influence is often present but never crucial in O'Casey's plays. In 1924 O'Casey's published *Shadow of a Gunman* included the character Donal Davoren, a self-styled "poet and poltroon." A stage direction describing Davoren's point of view quotes directly from Louis Dubedat's artistic credo from *The Doctor's Dilemma*. Captain Boyle in *Juno and the Paycock* (1924) superficially resembles Captain Shotover from *Heartbreak House*, O'Casey's favorite of Shaw's plays: Boyle, often in his cups, frequently comments that "Ireland sober is Ireland free" and is convinced that the world is "in a terrible state of chassis." *The Plough and the Stars*

(1926) takes Andrew Undershaft's statement from *Major Barbara*—"My sort of blood cleanses, my sort of fire purifies"—to direct a thrust, not at the Salvation Army, but at the Irish Citizen Army. One of the ruthless officers argues to a crowd that "Bloodshed is a cleansing and sanctifying thing, and the nation that regards it as the final horror has lost its manhood. . . ." Undershaft also ties bloodshed to manhood when he remarks that killing "is the final test of conviction" and that "The history of the world is the history of those who had courage enough to embrace this truth."

In *The Purple Dust,* published in 1940, O'Casey reveals only a limited indebtedness to *John Bull's Other Island* despite its Irish rural setting, attention to contemporary and social issues, and heavy-handed satire of "stage Englishmen" whose obtuseness contrasts sharply with Irish common sense. Although O'Casey often professed his admiration for Shaw's Irish play, *Heartbreak House* has been more influential here. Stanley Weintraub has called *The Purple Dust* "a try at social criticism through a symbolic decaying country house and characters who might have come out of *Heartbreak House*."[7] For R. F. Dietrich, who cites O'Casey's "pointing to his encounter with Shaw's work as the great awakener," O'Casey emerges as "one of the greatest celebrators of the Life Force."[8]

In terms of general influence and by virtue of their long theatrical association, Granville Barker, in his writing of "naturalistic social drama" and his use of the stage as an educational vehicle, also is one of Shaw's inheritors. In *The Voysey Inheritance* (1905), Granville Barker is realistic in the Shavian sense when a family of solicitors discovers that its wealth has derived from fraud. A. B. Walkley, pointing to "spare emotional content," "sardonic irony," "its willingness to question the assumptions upon which the lives of its audiences were based," and other Shavian traits, has called *Voysey* "*triple extrait de Shaw*."[9] This influence, however, is not entirely one way—*The Apple Cart* owes something to Barker's play *His Majesty* (written between 1923 and 1928).

James Gindin has noted in Shaw's contemporary John Galsworthy a focus on "the force of a conflict in which neither side is right,"[10] and R. F. Dietrich has commented that Galsworthy's "documentary realism contributed to the cause—inherited from Ibsen and Shaw—of democratically leveling heroes and villains, to the end of emphasizing the mixed humanity of all."[11] Daniel Leary cites James Bridie's *Sleeping Clergyman* of 1933 for putting "one in mind of George Bernard Shaw, some of whose social concerns, techniques, and philosophical-religious views seem to be echoed or paralleled in the younger dramatist." Bridie's 1950 drama *The Queen's Comedy* reminds Leary of *Back to Methuselah:* "Like Shaw's Lilith in the closing scene of *Back to Methuselah*, Jupiter at the close of *The Queen's Comedy* speaks of himself as a creator, an author driven by an urge not under his control to engender a creation beyond his comprehension."[12] One can find Bridie's own assessment of Shaw's contribution to British drama in his obituary tribute to Shaw, published in *The New Statesman and Nation* on 11 November 1950.[13] For Audrey Williamson, Gordon Daviot's *Richard of Bordeaux* (1932) reflects Shaw's approach to dramatizing history in its "wit, political irony, and . . . clear modern forms of speech."[14] Like Shaw, Daviot creates characters who articulate their understanding much more clearly than they might have done in real life, thus using the method Shaw defended in his Preface to *Saint Joan*.

Several playrights reveal their indebtedness to specific plays. *Man and Superman*'s Henry Straker seems to have helped inspire John Galsworthy's Lemmy in *The Foundations* (1917). In Stanley Houghton's *Independent Means* (1909), one woman's "marital rebellion begins when her husband forbade her to see *Man and Superman*," but, as J. L. Wisenthal points out, "the plot is too neat and contrived."[15] *Pygmalion* has inspired Louis D'Alton's character Bartley Murnaghan in the 1947 play *They Got What They Wanted*. Like the immortal dustman Alfred Doolittle, Murnaghan "undergoes a sudden transformation from a shirker of work and of responsibility to an ingenious man of business," and D'Alton's *This Other Eden* (1953) is "an updated *John Bull's Other Island*."[16] *Heartbreak House*, in addition to its influence on Coward and O'Casey, has attracted the attention of several playwrights. T. F. Evans has said of St. John Hankin's 1908 play *The Burglar Who Failed* that Hankin stands the burglar on his head in a way similar to Shaw's treatment of Billy Dunn in *Heartbreak*.[17]

T. S. Eliot was decidedly reluctant to inherit anything from Shaw. His remarks on *Saint Joan* in the April 1926 issue of the *Criterion* hardly reflected admiration: he called Shaw's Joan "one of the most superstitious of the effigies which have been erected to that remarkable woman."[18] In 1935, however, Eliot's *Murder in the Cathedral* has the murderers address a political apologia to the audience in a way reminiscent of the Epilogue of *Saint Joan*, and Eliot confessed some fifteen years later, "I may, for aught I know, have been slightly under the influence of *St. Joan*."[19] Eliot's "The last temptation is the greatest treason: / To do the right deed for the wrong reason" recalls *Major Barbara*'s Andrew Undershaft, whose wife declares, "Thats Andrew all over. He never does a proper thing without giving an improper reason for it."[20] Robert Brustein in *The Theatre of Revolt* suggested in 1964 "that the ritual chant of multiple voices at the close of the first act of *Heartbreak House* foreshadowed the choral technique employed by Eliot in *The Family Reunion* (1939), while his later, more accessible, comedies employ wit and satire suggesting Wilde and Shaw."[21] As Eric Bentley has commented, although Eliot began his career as a playwright "in strong opposition to the drama in prose, drama of ideas, and drama by Bernard Shaw; *The Confidential Clerk* has all the earmarks of Shavianism as described by the early Eliot, without the merits of the real Bernard Shaw. . . ."[22]

Shaw's more recent inheritors owe less to his specific plays than to his general philosophy and to his "opening a wedge" to increase the recognized possibilities of the dramatic medium. John Osborne, for example, whose *Look Back in Anger* changed theater forever in 1956, seems an extremely unlikely inheritor of Shaw. Osborne loathed Shaw, and his vitriolic, acerbic, and even hateful tone when dramatizing social evils is the very antithesis of Shaw's. Still, his drama has some Shavian affinities, as Katharine J. Worth has pointed out. These include the socialist element in Osborne's drama, "the wide range of Jimmy Porter's criticisms . . . recalling Tanner's discursive onslaughts in *Man and Superman*," and "the ability to distribute argument convincingly, on which the dramatic life of rhetorical drama depends."[23] In *The Entertainer* (1957), the decaying music hall which is a metaphor for English decline recalls Shotover's ship-house, which performed the same emblematic function. In the 1960 BBC play *A Subject of Scandal and Concern*, Osborne depended upon original transcripts from the last trial by jury for atheism in England as Shaw had drawn from the historical record of Joan's trial. In *Luther* (1961), Osborne's balancing of the argument between Cajetan (who argues with moderation) and Luther suggests the similar balance between Cauchon and Saint Joan. Osborne's *Blood of the Bambergs* (1962), in compensating a ruler for having to undergo the tedium of government, recalls features of *The Apple Cart*. While none of Osborne's plays could be called derivative in the sense of being possible only in response to or imitation of Shaw, the affinities make Osborne one of Shaw's inheritors.

My nominee for the most Shavian of contemporary playwrights is one whose *Dictionary of Literary Biography* entry, written by Shavian scholar Anne Wright, links him with practically everybody *but* Shaw.[24] I refer, of course, to Tom Stoppard, who rivals Shaw in his devotion to the theater of ideas, his tactic of using drama to "ambush" the audience into recognition, his imaginative adaptation of others' thoughts and works, and his knack for combining paradox, brilliant and witty debate, and absurd situations into "serious farce." Stoppard, like Shaw, spent some time as a theater critic, but his apprenticeship was severely compressed—in 1963 he reviewed 132 plays in seven months.

Reminders of Shaw's plays abound in Stoppard's work. The deliberate, historically leveling anachronisms in *Rosencrantz and Guildenstern Are Dead* (1966) serve a Shavian function—to convey to the audience that people of bygone times were not materially different from ourselves. In *The Real Inspector Hound* (1968), Stoppard spoofs the critics as Shaw had in *Fanny's First Play*. For Clive Barnes, *Jumpers* (1972) "suggests the Shaw of *Man and Superman.*"[25] T. E. Kalem's review calls *Travesties* (1974) "a tinder-box of a play blazing with wit, irony, and yes, ideas. It is exhilarating, diabolically clever. The bloodline of Wilde and Shaw is not extinct while Tom Stoppard lives."[26] And in *The Real Thing* (1982), a character's remark about "the impossible competition" that every major dramatist feels with Shakespeare recalls the focus of *Shakes vs. Shav,* the last of Shaw's plays to be performed in his lifetime.

Shaw's legacy of "serious farce" continues in the work of Alan Ayckbourn, Henry Livings, and Peter Nichols, and the vigor of contemporary "agitprop" and absurdist drama is also part of the Shavian bequest to the contemporary stage. Shaw's strenuous opposition to the oppressive stage censorship that prevailed until 1968 and his efforts to bring into being a National Theatre are also parts of the Shavian inheritance, but the most valuable contribution of Shaw has been to break trail for a theater that is worthy of a thinking audience, that can improve the quality of modern life, and that can challenge the imagination. Shaw's influence has been pervasive in ways that are hard to pinpoint, perhaps for the same reason that Shaw once offered to explain why water has no taste—because it is always in our mouths.

Shaw's encouragement of budding dramatists and his influence on them have had their effects, even when not fully apprehended by the playwrights. Two have eloquently described Shaw's influence on them. Peter Terson has commented, "I was the son of a joiner whose only concession to culture was a *Daily Herald* edition of George Bernard Shaw and a set of Shakespeare which was never opened."[27] Early reading of Shaw shaped Terson's perspective beyond his understanding. Denis Johnston has considered both the extent of Shaw's influence on himself and the rather ironical consequence of that influence: "During my formative years I was influenced greatly by H. G. Wells, particularly by his *Outline of History.* I was also influenced by Wilde and, of course, enormously by Shaw, as most of us were. We were all standing on Shaw's shoulders. Having got over the initial annoyance of not knowing quite what he was talking about, one realises that Shaw is so plain and obvious that nowadays one finds him a bore."[28]

This is surely what Shaw himself might have wished, as Stanley Weintraub indicated when he wrote,

> Shaw would not have been downcast at leaving no school. "It is my hope," he had written in 1921, when he was sixty-five, "that a hundred apter and more elegant parables by younger hands will soon leave mine as far behind as the religious pictures of the fifteenth century left behind the first attempts of the early Christians at iconography."[29]

This has hardly happened to *that* extent, as the continuing vitality and relevance of Shaw's plays make clear. However, Shaw would have found it gratifying to learn that some dramatists of a later generation would see his conclusions as self-evident, particularly after he had worked for years as novelist, pamphleteer, critic, and playwright to pound the Shavian viewpoint into the thick skulls of his benighted contemporaries. He would surely have realized that inheritors of the Shavian perspective reflect greater credit on his work than would a school of self-styled Shavians forever in his shadow.

Notes

1. Frederick Lumley, *New Trends in 20th Century Drama: A Survey Since Ibsen and Shaw* (New York: Oxford University Press, 1972), p. 36.
2. TPCS, Dan H. Laurence to Fred D. Crawford, 12 January 1990.
3. Enoch Brater, "Noel Coward," *Dictionary of Literary Biography, Volume 10: Modern British Dramatists, 1900–1945, Part 1: A–L,* ed. Stanley Weintraub (Detroit: Gale Research, 1982): 119.
4. Richard F. Dietrich, *British Drama 1890–1950: A Critical History* (Boston: Twayne Publishers, 1989), p. 168.
5. Noël Coward, *Private Lives: An Intimate Comedy* (London: Samuel French, 1947), pp. 25, 43, 49, 13.
6. Quoted in Stanley Weintraub, *The Unexpected Shaw: Biographical Approaches to G.B.S. and His Work* (New York: Frederick Ungar, 1982), p. 211.
7. Ibid., p. 218.
8. Dietrich, *British Drama 1890–1950,* p. 208.
9. Stanley Weintraub, "The Royal Court Theatre and the New Drama," *DLB* 10, Part 2: 305.
10. James Gindin, "John Galsworthy," *DLB* 10, Part 1: 198.
11. Dietrich, *British Drama 1890–1950,* p. 152.
12. Daniel Leary, "James Bridie," *DLB* 10, Part 1: 69–70.
13. T. F. Evans, *Shaw: The Critical Heritage* (London: Routledge & Kegan Paul, 1976), pp. 389–91.
14. Audrey Williamson, "Gordon Daviot," *DLB* 10, Part 1: 140.
15. J. L. Wisenthal, "Stanley Houghton," *DLB* 10, Part 1: 232.
16. Heinz Kozok, "Louis D'Alton," *DLB* 10, Part 1: 131, 132.
17. T. F. Evans, "St. John Hankin," *DLB* 10, Part 1: 224.
18. T. S. Eliot, "Books of the Quarter," *Criterion* 4 (April 1926): 389.
19. Quoted in Louis L. Martz, "The Saint as Tragic Hero," in Saint Joan *Fifty Years After: 1923/24–1973/74,* ed. Stanley Weintraub (Baton Rouge: Louisiana State University Press, 1973), p. 155.
20. T. S. Eliot, *Murder in the Cathedral,* in *The Complete Poems and Plays, 1909–1950* (New York: Harcourt, Brace & World, 1962), p. 196; Bernard Shaw, *Major Barbara,* in *Collected Plays with Their Prefaces* 3:143.

21. Robert Brustein, *The Theatre of Revolt: An Approach to Modern Drama* (Boston: Little, Brown, 1964), p. 222.

22. Eric Bentley, "Old Possum at Play," in *What is Theatre?: Incorporating the Dramatic Event and Other Reviews, 1945–1967* (New York: Atheneum, 1968), p. 144.

23. Katharine J. Worth, "Shaw and John Osborne," *Shavian* 2.10 (October 1964): 29, 31.

24. Anne Wright, "Tom Stoppard," *Dictionary of Literary Biography, Volume 13: British Dramatists Since World War II,* ed. Stanley Weintraub (Detroit: Gale Research, 1982): 482–500.

25. Clive Barnes, review of *Jumpers,* by Tom Stoppard, *New York Times* (23 April 1974), quoted in Susan Rusinko, *British Drama 1950 to the Present: A Critical History* (Boston: Twayne Publishers, 1989), p. 68.

26. T. E. Kalem, "Dance of Words," *Time* (10 November 1975), quoted in Rusinko, *British Drama 1950 to the Present,* p. 67.

27. Quoted in Gillette Elvgren, "Peter Terson," *DLB* 13: 514.

28. Des Hickey and Gus Smith, *Flight from the Celtic Twilight: Irish Playwrights, Directors, and Actors Speak Frankly About Their Careers In and Out of Ireland* (New York: Bobbs-Merrill, 1973), p. 69.

29. Stanley Weintraub, "Foreword," *DLB* 13: x.

A. M. Gibbs

HEARTBREAK HOUSE: CHAMBER OF ECHOES

Heartbreak House is the site of a remarkably complex convergence of creative impulses and influences.[1] The play reflects an intricate intertwining of some of Shaw's personal experiences in the pre–World War I period with his responses to literary and dramatic texts. These experiences and responses became linked, in turn, with the larger "text" of early twentieth-century history. As Europe was stumbling toward the most destructive war, up to that time, in human history, certain turbulent situations were developing in Shaw's private life which were to shape some of the central thematic concerns and images of *Heartbreak House,* especially with regard to the treatment of sexual and filial relations in the play.[2] In the same period, Shaw had his one meeting with Strindberg, whose treatments of marital relations in his plays and stories find parallels in *Heartbreak House,* and saw the first London production of one of Strindberg's plays about that subject, *Creditors.* He was also extolling the virtues of Chekhov, one of the Russian masters alluded to in the subtitle of *Heartbreak House: A Fantasia in the Russian Manner on English Themes*— "everything we write in England seems sawdust after Tchekhov," wrote Shaw later to H. G. Wells[3]—and was helping to get Chekhov's work launched on the English stage. Evidently during this period he was also re-immersing himself in the texts of *Othello* and *King Lear,* plays which figure prominently in the intertextual relations of *Heartbreak House.*

This essay does not aim at an encyclopedic account of the numerous echoes of other texts which are present in *Heartbreak House.* Nor does it set out to deny that the play is very much preoccupied with the kinds of "public" themes—the predicament of "cultured, leisured Europe before the war,"[4] the disastrous separation of culture and power in English and European societies, the failure of the intellectual elites, and their part in the "drift to the abyss" (21)—which are so much highlighted by Shaw in his 1919 Preface. The principal aim here is to explore the patterns of intertextual play and creative dialogue with other texts, especially dramatic texts, that are discernible in *Heartbreak House,* and to throw light on certain characteristics of Shaw's dramatic artistry in these processes of textual interaction.

Some of Shaw's experiences of other dramatists in the period leading up to World War I would have brought art into very close relation with events in his own life. As he was becoming acquainted with the charming, dangerous heroines of Chekhov's *Uncle Vanya* and Strindberg's *Creditors,* who wreak havoc and destruction among the menfolk in their plays, havoc was being wrought in his own life by his infatuation with the "perilously bewitching" Stella Campbell.[5] Like Tekla in *Creditors* and the Shotover daughters in *Heartbreak House,* Stella represented a fatally attractive combination of mother-figure and siren. She conjured up for Shaw virtually the whole gamut of male fantasies about, and stereotypes of, the feminine, ranging from *The Vampire*—the title of a painting by Philip Burne-Jones for which Stella was recognizably the model—to the Madonna, or "mother of Angels," as she was rapturously addressed by Shaw in a letter written on New Year's Eve, 1913.[6] Shaw's affair with Stella Campbell, and her eleventh-hour evasion of what was clearly, in Shaw's mind at least, an assignation for its physical consummation after a long period of flirtation and dalliance, probably brought him as close to the experience of heartbreak as he ever came. Like his character, Randall, he had been a servant-lover bilked of his reward "when pay-day [came] round" (156). *Heartbreak House,* with its rather Irish view of heartbreak as ultimately a beneficial experience, can be seen in part at least as being an exorcism of what had been for Shaw a painful and humiliating episode of his life. The images of sexually magnetic, destructive women in the plays of Chekhov and Strindberg would have combined with his own experiences to cast a powerful spell over the composition of *Heartbreak House* and the creation of the "demon daughters" (156) of Shotover.

In the fictional world of *Heartbreak House,* the maternal sirens of the household are destructive and emasculating forces. As such, they resemble the character of Laura, the wife in Strindberg's play *The Father,* who came into her husband's life as "his second mother,"[7] and who in the course of the play reduces him to tearful and impotent childishness and finally brings about his complete destruction, with the help of the maternalistic ministrations of an old family nurse. Strindberg makes Laura the definer of her own—to her, repugnantly ambiguous—situation as her husband's lover/mother in the remarkable scene at the end of Act II in which she announces his defeat at her hands in the duel of sex. In March 1912 Strindberg's *Creditors,* another play about a wife who treats her husband as her child and brings about his destruction, was presented by the Stage Society in London. Shortly afterward, Shaw wrote a Preface to a new edition of *The Quintessence of Ibsenism* in which he described *Creditors* as "the terrible play with which Strindberg wreaked the revenge of the male for A Doll's House [in which] it is the man who is the victim of domesticity, and the woman who is the tyrant and soul destroyer."[8] The description by Strindberg ("Ibsen's twin giant," as Shaw describes him in the same Preface)[9] of his creation of the charming tyrant mother-wife, Tekla, in *Creditors* serves to underline the kinship between Shaw's portrayal of female characters in *Heartbreak House*, especially Hesione, and that of Strindberg in his powerful and disturbingly probing plays about marriage. "You will find the vampire wife," Strindberg wrote about Tekla in a letter of 26 June 1892, "charming, conceited, parasitical . . . loving (two men at once!), tender, falsely maternal, in a phrase, woman as I see her!"[10]

The main paradigm of female-male relations in *Heartbreak House* is a pattern of female domination involving, first, mutual flirtation and sexual negotiation between male and female figures, followed by exposure, humiliation, and rejection of the male and his reduction to abject states of frustration and childishness.[11] Ariadne's reduction of Randall to "crybaby" status, Hesione and Ellie's reduction of Mangan to a howling mess ("I like him best when he is howling" [171] says Ellie of Mangan), and the lap-dog status of Hector in *Heartbreak House* are exemplary of the way in which female attractiveness and power are exerted in Shaw's fictional world of men and women leading "foolish lives of romance and sentiment and snobbery" (146) in this play. The acerbic view of the duel of sex which Shaw's play presents was nurtured in a complex matrix of personal and literary experience in which other dramatists played an important role.

Of all writers, Shaw presents himself as one of the least perturbed by the anxiety of influence. He cheerfully acknowledged his extensive pillagings from other authors—"all is fish that comes to my net"[12]—and sometimes obligingly conducts his own *Quellenforschung* in prefaces and letters. But the interaction of Shaw's plays with other texts is generally more complicated than some of his statements, suggesting primitive and unmediated piracy ("I was finding that the surest way to produce an effect of daring innovation and originality was . . . to stick closely to the methods of Moliere; and to lift characters bodily out of the pages of Dickens"),[13] would lead us to think. To invoke the Bakhtinian model of the generation of meaning, his plays can be said to create a dialogic, and very frequently oppositional, relation with other texts with which they connect.[14]

Heartbreak House is one of the most densely allusive of all Shaw's works. The play echoes, often in ways which are far from simple, a very large number of other texts, ranging in time from Homer to Chekhov. Allusion occurs in the play in both explicit and implicit ways. For example, Shakespeare's *Othello* is directly referred to, or alluded to, on several occasions, but *King Lear* is an implied textual presence in the background of the play, evoked by the image of the raging old man and his two "demon daughters" (156) and in various other indirect ways. Ironies are created by clashes between Shaw's text and the texts which are echoed within it. The ending of the play, for example, might call to mind the tumultuous close of Wagner's *Twilight of the Gods*, or the fall and burning of Troy in classical legend. But such heroic images come into comic tension with the comparatively anticlimactic conclusion of the play and with Randall's amateurish tootling on the flute.

Characteristically, Shavian dramatic texts bear an ironic and parodic relation to the other texts and literary motifs that they echo. In *Heartbreak House* this principle can be illustrated by the play's relation to a tradition in English nondramatic literature in which "houses" are employed metaphorically for critical exploration of, and satire upon, existing social orders and mores. Shaw's first completed play, *Widowers' Houses*, is related to this tradition. The *topos* of the "house-as-ship" can be described as a subset of the larger category of these literary houses of fame, or ill-fame, and the relationship of *Heartbreak House* to the English nineteenth-century fictional tradition of ship-like houses, and to the similarly named *Bleak House* of Dickens, supplies a model of the contrapuntal, asymmetrical way in which the play echoes the texts with which it interacts.

As an avid reader of Dickens in his boyhood, Shaw would very early have come across the converted barge, situated on dry land on the foreshore, in which Mr. Peggotty and his family live at Yarmouth in *David Copperfield*. The "sort of ark" in which the good-natured Peggottys live is "beautifully clean inside, and as tidy as possible,"[15] and the Peggottys themselves are the soul of hospitality as they attend to the needs of their young guest and conduct him to his enchanting bedroom in the stern of the vessel. In *Dombey and Son,* Florence Dombey leaves the sterile dwelling of her father and finds happiness in the ship-like house-cum-shop of the nautical instrument maker, Solomon Gills. Everything is so compactly stowed and organized in this place, where Solomon Gills lives "in skipper-like state," that "the shop itself . . . seemed almost to become a snug, sea-going, ship-shape concern, wanting only good sea-room . . . to work its way securely to any desert island in the world."[16] It is here that Florence is given a home by the hospitable friend of Gills, Captain Cuttle, in a garret "transformed into a species of land-cabin."[17] Similar in character to these Dickensian ship-like houses and havens is the orderly, small, but well-fitted-out house belonging to the retired

Captain Harville in Jane Austen's *Persuasion* that becomes the sanctuary for Louisa's convalescence after her fall at the Cobb in Lyme Regis. This house, with its "ingenious contrivances and nice arrangements" for which Captain Harville is responsible, looks out to sea from near the foot of an old pier.[18] In an analysis of this house in his study of *Persuasion*, Tony Tanner remarks on the special quality of hospitality, in the best tradition of the Navy, that characterizes the ordering of affairs in the Harville house.[19]

The Shotover house in Shaw's play is a travesty of these ship-like houses of order and hospitality in nineteenth-century fiction. The play gives a number of sardonic twists to the fictional tradition to which it belongs. In the opening scene of *Heartbreak House*, an already observed but ignored guest sits reading Shakespeare in a setting that includes a carpenter's bench in the living quarters of the house and a floor "*littered with shavings, overflowing from a waste-paper basket*" (59). The guest's luggage has been left on the front steps of the house "for everybody to fall over" (62). The considerate, kindly welcomes accorded David Copperfield, Florence Dombey, and Louisa Musgrove in the houses in Yarmouth, London, and Lyme Regis are here replaced by careless neglect. The first of the many comments in the play on the house and its Fawlty Towers-like management comes from an angry Captain Shotover, whose understanding of the "commonest decencies of social intercourse" (62) does not necessarily make him an exemplary practitioner: "This is a pretty sort of house, by heaven! A young and attractive lady is invited here. Her luggage is left on the steps for hours; and she herself is deposited in the poop and abandoned, tired and starving. This is our hospitality. These are our manners. No room ready. No hot water. No welcoming hostess. Our visitor is to sleep in the toolshed, and to wash in the duckpond" (62). Shortly afterward, Lady Utterword, who has had an equally unsatisfactory reception, extends the opening images of domestic chaos to deeper levels of criticism. Beneath the failings of ordinary household management she finds, on her return to "this house, this house!" after a twenty-three-year absence, "the same disorder in ideas, in talk, in feeling" (65–66). The last term in this trilogy of disorders (from which Ariadne herself is, ironically, not immune) suggests a peculiarly deep-seated disorientation in the household, as if its inhabitants have lost track of basic codes of behavior.

In the larger tradition of fictional houses, *Heartbreak House* bears some resemblance to such satirical novels of Thomas Love Peacock as *Nightmare Abbey*, *Crotchet Castle*, and *Headlong Hall*. Set in substantial country houses owned by enthusiastic patrons of general intellectual inquiry, Peacock's novels bring together groups of amiable eccentrics who, while drinking many bumpers of wine, engage in vehement debate, collectively creating in each work, as one commentator aptly puts it, "a mad-house . . . where there is a bee in every bonnet, but every bonnet has style."[20] Passages in *Heartbreak House*, such as Ariadne's dogmatic discourse about the advantages of houses with horse stables over those that lack this amenity, have a distinctly Peacockian flavor. More influential on *Heartbreak House*, however, was a novel that Shaw had known and admired since his teenage years and to which he made frequent reference in his nondramatic writings, Charles Dickens's *Bleak House*.[21] The dwelling known as Bleak House in the novel belies its name: it is in fact the most cheerful house of the many portrayed in the work. But the name of the house becomes a metaphor for the condition of the whole of England, as Dickens saw it in the mid-nineteenth century, as a land of human degradation where grinding poverty exists side by side with conditions of great wealth, and as a society in the grip of deeply corrupt and incompetent legal and political systems of management that cause widespread misery and heartbreak. Leadership in the land has failed under the direction of aristocratic personages with such ludicrous names as Coodle, Boodle, and Noodle, and the principal aristocrat in the work, the wooden Lord Dedlock, is nicknamed "Sir Arrogant Numskull," a title which probably remained in Shaw's mind when he had Shotover refer to Sir Hastings Utterword as a "numskull" (72).[22] Maritime imagery about the state of England recurs in *Bleak House*, as when Lord Boodle describes the whole country as "shipwrecked, lost and gone to pieces."[23] In a late passage in the novel, England is seen as a ship drifting without a pilot. In the same passage, Dickens likens the people of England to the careless souls in the days of Noah before the apocalyptic moment of divine intervention and destruction with the Flood: "England has been some weeks in the dismal state of having no pilot . . . to weather the storm; and the marvellous part is that England has not appeared to care very much about it, but has gone on eating and drinking and marrying and giving in marriage, as the old world did in the days before the flood."[24]

The dialogue that occurs just before the explosion in Act III of *Heartbreak House* contains several ideas and images that recall such passages in Dickens's novel as those referred to here. England is again a ship, as in Hector's questioning speech, "And this ship we are all in? This soul's prison we call England?" (177). The Captain has just been talking about the dangers of a "drifting skipper" and is about to bark out his command about the proper business of an Englishman: "Navigation. Learn it and live; or leave it and be damned" (176, 177). Mazzini Dunn encapsulates the whole tendency of the inhabitants of Heartbreak House to avoid facing reality when he says, a second before the first explosion is heard, "I assure you nothing will happen" (177).

But for all its clear echoes of *Bleak House,* the temper of *Heartbreak House* is finally very different. Despite the ruin and death of Richard Carstone and the melodramatic demise of Lady Dedlock, Dickens's novel ends on a strongly upbeat note with the happy marriage of Esther Summerson and the continued companionship of the benevolent Jarndyce. It is almost as if "there is hope for the old ship yet," to quote an ironical comment from the author/narrator in Chapter 40.[25] But no such redemptions through love, benignity, and good-fellowship are suggested by the ending of *Heartbreak House.* The pattern of Dickensian echoes is broken by the powerful counter-thrust of the completely unsentimental final movement of Shaw's *"Fantasia."*

Shaw's dialogue with other dramatists in *Heartbreak House* is similar in character to his dialogue with previous makers of fictional houses. It is creative, active, counter-directional. In the chamber of Shaw's fictional house of social disorder the echoes of other dramatists, while remaining recognizable as echoes, are quite different in sound, mood, and significance from their originals. Shaw's role in his relationship with other dramatists in the play is not that of a passive imitator. Rather, he engages in exuberant, interactive games with previous players in the fields of discourse and interest to which the play relates. To speak simply of "debts" and "borrowings" or, in the case of Chekhov, attempted imitation is to misapprehend the nature of the relationship of the play with other dramatic texts. The main intertextual conversations of *Heartbreak House* are with Shaw's old foe Shakespeare and his new rival in the early years of the twentieth century, Chekhov, two predecessors in Shaw's explorations of heartbreak.

Shaw's dramatic and nondramatic writings show an abiding interest in, and sharp critical response to, the works of Shakespeare. He was an eccentric but alert and engaged reader of Shakespeare, and throughout his life the Bard remained a major presence in Shaw's imagination. Works such as *The Doctor's Dilemma* and *The Dark Lady of the Sonnets* make splendid comic play with Shakespearean texts. Yet as the tide of reverence in which Shakespeare and his works were held rose to a peak in the late nineteenth and early twentieth centuries, Shaw, the inventor of the term "bardolatry" (in the Preface to *Three Plays for Puritans,* 1901), took great delight in shaking the pedestal upon which contemporary John Bulls were placing their major cultural icon.

In his final joust with Shakespeare, in the form of a puppet play called *Shakes versus Shav* (1949), Shaw introduced, in explicit reference to *Heartbreak House,* a tableau based on a painting by Millais of a young woman of virginal beauty sitting at the feet of an ancient sea-captain, about which Shav declares, "Behold, my Lear" (7:475).

For the reader of *Heartbreak House,* an allusion to Shakespeare occurs even before the dialogue begins in Act I. The opening stage direction of the play tells us that the young lady, Ellie, while impatiently waiting for some attention in the Shotover household and before she falls asleep, is passing the time by reading a copy of the Temple Shakespeare. In the play itself, a complex pattern of Shakespearean echoes is developed in which *Othello* is gradually displaced by *King Lear* as the dominant point of reference. As we learn in her first dialogue with Hesione, Ellie's perception of her romantic encounters with Hector is largely shaped by the account, in Act I, scene iii of *Othello*, of the wooing of Desdemona by Othello with his enchanting tales of dangerous exploits and strange adventures. Ellie has been similarly enchanted by Hector's tales of his derring-do. Through Hesione, Shaw deliberately deploys the allusions to *Othello* in this scene to cast doubt on Hector's stories ("Ellie darling: have you noticed that some of those stories that Othello told Desdemona couldnt have happened?" [79]) and more generally to destabilize the margins between fiction and reality in *Heartbreak House*. In the course of the dialogue, Ellie displays a naïve faith in both Othello and Shakespeare as truth-tellers: "Othello was not telling lies. . . . Shakespear would have said if he was" (79). Hesione's dominance over the still ingenuous Ellie in this scene is partly defined by her obviously more intelligent, skeptical approach to the reading of Shakespeare.

The echoes of *King Lear* in *Heartbreak House* take the form of a kaleidoscopic series of refracted images, motifs, and character portraits from Shakespeare's play. It is not to the point to argue that *Heartbreak House* is some kind of botched attempt on Shaw's part at writing a Shakespearean, or any other form of, tragedy. Nicholas Grene's project of seeing "how well the post-Chekhovian mode of the play's form and technique suited Shaw, and whether we can find in it the signs of a new tragic vision in his work," seems to propose critical questions which the play itself does not strictly invite. *Heartbreak House* deals with somber and violent themes, but it remains essentially a comic creation. The play was recognized by one of its earliest reviewers as being among "the larkiest and most amusing" of Shaw's works, and Shaw himself formally presents it not as a tragedy but as "*A Fantasia.*"[26] Kent's poignant utterance in the last moments of *King Lear*, "break heart, I prithee break" (V, iii, 311), may be echoed in Shotover's command, "let the heart break in silence" (171). But Shaw's treatment of the theme of heartbreak is essentially comic in character, and the mood and temper of *Heartbreak House* are obviously quite remote from the spirit of *King Lear*. The relation between these Shavian and Shakespearean texts is more often parodic than imitative.

The relationship between children and parents is one of several thematic loci which call for analysis in discussing the *King Lear* connections of Shaw's play. *King Lear* presents a series of radical disruptions of cul-

FIG. 4. The 1990 Milwaukee Chamber Theatre production of *Heartbreak House* at the MCT's Eighth Annual Shaw Festival, directed by Montgomery Davis: Laura Kohler as Ellie Dunn and Richard Halverson as Captain Shotover. Photograph by Mark Haertlein. Reproduced by permission of The Milwaukee Chamber Theatre.

tural norms in the matter of child-parent relations. Lear foolishly casts off his "joy," Cordelia, and is in turn cruelly humiliated and rejected by the "tigers, not daughters" that Goneril and Regan turn out to be. Edmund shows from the outset a contemptuous and predatory attitude toward his father, Gloucester, and sides with those who put out his eyes. The tragic pattern of *King Lear* depends on deep-rooted cultural assumptions about the "natural" relations of love and reverence that should exist between parents and children.

There is, of course, a quite straightforward reflection of *King Lear* in the images of the octogenarian Captain Shotover raging ("is there no thunder in heaven?" [104]) and his two demoniacal daughters, Hesione and Ariadne. But the interaction of Shaw's text with that of *King Lear*, with respect to the treatment of the parent-child relation, is more complicated. Early in Act I, a disconcertingly comic questioning of conventional assumptions about parent-child relations is introduced with Captain Shotover's precise assertion that "the natural term of the affection of the human animal for its offspring is six years" (64). In one of his speeches in Act III, Shotover speaks of his deep hurt, long ago in the past, at Ariadne's running away from home when she was nineteen: "you left because you did not want us. Was there no heartbreak in that for your father?" (172). But the Shotover of the play's present, so far from showing a Lear-like craving for love and affection from his daughters, wishes himself rid of one and is savagely critical of the other. His railing is not about his mistreatment by his daughters, but about what he sees as their wasted, foolish, and destructive lives. Like Lear, he sees his two daughters as demonic, and there are echoes of Lear's misogyny in Shotover's characterization ("they bring forth demons to delude us, disguised as pretty daughters" [102], says Shotover in Act I). But Shotover's rage is much less focused on his own misfortune than is that of King Lear.

Hesione and Ariadne are also significantly different from their Shakespearean counterparts, the two fiendish daughters of Lear. Goneril and Regan are presented by Shakespeare as fairy-tale-like figures of evil, monsters of deceit, disloyalty, lust, and cruelty. The ruthless and cruel qualities of Hesione and Ariadne are very much in evidence in Shaw's play. But unlike Goneril and Regan, the two characters are entirely without criminal leanings, and they are also endowed with attractive, amusing, and socially adroit qualities which clearly distinguish them from the Shakespearean figures that in some respects they recall. Shaw's portrayal of Hesione and Ariadne serves to underline, by contrast, the melodramatic qualities of Shakespeare's Goneril and Regan. Hesione and Ariadne are also quite different in their attitude toward the father figure. Like Lear, Shotover suffers the "casual impudence" (66) of a servant, but there is no real threat to his place in the household. Ariadne seeks Shotover's recognition and affection, and she is deeply hurt by his harsh response and by *his* poor hospitality: in this case, the tables of *King Lear* are turned. For her part, Hesione affectionately recognizes Shotover's patriarchal authority by addressing him as "daddiest" (102).

The distribution of Shakespearean echoes in the characterization of *Heartbreak House* resembles in its complexity the way in which the prewar events in Shaw's personal life are reflected in the play. Ellie Dunn, for example, can be seen to undergo several Shakespearean metamorphoses in the course of the play. At the beginning, as we have seen, she is closely identified with the romantically spellbound Desdemona evoked in Act I, scene iii of *Othello*. Following her disillusionment about "Marcus Darnley," however, a new, harder, rationalistic, and more cynical persona emerges: she becomes "as hard as nails" (122) and begins to seem more like the

Goneril and Regan of *King Lear* than the Desdemona of *Othello*. In her Act II discussion of marriage with Mangan, she is completely unromantic ("it's no use pretending we are Romeo and Juliet" [107]). When she and Hesione callously discuss Mangan as he sits on a chair hypnotized and, as it were, blinded by Ellie, a disturbing echo is created of the scene in *King Lear* when Goneril and Regan attend and assist in the putting out of Gloucester's eyes while he sits bound to a chair. In the last act of *Heartbreak House*, after Ellie has announced her spiritual marriage with Captain Shotover, there are echoes of the scenes of love and reconciliation between Lear and Cordelia in Acts IV and V of *King Lear*.

The character of King Lear himself is recalled in *Heartbreak House* in several different ways. Shakespeare's protagonist is most obviously echoed in the portrayal of Captain Shotover in ways which have already been observed. But Shaw creates a strange Shakespearean coupling in the play by introducing equally strong recollections of Lear in the unlikely person of the *"entirely commonplace"* (86) Boss Mangan. Both Shotover and Mangan echo Lear's cry of "Howl, howl, howl, howl!" from the last scene of *King Lear*, Shotover with his *"strange wail in the darkness"* (104) as he rails at his daughters at the end of Act I, and Mangan with his "howling" in Act III. But Shaw allots to Mangan alone two of the most specific reminiscences of Lear in the play. In Acts I and II of *King Lear*, Shakespeare gives Lear two premonitions of his own insanity. Near the end of Act I, he exclaims, "O! let me not be mad, not mad, sweet heaven" (I, v, 43), and shortly afterward, in Act II, he feels the swelling within him of *"hysterica passio"* (II, iv, 55), a disorder which had the curious alternative name in Elizabethan times of "the suffocation of the Mother" because its symptoms included a choking in the throat that was popularly associated with the idea of suffocation in the womb.[27] Lear alludes to this alternative name when he says, "O! how this mother swells up toward my heart" (II, iv, 54). Mangan, the victim of "mothering tyranny" (167) in *Heartbreak House*, has a similar frenzied apprehension of encroaching madness when he is being tormented by the brazen candor of Ellie Dunn in the opening scene of Act II. Like Lear, Mangan admits his need of feminine tenderness and love, but in doing so he makes himself vulnerable to cruelty and contempt: "[*clutching at his bursting temples*] Oh, this is a crazy house. Or else I'm going clean off my chump . . . [*throwing himself into the chair distractedly*] My brain wont stand it. My head's going to split. Help! Help me to hold it. Quick: hold it: squeeze it. Save me" (112).

Anne Wright draws attention to the "unmistakable [further] echo of *King Lear*" which occurs in Act III of *Heartbreak House* when Mangan begins to strip off his clothes, as does Lear during the storm on the heath. Wright considers that this echo "points to the centrality of Mangan not only as a comic butt . . . but also as a potentially tragic figure and sacrificial victim."[28] Mangan is certainly victimized, but, as with so many other echoes in the play, the significance of the recollections of Lear in the portrayal of Mangan is defined as much by difference from as by resemblance to the original. Mangan and Lear strip for very different reasons, and with very different dramatic effects. Lear is confronted on the heath by the naked Edgar, "unaccommodated man" (III, iv, 104–5), and wants to imitate his state. His action can be seen not only as a moment of empathy with suffering and degradation, but also as an extremely powerful expression of his demotion in the play, his loss of kingly rank, dignity, and distinction. Mangan begins to strip off his clothes as a desperate and impotent gesture of protest at the cruel games of stripping away masks and exposing weaknesses at which the clever conversational duellists of Heartbreak House are certainly expert. It is a moment of bathos rather than pathos, and Hesione's maternal reproof (which contains another reminder of Lear's madness) extends an exquisitely comic moment: "Alfred: for shame! Are you mad?" (166). Mangan is not even remotely a figure of tragic stature, and the parodic echoes of Lear in his character portrayal by Shaw serve rather to emphasize this, and perhaps also to stir at the roots of our understanding of the tragic, as elsewhere the play questions conventional ideas of heartbreak. Mangan's portrayal can be seen to exemplify one of the many ways in which tragic experience undergoes a sea change in Heartbreak House.

A further dimension of the intertextual connections of Heartbreak House with King Lear can be seen in the treatment of sexual relations in the two plays. In the course of King Lear, Goneril comes to regard her recently acquired husband, Albany, as "milk-liver'd" and as an over-scrupulous "moral fool" (IV, ii, 50, 58). Her assumption of domination over him is likened to the treatment of Hercules by Omphale in classical legend in which the great hero is reduced to effeminacy and set to work on the distaff by the woman of whom he has becomed enamored in one of his journeys: "I must," says Goneril to Edmund, "change arms at home, and give the distaff / Into my husband's hands" (IV, ii, 17–18). As we have seen, Hector is another husband reduced to abject subordination by a woman. He also resembles Albany in his capacity for moral idealism and compassion. It is fitting therefore that Shaw should have Hector nearly quote the words "Fall and cease" that Shakespeare gives to Albany at a moment of intense emotional crisis in the last scene of King Lear (V, iii, 263). In his exclamation, Albany is calling on the heavens to fall and bring all things to an end, to bring about an apocalyptic moment. Hector, at the end of Act II of Heartbreak House, in a moment of unbearable frustration at "women! women! women!" likewise calls on the heavens to "Fall and crush" (157). But, again, the echoes are far from straightforward. Hesione wins dominance over Hector by much more subtle means than those employed by Goneril with Albany. Goneril's ferocious and overt attack on Albany's "manhood" is not at all recalled in Hesione's relation with Hector, which is, on the contrary, loving, solicitous, and affectionate. The resultant effects of male subordination and emasculation may be similar, but the means by which they are obtained are different. Shaw refines and sophisticates the Shakespearean portrayal of female cruelty and tyranny.

Discussion of the connections between *Heartbreak House* and the Russian works alluded to in the subtitle, *A Fantasia in the Russian Manner on English Themes,* and specifically cited in the Preface as earlier portraits of "Heartbreak House" has understandably tended to concentrate on the relationship with Chekhov's *Cherry Orchard,* a performance of which Shaw attended in May 1911.[29] There are indeed many significant links with *The Cherry Orchard* in *Heartbreak House.* The "feckless, unbusiness-like, queer people" (as Lopakhin calls them)[30] who make up Ranyevskaia's circle in *The Cherry Orchard* together represent a social order which has lost control of its own destiny and which is under threat of destruction, mainly self-induced. As in *Heartbreak House,* a sense of impending doom is increasingly felt as Chekhov's play develops. The Cherry Orchard and Heartbreak House are places under threat of annihilation. "I keep expecting something dreadful to happen . . . as if the house were going to fall down on us," says Ranyevskaia in Act II of *The Cherry Orchard* (Chekhov 359). Similar expectations of catastrophe permeate Act III of *Heartbreak House,* beginning with Mangan's presentiment of his death and Hesione's report of hearing a mysterious "splendid drumming in the sky" (159). In both plays, the place evoked in the stage setting becomes explicitly a metaphor for a national social predicament: "the whole of Russia is our orchard" (Chekhov 367), says the idealistic student, Trofimov, in his outcry about the wasteful and useless lives of the indolent owners of the Cherry Orchard. And reference has already been made to Hector's speech in Act III of *Heartbreak House,* in which the ship/house of the play's setting is metaphorically identified with England (177).

But many of the links between *Heartbreak House* and *The Cherry Orchard* display the same kind of *discordia concors* as those between Shaw's play and *King Lear.* Echoes of *The Cherry Orchard* are modified and Shavianized in *Heartbreak House* in such a way as to effect a complete transformation of the Chekhovian motifs. Shortly after the opening of Chekhov's play (following Lopakhin's report of his having fallen asleep over a book, which anticipates the first glimpse of Ellie Dunn in *Heartbreak House*), Ranyevskaia, returning home after a long absence, bursts onto the scene with joyous cries about the nursery, which brings back ecstatically happy memories of her childhood: "The nursery, my dear, my beautiful room! . . . I used to sleep here when I was little. . . . [*cries.*] And now I feel as if I were little again" (Chekhov 336). Ariadne's entry shortly after the beginning of *Heartbreak House* conveys the impression of a theatrical quotation from Chekhov. She is also returning home after a long absence, and her first words in the play are addressed to the Nurse. But Shaw has his character convey a much more astringent view of childhood and its associations than that expressed in Ranyevskaia's opening speeches. In place of the latter's tearfully joyous revisiting of the nursery and recognitions of loved ones, we have Ariadne thinking Ellie must be one of her nieces, failing to be recognized by her own father, railing against the disorder of the house of which she has only unhappy memories, and, especially, not wanting to be accommodated in her childhood bedroom. When Shotover, still infuriatingly refusing to acknowledge that it is Ariadne he is addressing, proposes to her that she sleep in "Ariadne's old room," her indignant reply conveys feelings of deep animosity toward this room:

> THE CAPTAIN . . . You shall sleep in Ariadne's
> old room.
> LADY UTTERWORD. Indeed I shall do nothing of
> the sort. That little hole! (72)

Hesione's report, early in Act III of *Heartbreak House*, of a "splendid drumming in the sky" (159) recalls, in several details, the episode in *The Cherry Orchard* in which a sound, as of a string snapping, breaks a silence which has descended on the characters near the end of Act II. In each case the sound comes "*out of the sky*" (Chekhov 365) from a distance and then dies away. In each case there is speculation about the source of the sound (with the two prosaic men, Lopakhin and Mangan, giving similarly commonsensical explanations), followed by discussion about what the sound might signify. But here again, Shaw gives this Chekhovian echo distinct inflections that have the effect of radically adjusting the meaning of the original. Chekhov clearly wanted the strange sound in his play to convey a mood of almost indescribable sadness: the stage direction calls for the sound to fade in a melancholy diminuendo, "*slowly and sadly dying away*" (Chekhov 365). A quite different impression about the distant sound in the sky is created in *Heartbreak House*. Hesione's description of the sound as "a sort of splendid drumming in the sky" (159) conveys a sense of excitement and exhilaration. When the sound returns at the end of the play, she again calls it "splendid" and says that it is "like Beethoven," a comparison that is underlined in Ellie's response, "By thunder, Hesione: it is Beethoven" (178). The exquisite sadness and foreboding which surround the snapping of the string in Chekhov's play are replaced by a mood of fierce exuberance in *Heartbreak House*.

Shaw also diverges from his Russian model when the question of the

FIG. 5.   The 1990 Milwaukee Chamber Theatre production of *Heartbreak House* at the MCT's Eighth Annual Shaw Festival, directed by Montgomery Davis: (Left to right) Durward McDonald as Mazzini Dunn, Richard Halverson as Captain Shotover, Laura Kohler as Ellie Dunn, Michael Duncan as Hector Hushabye, and Carrie Hitchcock as Ariadne Utterword. Photograph by Mark Haertlein. Reproduced by permission of the Milwaukee Chamber Theatre.

possible significance of the sound is discussed by the characters. In the open country scene of Act II of *The Cherry Orchard,* the mysterious sound elicits from Ranyevskaia a shudder and a vague sense of uneasiness: "it sounded unpleasant, somehow. . . ." (Chekhov 365). After another pause in conversation the old servant, Feers, calls to mind similar ominous sounds heard in the reign of Tsar Alexander II before the emancipation of the serfs, to which he ironically refers as "the misfortune" (Chekhov 365). Feers's speech provides a hint that another profound change in the social order of Russia may be heralded by this sound. But in the garden scene of Act III of *Heartbreak House* the sound is specifically related, in a speech by Hector, to the possibility of an apocalyptic moment in human history, a divine intervention and punishment. The sound is "Heaven's

threatening growl of disgust at us useless futile creatures. . . . Either out of
that darkness some new creation will come to supplant us as we have
supplanted the animals, or the heavens will fall in thunder and destroy us"
(159).

Of the two other Chekhovian portraits of houses of heartbreak to
which Shaw refers in his Preface, *The Seagull* and *Uncle Vanya*, the latter
play has the closer links with *Heartbreak House*. *Uncle Vanya* was performed in London by the Stage Society, at Shaw's urging, in 1914. The
household of the aged and irritable Professor Serebriakov in *Uncle Vanya*
is a place in which, as we are told by his charming and attractive young
wife Yeliena, "things have gone to pieces" (Chekhov 205). Like the abode
of Shotover, that of Serebriakov is a house of disorder and heartbreak.
The main occupation of the characters who are portrayed in this suffocat-
ing Chekhovian hothouse is their indulgence in fruitless and destructive
amatory negotiations like those in *Heartbreak House*.[31] At the center of
these negotiations is the sexually magnetic Yeliena, who is hopelessly
courted by both Uncle Vanya and the frequently visiting Doctor Astrov.
Yeliena, who has been described by an English theater critic as "a Russian
Hedda Gabler,"[32] has much in common also with the dangerously attractive daughters of the Shotover household. Referring to the way Yeliena
distracts Astrov from his practice and his forestry, her stepdaughter
Sonia declares, "You must be a witch" (Chekhov 218), and Astrov himself
describes her as "a charming bird of prey" before saying to her, in com-
plete submission to her powers, "Here I am, devour me" (Chekhov 224).
(Shaw can hardly have failed to be reminded by this dramatic moment in
Uncle Vanya of his own Ann Whitefield in *Man and Superman* who, as Jack
Tanner claims in an admonitory speech to Octavius, gobbles up her male
prey like a boa constrictor.)[33]

A view of Chekhov as philosophically and politically uncommitted, as a
compassionate and humane fatalist who makes no judgments about his
characters, is strongly entrenched in the critical tradition surrounding his
work. But such a view is particularly difficult to sustain in the cases of *The
Cherry Orchard* and *Uncle Vanya*.[34] Despite the complexities of characterization and action and the more than occasional glimpses into metaphysical
voids of absurdity, these plays contain powerful and incisive critiques of
contemporary society. The landowning class is portrayed as idle, selfish,
and feckless. The intellectuals of Chekhov's Russia are hopelessly ineffec-
tual and remote from issues that concern the common weal. Near the end
of *The Cherry Orchard*, great concern is expressed about the failing health
of the old loyal servant Feers. But within a few minutes' playing time, he is
simply forgotten by his employers and left alone on stage to make his sad
closing soliloquy. Ranyevskaia and her entourage, having visited the estate
like a flock of birds to feed on memories, abruptly and insouciantly de-

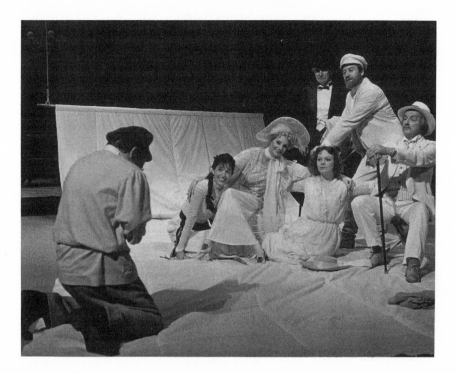

Fɪɢ. 6. The 1980 Shaw Festival Theatre production of *The Cherry Orchard* at Niagara-on-the-Lake, directed by Radu Penciulescu. Photograph by David Cooper. Reproduced by permission of The Shaw Festival Theatre.

part, apparently without any further thought for the major human problem they have left behind. Serebriakov, the retired professor and owner of the estate on which *Uncle Vanya* is set, is presented as a monster of self-engrossment and hypochondriacal irritableness who "for twenty five years has been chewing over other people's ideas about realism, naturalism and all that sort of nonsense" (Chekhov 191). Astrov, the play's man of action and vision, talks of an intellectual class that is "positively rotten with introspection and futile cerebration" and sees around him in the district "a picture of decay . . . caused by inertia, by ignorance, by utter irresponsibility" (Chekhov 211, 223).

Shaw was justified in seeing Chekhov's portrayals of social decay and helpless irresponsibility in Russia as precursors of his own presentation in *Heartbreak House* of a cultivated intelligentsia that has lost control of its destiny and plays dangerous and foolish games of love as civilization drifts toward self-destruction. But in Shaw's play the auguries of doom are much more strongly stressed. The sad music of the snapped string gives way to the tumultuous sound of drums and explosions and to intimations of the possible demise not simply of a social order, but of human civilization itself.

By the time he came to write the Preface to *Heartbreak House* for its publication in 1919, the play had clearly become, in Shaw's publicly presented account of it, a dramatized treatise about a critical moment in human history. The Preface includes no hint of the personal experiences from which Shaw was drawing in the play and gives very little idea of the depth and complexity of its literary relations. Although it is a powerful essay and has clear validity as an account of the social themes of the play, the Preface bears a distinctly ironic relation to some of the less philosophical matters involved in the genesis of *Heartbreak House*. In extreme reaction to late nineteenth-century notions of *l'art pour l'art*, Shaw rejoiced in carrying out regular demolitions of his "literary" reputation as a dramatist by insisting, in the superbly written prefaces, that his plays were strictly to be regarded as sociological essays, cast in dramatic form and designed for the instruction and improvement of humankind, especially for those members of the race living in the southern counties of England. Analysis of the play as a chamber of personal and literary echoes does not deny the strength of its social critique, but it does show *Heartbreak House* to be at once a more autobiographical and a more typically modernist play than might otherwise be apparent.

Notes

1. Although the arguments in this essay take different directions from theirs, I am indebted to the writings on *Heartbreak House* of Stanley Weintraub and Anne Wright. Weintraub's *Bernard Shaw 1914–1918: Journey to Heartbreak* (London: Routledge & Kegan Paul, 1973) is an excellent study of Shaw's life during World War I and includes a discussion of the biographical background of *Heartbreak House* and an essay on the play's connections with *King Lear*. Wright makes an extensive study of the play in *Literature of Crisis 1910–22* (London: Macmillan, 1984) and collaborated with Weintraub in the introductory essay to the facsimile edition of the typescript of the play, *Bernard Shaw, Heartbreak House: A Facsimile of the Revised Typescript* (New York and London: Garland, 1981).

2. The biographical background of the play is treated in more detail in my forthcoming book, *"Heartbreak House": Preludes of Apocalypse*. The influence of the Shaw-Cotterill affair on the composition of *Heartbreak House* is one of the subjects examined in this book. The idea of a "spiritual marriage" between Ellie and Shotover and the treatment of parent-child relationships in *Heartbreak House* were both influenced by Shaw's marriage-threatening relationship with Erica Cotterill.

3. *Bernard Shaw: Collected Letters 1911–1925*, ed. Dan H. Laurence (London: Reinhardt,

1985), p. 439. Subsequent references to Shaw's correspondence in the text are to the four-volume Laurence edition.

4. Bernard Shaw, Preface to *Heartbreak House*, in *Collected Plays with Their Prefaces*, ed. Dan H. Laurence (London: Reinhardt, 1970–74), 5:12. Subsequent references to Shaw's plays and prefaces are to this edition and appear in the text.

5. Shaw's description, *Saturday Review*, 30 April 1898. See *Our Theatres in the Nineties by Bernard Shaw* (London: Constable, 1932), 3:373.

6. See *Bernard Shaw and Mrs Patrick Campbell: Their Correspondence*, ed. Alan Dent (London: Victor Gollancz, 1952), pp. 154–55.

7. This description occurs in a highly charged passage of dialogue in Act II of *The Father*, in which Laura expresses her revulsion at her dual role of being both the mother and the mistress of the Captain, and which concludes with her cruel dismissal of him as "no longer needed." See *August Strindberg: The Plays*, intro. and trans. Michael Meyer (London: Secker & Warburg, 1975), 1:68–71.

8. Bernard Shaw, Preface to the 1913 edition of *The Quintessence of Ibsenism*, in *Shaw and Ibsen: Bernard Shaw's* The Quintessence of Ibsenism *and Related Writings*, ed. J. L. Wisenthal (Toronto: University of Toronto Press, 1979), pp. 101–2.

9. Ibid., p. 102.

10. Strindberg to Charles de Casenove, 26 June 1892, cited in Michael Meyer, *Strindberg: A Biography* (New York: Oxford University Press, 1987), p. 246.

11. As Anne Wright says in *Literature of Crisis*, the men of *Heartbreak House* are "*infantilised*" by the women (93).

12. Bernard Shaw, "Mr Shaw's Literary Morals" (statement for *The Observer*, 11 January 1914). "My plays are full of pillage," Shaw says in the same statement, made in reply to a charge that he had stolen the plot of *Pygmalion* from Smollett's *Peregrine Pickle* (which he had not read). See *Collected Plays with Their Prefaces* 4:799.

13. Bernard Shaw, Preface to *Back to Methuselah*, in *Collected Plays with Their Prefaces* 5:258.

14. John A. Bertolini identifies a pattern of reverse parallel in his discussion of the relation of Shaw's *Caesar and Cleopatra* with Shakespeare's *Antony and Cleopatra* that exemplifies the principle referred to here. See *The Playwrighting Self of Bernard Shaw* (Carbondale: Southern Illinois University Press, 1991), pp. 9–26.

15. Charles Dickens, *David Copperfield* (Harmondsworth: Penguin, 1966), pp. 79, 82. Some of the Dickensian echoes that are discussed below were noted by Martin Quinn in his essay "The Dickensian Presence in *Heartbreak House*," *Shaw Review* 20.3 (September 1977): 119–25. Quinn does not comment on the transformations which occur in Shaw's handling of Dickensian themes and motifs.

16. Charles Dickens, *Dombey and Son* (Harmondsworth: Penguin, 1970), pp. 88–89.

17. Ibid., p. 789.

18. Jane Austen, *Persuasion* (London: Penguin, 1965), p. 119.

19. Tony Tanner, *Jane Austen* (London: Macmillan, 1986), p. 224.

20. This remark, by a Mr. Earle Welby, is quoted by James Agate in a review of the 1932 revival of *Heartbreak House* at the Queen's Theatre, *Sunday Times*, 25 April 1932.

21. Shaw's numerous comments on *Bleak House*, which show a detailed and intimate acquaintance with the work, are recorded in *Shaw on Dickens*, ed. Dan H. Laurence and Martin Quinn (New York: Frederick Ungar, 1985). The novel must have been very much on Shaw's mind in 1913 when he wrote a playlet, "Beauty's Duty," which includes a character based on the legal clerk, Mr. Guppy, in *Bleak House*. See *Shaw on Dickens*, p. xliv.

22. Charles Dickens, *Bleak House* (Harmondsworth: Penguin, 1971), p. 299. Shaw refers to the "arrogant numskull" Dedlock in the draft of an essay "From Dickens to Ibsen," written in 1889. See *Shaw on Dickens*, p. 20.

23. Dickens, *Bleak House*, p. 211.

24. Ibid., p. 619. Dickens alludes here to the telling of the story of the Flood and Noah's ark in Matthew 24:38 ff.

25. Ibid.

26. See Nicholas Grene, *Bernard Shaw: A Critical View* (London: Macmillan, 1984), p. 115; and an anonymous review of the 1920 premiere in New York entitled "The New Shaw Play," Billy Rose Theater Collection, Lincoln Center, New York.

27. Coppelia Kahn shows the significance of this passage and of ideas about the mother and maternal nurture in the play in "The Absent Mother in *King Lear*," in *Rewriting the Renaissance: The Discourses of Sexual Difference in Early Modern Europe*, ed. Margaret W. Ferguson, Maureen Quilligan, and Nancy J. Vickers (Chicago: University of Chicago Press, 1986), pp. 33–49. I am indebted to Kahn's discussion of Lear's simultaneous craving for maternal tenderness from his daughters and fear about the usurpation of his manhood by "womanish" feelings.

28. Wright, *Literature of Crisis*, pp. 99–100.

29. *The Cherry Orchard* was presented by the Stage Society at the Aldwych Theatre on 28 May 1911. It was not well received, but Shaw was deeply impressed by Chekhov's dramatic artistry, and later, in 1911, he reported to George Moore, with reference to the Stage Society production, that "an exquisite play by Tchekoff was actually hissed" (*Collected Letters 1911–1925*, pp. 52–53).

30. *Plays: Anton Chekhov*, trans. Elisaveta Fen (Harmondsworth: Penguin, 1959), p. 358. Subsequent references to Chekhov's plays are to this volume and appear in the text.

31. The motif of suffocation recurs in *Uncle Vanya*. Uncle Vanya himself feels "suffocated" by the thought that his life has been "irretrievably lost" (205), and Doctor Astrov says that he could not stand being in the Serebriakov house for a month: "I should be suffocated in this atmosphere" (210).

32. Michael Billington, in a review of a London production of *Uncle Vanya*, "Missing the Magic," *Guardian Weekly* 145.9 (week ending 1 September 1991): 26.

33. *Uncle Vanya* (1899) predates *Man and Superman* (1901–3), but Shaw's awareness of Chekhov's work apparently dates from 1905. See letter to Laurence Irving, 25 October 1905: "I hear that there are several dramas extant by Whatshisname (Tchekoff, or something like that)—the late Russian novelist who wrote The Black Monk &c.," *Collected Letters 1898–1910*, p. 569.

34. John Tulloch argues persuasively against this tradition of Chekhovian criticism in *Chekhov: A Structuralist Study* (London: Macmillan, 1980).

Christopher Newton

NOTES ON DIRECTING SHAW AND A FEW CONTEMPORARIES

Screaming. Shouting. Programs thrown in the air. Shaw never saw much of this. He had his triumphs, but they were never anything like the reception for Coward's *Cavalcade* or *My Fair Lady*.

Why? Because he never asked the audience to be swept up in his plays, never demanded that they give themselves to the play by wallowing in an ecstasy of bright lights and large emotions which preclude thought. With all his posturing, all his running after attention from the newspapers and later from radio and film, he never compromised the plays.

The plays are tough, but they operate in disguise. An audience wants a good story and interesting characters. Ideas are acceptable if nicely coated in laughs or held in a tight vice within the plot. Shaw knew all this. His plays are hard to do, sometimes hard to understand, and certainly tough-minded.

A text is a code. What it means is more than it conveys on a superficial reading. To be somewhat infantile in my illustration, if I wrote down everything that was said at a lunch for four people, I would end up with a sort of a text. In order to restage the lunch I would have to ask a lot of questions—not of the people who were there, they would have disappeared—but of myself as the director and of the actors. The actors' basic questions are "why am I here?"; then "where have I come from?"; then "what am I doing?"; then "where am I going?" We are looking for objectives, and we are trying to find a way to place the lunch in a longer continuum. After this we can begin to ask questions about the relationships between the people. "How well do they know each other?" Here we will have to make guesses working from the minute clues in the text. "Why doesn't this person speak for five minutes?" "Is she in pain?" "Is she thinking of something else?" If so, what? The actor will have to reproduce this silent thinking. It will affect her part and the attitude of those around her. This method holds true for any play. The complexity of the answers varies with the density of the text.

Because I have been obsessed with Shaw for the last twelve years and because I have had to invent a method of piecing together the clues and bringing the texts to life—a method partially based on Granville Barker's ideas, partially on the ideas of my old teacher G. Wilson Knight, and partially, I suppose, on William Empson—I often wonder, half jokingly, if there is a connection between Shaw's development as a playwright and the fact that in his formative years *The Strand* magazine was thrilling its readers with the adventures of Sherlock Holmes. The texts of the plays have all the clues in them for the director and actors to be able to disentangle the various elements, understand and take note of them, then put them aside and act out a dense and lovely yarn—but they are often very difficult clues, and the inexperienced director can get into a lot of trouble if he comes up with the wrong solutions.

Some years ago I was mildly chastised by a scholar, whom I very much respect, for leaving out the horse trough from the second act of *Major Barbara*. Shaw wants a horse trough down left. Because of the exigencies of the stage and because I wanted to set the Salvation Army hostel under the arches of a railway viaduct (contrasting the noisy violence of the east end of London with the peace of Perivale St. Andrews), I left out the horse trough. I realized, listening to my complainant, that for some people the texts as set down are pretty much the end of the matter. This happened with Shakespeare. When I was a young man one teacher in all seriousness said to me, "The problem with Shakespeare is the actors." (I hasten to add it was not Wilson Knight—I laced him into his corset when he played Othello.) Well, the joy of Shaw is the actors. He is very, very hard to play well. And the actors need settings which connect with a modern audience—thus the noisy viaduct and the subsequent lack of space for the horse trough. Interestingly, the plays do not need Shaw's exact settings. They need intelligent interpretation.

Before I took over the Shaw Festival, I disliked Shaw. I had played Higgins and Hector Hushabye, but I was deeply dissatisfied by both performances. Practically every Shaw production I had ever seen twittered along about five feet above the stage: silly British accents, clever witticisms, self-conscious opera laughter, and, above all, like the Shaw on the radio I remembered as a boy, too clever by half. Nothing seemed to connect. Actors did not talk to each other. They did not own the text or inhabit their characters. Their only relationship was with the preconceived notions of the audience.

This was not what the old boy wanted. Why did he ask Irving to do his plays? Why did he want Beerbohm Tree? Because he wanted the old-style grand passions, the big theatrical gestures, but he wanted the actors to think at the same time. That is what is important in playing Shaw. You have to combine the big gestures and the swiftest, most subtle thinking. Most actors cannot do this. One or the other gets forgotten. You either end up with a lot of unconnected shouting or British twittering, or, worst of all, you end up with ponderous wallowing in half-understood ideas.

With Shaw's contemporary Arthur Wing Pinero you really do not have to think at all. There are very few ideas to exercise the intelligence, and the characters hardly ever have to articulate anything other than the simplest precepts. Pinero is concerned with feelings first and foremost and the relationships between the world as perceived by his characters and the world as perceived by the audience. Two separate existences. Intellectually, Pinero's plays exist inside the proscenium arch; no sharp intellectual hooks are ever cast toward the audience. Those in the audience are only engaged on a level of sensory perception—if they are lucky. They are bamboozled into thinking that serious matters are being dealt with in a flurry of minor excitements.

Pinero does not really stand up today. The plays seem flat, two-dimensional pieces. They do not carry truths across the barrier of time. If in rehearsal you ask questions about what is going on, usually the answer is nothing other than what is obviously apparent. For a sensitive modern actor, they are awful pieces. For a star, they can sometimes provide vehicles. *The Magistrate* is a good example—but there is no density to intrigue an audience, no ambiguity to beguile the performers.

Shaw cries out for illustrations and explorations. Try to illustrate or even explore Pinero and you will find yourself in a wasteland. There is nothing underneath. It is all underneath in Shaw, but it is hard to get at.

In some ways what is underneath is all too easy to get at in Chekhov. The temptation is to play the half-stated connections rather than the plot. It is easy to imagine these characters in other situations. There is space around the character for the actor to fill. The difficulty is to play specifically what is written. It was not very long ago that I finally clued in to Vanya. He is so pathetic, so charming, so strangely grand (and here I must admit that I have always had the image of William Hutt's Vanya in my mind) that I never asked what "Vanya" meant. It was not until a Russian told me that it is a somewhat dismissive form of the name that the play came to a focus. So it is "Uncle Jimmy"—not Uncle James or even Uncle Jim, but Uncle Jimmy. And there it was all the time. If you do not move too far away from what is actually there in front of you, usually, as long as the dynamic is maintained, Chekhov makes it easy.

On the other hand, Shaw does not make it easy. Look at the great moment in *Man and Superman* that ends, "If we two stood now on the edge of a precipice, I would hold you tight and jump." Ecstasy. It has been led up to relatively quickly and passionately. I have seen the passage "I tell you, no, no, no" / "I tell you, yes, yes, yes" actually played for laughs. How stupid! How can you get to the last moment like that? There is an example of a piece of bad direction, the kind that caused many of us to dismiss Shaw much too easily in the past. This passage should sweep along. Jack and Ann must be crying, clutching, gripped in something larger than either of them.

That is what the play is about. It must be *Tristan and Isolde*. Shaw really does not give us much time to get there, and when we are at the top, the two of them sobbing and hitting each other, we are in a moment so sexually tense, so extraordinary, so orgasmic that the audience must be as exhausted as the players.

You see this is a kind of poetry built of curious juxtapositions of ideas and places. There is none of the strange, allusive naturalism of Chekhov. This is hard-edged and poetic with a richness of texture that takes time and energy, hard thinking and big emotions.

Interestingly, although Shaw talked a good musical line, his plays seldom approach the sophisticated musicality of Coward at his best (the second act of *Private Lives,* for instance). In Coward the shape is always perfect. He would never contract a love scene into something almost unplayable. He knew, down to the second, how to connect with an audience. Certainly Shaw knew how to make an effect. His directorial notes are exceptionally perceptive, but only from the outside. Granville Barker and Coward knew from inside the playing space; Shaw knew only from the stalls.

And now back to the horse trough for a moment. We all know that the texts were meant to make money. All Shavian directors know how irritating it is to read "The Man." "Who is this? Where is the cast list? Please be helpful." And, yes, we all know the plays are meant to be read like novels. Here is a clue. My internal picture of Barsetshire is unlike anyone else's even though Trollope is pretty precise in his descriptions. Word. Action. Time. Communication. My Barchester is as alive as anyone else's even though I may forget a bellpull or a flowerpot. The horse trough does not have to be there to make a picture for today.

When we did *Saint Joan* in 1981, I got into a bit of trouble not only because I tried to cut the Epilogue—I am still ambivalent about it, and I understand that Archibald Henderson encouraged Shaw to drop it (perhaps that is why it is still there)—but also because I took the riverbank scene to be a serious scene about soldiers waiting for something to happen. When soldiers are close to water, they wash simply because they may not get another chance (remember all the reports about showers in the Gulf war). So Dunois was shaving and the page swimming in the river. In the Middle Ages there was not much in the way of underwear or bathing suits, and because Dunois and the page are both men I assumed that the page would swim without clothes. This helped me establish the unique moment when Joan appeared in men's armor. The page naturally took her for a man. He had never seen a woman in men's clothes.

I loved this little scene. It was about soldiers and war. I knew that I had thrown the horse trough into the river, but the scene remained true to the words the actors say, true to the ideas, and, most important of all, close to a modern audience.

What I am ultimately suggesting is that Shaw's texts are far richer, far more dense than can be imagined by a reader. They need an actor's life-giving touch, but not just any actor's. These plays need particular skills. You cannot come at them as you might Pinero (if you bother) or Coward or Chekhov. And you must admit the faults to get at the real qualities. For instance, the argument in *Don Juan in Hell* is appallingly structured, but somehow it works on a level of theatrical hypnosis not unlike the incantatory nature of blank verse. (If the Commander can cross the divide between Heaven and Hell so easily, why does Don Juan have to go on talking?)

Directorially Shaw's plays can be explored through three avenues. First, the settings should have a hard modern light shone onto them as in *Major Barbara*. Second, what the characters are spending their time doing can suggest a whole series of new ideas (the riverbank in *Saint Joan*). And third, the rapid shifts within the text can be illuminated to reveal far more than we initially imagined, as in the ecstatic scene between Jack and Ann in *Man and Superman.* No exploration is unique, and none is exclusive of others.

Shaw is a poet of the theater. It does not matter that he writes in prose. His thinking is fast and accurate for the most part, and the faster the actor can think, the more room he has to explore the huge emotions that stir beneath the text. Shaw is very difficult to play, and it has taken me years to develop this lithe ensemble of one hundred actors at the Shaw Festival who have some understanding of what he needs. To paraphrase that enigmatic line from Dryden which has always haunted me, "My chase has a beast in view."

Gwyn Thomas

THE GHOST OF ADELPHI TERRACE
(Edited by R. F. Dietrich)

[Gwyn Thomas (1913–1981) was a Welsh novelist, playwright, and radio and television personality known for his satirical wit and dazzling linguistic acrobatics. Most of his works depicted and commented upon the economic and cultural death of South Wales in his time.

Rather different is his teleplay, *The Ghost of Adelphi Terrace*. Recorded for BBC-2 TV's "Centre Play" on 30 March 1975 and televised a few weeks later, this play depicts an attempt by Shaw to rescue his fellow playwright and Adelphi Terrace neighbor J. M. Barrie from his melancholy. Set in 1911, two years after J. M. Barrie's divorce following a marriage not consummated due to Barrie's impotence, and one year after the death of his mother-surrogate Mrs. Sylvia Davies, the model for Wendy's mother in *Peter Pan*, this play finds the lonely Barrie haunted by his long-dead mother, Margaret Ogilvy, whose biography he has written and whose emotional vampirism, begun in his childhood, continues to drain him. G.B.S. drops in and offers the perfect antidote to Barrie's mother-fetish in an attitude of irreverence toward parental ties, Mrs. Shaw's indifference toward her children having fostered in Shaw an independent spirit. The action of the play consists mainly of Shaw's attempt to exorcise Barrie's maternal ghost by taking him out for a night on the town.

In *The Listener* of 14 August 1975 (pp. 218–19), Gwyn Thomas explains how he was attracted to Shaw and Barrie as "among the last great literary men to come to London while the city still remained the capital of a confident world power." On all other points, however, he finds them to be opposites, and their opposition to be the natural stuff of drama.

The teleplay script has numerous directions for the camera that I have omitted, although I have spliced those referring to character or setting with the stage directions. I have also corrected a few misspellings and grammatical errors, and I have added and regularized the punctuation of the stage directions—R.F.D.]

SCENE 1

Early autumn, 1911. J. M. Barrie sits in his Adelphi Terrace flat [in which are many bookcases, a Peter Pan photo prominently displayed, a line of cricket caps, and a toy theatre]. He has the air of a man looking and sniffing around him for presences that have recently fled. The small, vulnerable body, the shadowed eyes, suggest a creature of unique loneliness. He is in a well of melancholy up and down whose walls he travels with perfect ease. The constant clouds of smoke from a large pipe underline the effect of hellishness.

BARRIE: ([*Seated before a fire, eyes closed, holding a glass.*] *Voice over.*) We have poison for mice, but not for memories. Mine scurry around my skull. The dead are insatiable. They make a royal feast of us. A great sucking legion.

GHOST OF MARGARET OGILVY: That is terrible, harsh talk to be hearing from you, Jamie.

BARRIE: Sorry mother. Another summer has gone and every thought is a nest of crows.

GHOST: I wish I could have gathered your wounds to me as they came. I put myself inside you and softened the stone overmuch.

BARRIE: You've done well, mother. You are immortal. The whole world knows about you. With and without my father's looms I wove your dreams into as pretty a web as words will ever make.

GHOST: Oh, you listened, Jamie. Not a breath, not a sigh of mine was ever missed. You bottled my tears for sale and that is a fine, crafty Scottish thing to do. I pity any woman whose tears go to waste in the hard ground.

BARRIE: (*Standing.*) It made a good brew, your tears, my fears, the long shadow of your spirit, the short shadow of my body.

GHOST: The smallness of your body was a meant thing. The good Lord needed someone to speak for the tiny, timid creatures.

(Barrie pours himself an undiluted whiskey.)

BARRIE: Oh, God, is that why it was? Never mind. I gave you to the world, Margaret Ogilvy. All my days have been a tribute to the love that grew to the level of genius between us. We concocted a rare old madness between us.

GHOST: Sadness for me is your only love now, Jamie boy.

(There is a knock at the door. Barrie goes to door but there is no one there. He looks outside. He turns and finds Shaw in [the] hallway. Shaw laughs.)

BARRIE: Oh, hello, Shaw.

SHAW: For pity's sake, Barrie, a burning peat-bog would be preferable to this. Little wonder your fancy has everlastingly crawled with fairies. They were your substitute for fresh air.

BARRIE: Have a drink.

(*Shaw points at Barrie's glass.*)

SHAW: What's that?

BARRIE: Whiskey.

SHAW: Whatever wrong the English did the Scots you got your own back with that stuff and the pipes.

BARRIE: Oh, spare us.

SHAW: My father was a whiskey tippler. In a haze of whiskey all his life, except for a short sober run for salvation at the finish. People never understood where he got it and kept it. Probably in his bowler. Wore big bowlers. Always seemed to my childish eye to be steaming. Probably had a still in there.

BARRIE: He paid for his sins. He begat a monster of awareness.

(*Shaw stands.*)

SHAW: Absolutely right. Some prickle with a sense of everlasting naked-ness. Others slip on a few thick blankets of booze. (*Barrie moves to fire-place. Shaw turns.*) James Barrie. You're in a mess.

BARRIE: Mr. Shaw, you're in a mess.

SHAW: Having got the geography of the matter out of the way, we can take a conducted tour of the ruins. We've turned fifty and have enough talent to bring the sky down on our heads. You bewitch the bourgeois with an incomparable string of loony illusions, and I preach the perfect-ibility of every lousy ragamuffin who can be persuaded to stay out of the grog shop long enough to read my tracts and get the grime out of his eyes. (*Barrie sits.*) So you're down today?

BARRIE: Dumped, below every conceivable sky-line.

SHAW: Why's that? I know the answer but I'd like you to give it to me. You invent despair with such an agreeable jingle. You are the Grimaldi of the boneyard.[1]

BARRIE: Another summer's gone. I hate winter. Winter memories of a weaver's cottage have arthritis in them.

SHAW: I can't think of anyone who's made such a poor job of solitude. If you'd have been Robinson Crusoe you'd have whipped Man Friday into napkins and gagged him with a pledge not to utter a word. Now if I were landed on Mars I'd have nominated a Martian to chair my first bumper meeting within the hour.

BARRIE: You would, I'm sure. We are on different planets. I'll wink to you when we pass a thousand years from now.

SHAW: (*Hanging cap on wall.*) In the puberty sense of the word your soul never dropped.

BARRIE: Tenderness is simply the safer bet.

SHAW: You, Barrie, are as tender as a vampire. A bit slower getting around to the victim and you read the proofs after every job, that's the only difference.

BARRIE: You are a social epileptic. Every wince, ache, outrage, you dance attendance on it. Some people can occupy an empty lighted circle within themselves, loving the loneliness, mocking at the pop-eyed world without.

SHAW: You are about as lonely as Charing Cross at noon. You are the most haunted fellow who ever knocked on the doors of the dead and invited yourself in for tea. Since Burke and Hare you are the Scotsman who has most kept the dead guessing as to their next port of call. No man has ever so diminished the significance of death in his stories and so allowed it to dominate the daylight of his life.

BARRIE: Don't be so damned flippant about other people's wounds. I've been dealt heavy, killing blows.

SHAW: Bereavements, divorce. A skittle-alley play. Love and life are clumsy, fallible contracts. To consider them seriously is to disgrace the mind and foul one's days. Cut the cords. Float free, for God's sake.

(*Shaw, [who] has not taken a chair, lopes around the room, staring at the pictures and decorative objects. Barrie relights his pipe and sends up monumental billows of smoke. Shaw's right hand scythes through the fumes.*)

SHAW: How do you stand under the new Factory Act? Is there a statutory limit to the number of places and people you are allowed to pollute with that damned article you suck at? (*Barrie is unperturbed.*) You've heard of the Life Force?

BARRIE: Yes.

SHAW: Well, it's never heard of you. You give your love only to things and to people that have strong signs of perishing on them.

BARRIE: Earlier this evening I told someone . . .

(*He trails off into silence.*)

SHAW: You won't be content until your existence has become a convention of phantoms, will you? How long has your mother been dead?

BARRIE: Sixteen years and twenty days.

SHAW: You keep as close a count as that?

BARRIE: I was the clock of her life. Her memory is the clock of mine.

SHAW: A deplorable method of telling the time. I can imagine no more destructive monster than a mother whose talent is to inspire worship in her young. My mother did not give the peeling of an Irish damn, and that's a thin-peeled sort, for any of her brood. She wanted to make a great stir on the musical stage. She was not a great singer. She was not a clever woman. Her life petered out into a thousand kinds of shabbiness and frustration, but she left her children gloriously free of her own dreams.[2] What was your mother's dream?

BARRIE: To see me shine. She came from a darkened world, piety, work as a short cut to the grave. She needed light.

SHAW: When a parent sets out to redress her own grievances, supplement her own inadequacies, that's the supreme crime. For every effusion of love and milk a mother expends on an infant she should receive a counter-injection of indifference. No child should grow up with the leaden certainty that something is *expected* of it. To breathe, to talk, to clean up the litter of political and sexual excitement, *that* is enough, but to be the exploited agent of a despot whose least whim you have been terrified and drugged into obeying from the cradle on. . . . (*He lifts his hand through the wide Shavian spectrum of exasperation.*) When I think of the most gifted kind of parental parasite I wonder why they made all the fuss about Jack the Ripper.

BARRIE: Would you like a game of draughts or a heavily drugged cocoa?

SHAW: I'm not letting you go so easily. This is a good day for me. When I get my teeth into the neck of a spinner of fairy-lore, it's a pleasant interlude in my rule of vegetarian abstinence. I shall stay with you until midnight. We shall go into and around the town, as the rakes used to say. (*He begins gathering Barrie's coat and scarf. Barrie sighs and prepares for the unwelcome jaunt.*)

BARRIE: My mother, wishing to purge me with fear, told me that one night a creature wild of eye, long of beard and dark of wing, would come and bear me away. Her description made you a little shorter.

SHAW: I can offer you a first-class vegetarian restaurant. They offer a dandelion and herb salad that would settle even *your* nightmares.

BARRIE: Over my dead body.

SHAW: On your diet that should be arranged in a predictably brief time.

BARRIE: What about the Café Royal?[3]

SHAW: Whenever I go there I am besieged by men claiming they were the first to give Oscar Wilde money when he stepped out of Reading Gaol. Reading must have been packed and Oscar smothered. (*They move off.*)

BARRIE: Funny fellow, that one.

SHAW: Wilde?

BARRIE: Exceedingly weird. I got a toothache every time I met him.

SCENE 2

A dining room at the Café Royal. Night. Barrie and Shaw sit at a table in a small mirrored dining room—a plush, Edwardian nook of great chic and privacy. They are perusing the menu.

SHAW: What did you eat for lunch today?

BARRIE: Four lamb cutlets. The club is good at them.

(*Mrs. Leonora Lennox, about forty, of great opulence, in full physical bloom, the last flower of picture-postcard beauty, advances toward them.*)

BARRIE: Oh God, that woman Lennox, Shaw. Leonora, in her own and almost everybody else's flesh. She's asked me for a part.

SHAW: Widen Peter Pan and make it a non-flying part.

BARRIE: Pretend we've changed our minds about the place and go.

(*Shaw holds him in position.*)

SHAW: Come on. She won't mind you not being too chipper. She's probably heard all about your troubles and bereavements.

(*Leonora approaches through pillars.*)

BARRIE: Why do some women have to become so awful?

SHAW: Self-degradation is our sport. You've got used to fishing. Put up with this.

(*Leonora Lennox surveys them through a lorgnette that isn't there with a baleful calm.*)

MRS. LENNOX: I was wondering when you two peculiar fellows were going to greet me. I've seen plenty of artificial rudeness in the best houses in London. But for sheer natural crassness you two could start a new sort of peerage.

SHAW: (*Nodding agreement.*) That's a fair point, Leonora.

BARRIE: Mrs. Lennox, could I ask you to share something with us!

MRS. LENNOX: There wouldn't be a wide range of choice with you two, would there?

SHAW: No. Monstrously limited.

MRS. LENNOX: No, I won't bother to presume on your courtliness, Mr. Barrie. But Shaw can get me a bottle of champagne.

SHAW: If you wish I will call the waiter and request him to go out into Piccadilly and buy you a modest bouquet of short, cut voilets [*sic*]. The colour of your eyes.

MRS. LENNOX: That exhausts you erotically for a month.

BARRIE: Waiter, a bottle of champagne.

MRS. LENNOX: Have you seen the comic double act at Collins Music Hall? Americans. Hanky and Panky. Clever but never clean. That's their billing.

SHAW: What is the relevance of Hanky and Panky to this encounter?

MRS. LENNOX: If they fail to weather the fog of London obtuseness, you two could be the next double act. Clever but never scrutable.

(*She smiles to waiter, who pours the champagne.*)

BARRIE: Your health, Mrs. Lennox.

MRS. LENNOX: I wouldn't gamble on it.

SHAW: Nor, my dear Leonora, would I. Without that stuff you would have been a reasonable actress. In that last play you damned nearly seduced the leading man in full view of the public.

MRS. LENNOX: That frigid ninny! Burst his starched front with panic. I should never have gone in for straight drama. I make everything too explicit.

SHAW: You are the alphabet, Leonora.

BARRIE: I don't really enjoy this kind of conversation.

(*Shaw and Mrs. Lennox are both so fascinated by each other they have clearly failed to hear Barrie.*)

MRS. LENNOX: But I did well enough.

SHAW: You stormed the castle. *Allons enfants du theatre bleu.*[4]

MRS. LENNOX: Married a titled solicitor twenty vital years older than myself. Went down the aisle with the best man on one side and a wilderness on the other. He sends me his best wishes by wire across the broadest landing in Mayfair.

BARRIE: He is a most distinguished man, Mrs. Lennox.

MRS. LENNOX: If I didn't have the ghastly bad fortune to be always running into monastic freaks, like you two, I'd make a run for it before the night sets in. He handles all the juiciest scandals in London—yet he's the most neck-breaking bore. (*To Barrie.*) He handled your business, the divorce. That was a weird affair. A real festival of frustration.

BARRIE: (*Half-rising.*) Please . . . !

SHAW: Leonora! If I were a coachman and you a horse you would feel my whip across your flanks.

MRS. LENNOX: A lying Irishman's idle promises. (*To Barrie.*) I met your wife. A dull little woman. She talked about dogs all the time. What do you think about that, Shaw? Talked about dogs all the time.

SHAW: If they didn't eat meat I could grow to respect them.

MRS. LENNOX: (*She points at Barrie incredulously.*) Do you know, Shaw, I saw him one day with a dog twice as big as he was. He seemed to be feeding his head to it to amuse some lads. Laughing their heads off, they were, stupid little brats. I understand you loved your mother besottedly, Mr. Barrie.

BARRIE: I don't think *you'd* understand, Mrs. Lennox.

MRS. LENNOX: I think I would. I'm an experienced traveller.

BARRIE: (*Sips his champagne.*) Yes, Mrs. Lennox, I did love my mother. Among a gallery of things that have hurt and shamed, that alone remains radiant and assuring. That is the one thing that has never made me weep.

MRS. LENNOX: You'd have been better off with a broken neck.

BARRIE: You're a monster.

SHAW: That's taken for granted. Add something to it.

MRS. LENNOX: Well put, Shaw. I second that.

BARRIE: The only people on earth I truly pity are women who cannot have children and children who have no mother to revere and cherish.
SHAW: You're talking bubbles.
MRS. LENNOX: You mean that bit of oratory for me, Mr. Barrie?
BARRIE: I wouldn't have wasted it on Shaw. His soul is inside his beard.
MRS. LENNOX: Well, let me tell you this, Mr. Barrie. I am now treading the cooling cinders of a second marriage. My first husband was a sporting gent called Melody McHugh, sweet-talking siren for credulous punters. He didn't put me on the streets simply because he was too drunk to know where they were. He gave me one son, the blessing who pitchforked me into marriage. The boy is as rude, predatory and unlovely as his unspeakable sire. My second husband, a man of matchless taste, could stand him no better than I could. Had we found the right travel agent we'd have tossed a coin to decide whether to deposit him on St. Helena or Elba. The choice of our heart would have been Tristan de Cunha.[5] He's nearer than that but safely repelled from our presence.
BARRIE: Your son, your only son?
MRS. LENNOX: Flesh of my flesh. Thorn of my thorn. Error begotten of error.
BARRIE: You are not . . . explicable.
MRS. LENNOX: I wish I weren't. To be understood is the final doom.
BARRIE: You are trying to conceal some passing little bitterness, one of those little tiffs that cloud the brightest love.
MRS. LENNOX: You exaggerate the amount of love in the world, Mr. Barrie. The affection between you and your mother was probably the greatest barrage of mutual flattery ever known. The Scots have a self-esteem that just pauses this side of rape.
(Shaw gets up.)
BARRIE: You build a wall of mud between yourself and life as Shaw builds a wall of mockery.
SHAW: Thank God for cheap materials.
BARRIE: I cannot endure this. I will leave you, madame.
(He rushes out.)
SHAW: How can you possibly be so stupidly cruel? Don't answer. You and I founded that particular Trade Union.
(Calling.) Wait for me! *(He leaves.)*
MRS. LENNOX: *(Finishing her champagne [after raising her glass in a toast].)* Well, here's to coolness, here's to the Kiddikins and a minimum of exposures.

SCENE 3

The Lady of Shallot Pub. Night. Barrie and Shaw sit in an alcove designed for four people. The pub is having a quiet night. The landlord, Gus, is a reflective man: polishes his glasses with the anxiety of a man intent on removing some primal stain. Barrie has ordered scotch for himself and cream soda for Shaw.

BARRIE: The woman is totally unnatural.

SHAW: A society that will not share its wealth will share its perversions. But don't fret. I'm pretty certain she never had a son.

BARRIE: You mean she'd lie about a thing like that!

SHAW: At some time or another we all melodramatise some humiliating farce that stained our existence.

(There is a great burst of laughter from two jovial and lavishly decorated trollops, Chrissie and Carrie. They lay predatory eyes on Barrie and Shaw.)

CARRIE: *(Calling over.)* You two gents look as if you could do with a bit of a laugh.

(Shaw makes a great clown's face. Barrie tries to make his way down through the woodwork.)

CHRISSIE: *(Under her breath, to Carrie.)* A dead loss, and his brother, if ever I saw one.

SHAW: *(An urgent whisper to Barrie.)* Courage. Grit your teeth. A couple of earth-mothers may be just what the doctor ordered.

BARRIE: Send them away. Send them away.

SHAW: Whatever evidence is piled up to the contrary, easy, pleasant relationships with women are not beyond our reach.

(Carrie and Chrissie have joined them.)

CARRIE: New to the district?

BARRIE: *(Making the effort.)* Yes.

CHRISSIE: You'll be in trade. There's a posh look about you in a quiet way.

SHAW: Yes. He sells trolls and I process Irish peat.

CHRISSIE: Business pretty good, I bet.

SHAW: The peat's a bit slow. Smokes a lot. But his trolls are going quite briskly.

CARRIE: He looks crafty. He could sell me anything. I'd think twice with you, though. I'd look twice at *your* peat.

SHAW: I venture you would.

BARRIE: And how do you ladies busy yourselves?

CHRISSIE: We do a bit in the chorus on Saturday night. *(Sings.)* "My old man said follow the van . . ."

(Carrie joins in.)

SHAW: *(To Barrie.)* This is about an eviction. Evictions are the heart-beat of the plebs.

BARRIE: *(To the girls.)* And what do you do the other nights?

CARRIE: We take whatever the wind blows our way. Trade winds we call them.

SHAW: Quiet tonight.

CARRIE: Big fight in the town.

SHAW: Elections?

CHRISSIE: No. The fancy. (*Winks.*) The other fancy. The ring. They hold fights there.

BARRIE: I don't suppose my father ever saw the inside of one of these places. My mother didn't even know they existed.

SHAW: My father's mouth was painted as a tribute on the crest of eighteen Dublin pubs.

CARRIE: My mother came from Dublin.

SHAW: Where did your father come from?

CARRIE: Wormwood Scrubs. My husband, too. And he went back there the day after the wedding. A brawling man. And weddings brought out the worst in him. Between the love and the drink it took twenty men to get him to the station.

BARRIE: And your man?

CHRISSIE: Slung his hook. Went to sea. Somewhere in the Cannibal Islands, consoling himself with coconuts. Thin, useless shaving of a man. The cannibals can have him. He won't take them long.

SHAW: Racial spites would give the snack a special relish.

BARRIE: SShh! (*To Carrie.*) You have children?

CARRIE: I had two. She had three.

BARRIE: They are beautiful—they are happy and sweet?

CHRISSIE: Don't know. They went away.

CARRIE: We were always moving from one room to another, looking for the rent and a new rainbow. They got as sick of us as we did of them. They just vanished.

BARRIE: Don't grieve. There are places that children vanish to. They don't die. Never think that. On some islands, by some lake, inside some hill in a golden haven, they wait. They do not change. They even grow in beauty as their love for their lost mother grows deeper. And one night in a dream the grieving mother sees where [her] children are waiting. She goes to them. And there is a great reunion of love, a healing of hearts and lives. Everything will be made up to you.

CARRIE: (*To Shaw.*) Does he always get like this?

SHAW: Worse sometimes.

CHRISSIE: It takes men worst [*sic*] than women, the spirits.

(*Singing is heard in the background.*)

CARRIE: Here comes Chanting Charlie.

SHAW: Why do you call him Chanting Charlie? This is music hall dialogue.

CHRISSIE: He chants. He sings. Not exactly a beggar. Sings for the love of it.

(*Chanting Charlie appears singing "The Children's Garden," a minor classic that*

bruised the Victorian tear-duct. He sings in an eroded but quite sincere style, hands joined, head upraised, a dense melancholy on his face.)
CHARLIE: (*Singing.*)

> "The high-born child and the beggar
> Pass homeward side by side,
> For the ways of men are narrow
> But the gates of heaven are wide."

(*As the singing goes on:*)
CHRISSIE: It's a real cleanser, this song.
CARRIE: "For the ways of men are narrow." Too bloody right they are. With my corsets off, I'm wedged.
(*Chrissie does a bit of passionate exegesis, mainly for Barrie's benefit.*)
CHRISSIE: They die, you see. The little beggar boy starves and passes over, as they do. And the little high-born girl, she's snatched away by consumption, for it hits rich and poor alike, the decline, the cough. And off they go to heaven.
CARRIE: All I hope is that heaven won't be a suck-in like Margate.
(*The song comes to an end.*)
CHRISSIE: (*Calls to Charlie.*) Let's have the one about mothers in heaven, Charlie.
SHAW: (*He looks at Barrie.*) Yes, that will fill the bill, I think.
(*He gives coin to Charlie, via Chrissie.*)
SHAW: (*To Barrie.*) Intelligent men make a fetish of their mothers in fiction, and before you know it people like Charlie are at it in public places.
CHARLIE: (*Singing.*)

> "Skylark, said a dear little boy
> Pray, where do you go when you fly so high?
> Skylark, say, is it true
> That you sing to the angels in the sky?
> If so, my mother's an angel up there,
> And we do miss her so, you see,
> So would you, please, the next time you go up,
> Take this message from Dad and me?"

CHORUS: [*Charlie is apparently joined by others:*]

> "Skylark, skylark, winging your flight so high
> Skylark, skylark, when you get up in the sky,
> If among the angels mother you should see,
> Ask her if she will come down again
> To poor dear Daddy and me."

(*Song continues.*)

> "Skylark, said a desolate man,
> Your message has robbed me of my dear boy."

(*Girls: Sniff, sniff.*)

BARRIE: These women appall me.

SHAW: Spirits of the pavement, the finest first-aid troops in the world. (*Girls: Sob, sob.*)

SHAW: They see you as a dark one and so you are, bewitched in a self-made bog. They are the great launderers, let them get at you. Have a try at love without pretensions or echoes. (*Girls: Ah, ah, ah, ah . . .*)

SHAW: You had a mother who won't let you go. You had a wife who only too willingly let you go. You have been impaled on two unbearable farces. Purgatives you need, my friend, and they are always crude and scandalous. (*Song continues.*)

BARRIE: There are moments, Shaw, when you can be profoundly offensive, more frightening than life. (*Barrie bolts out. The song breaks off.*)

CARRIE: (*To Chrissie.*) When he gets back I'm going to pluck out some of his thoughts. I bet he's got some very peculiar thoughts, that one. I'll have a proper go at him when he gets back.

SCENE 4

Adelphi Terrace. Night. Barrie's flat. He sits recessed in his armchair as we saw him at the play's beginning.

VOICE OF MARGARET OGILVY: Safe again now, Jamie. You were so fretful. I was so worried, afraid for you.

BARRIE: All's well again now, Maggie. Today some darkling elves danced on the patch of our private peace. And it ached and made me want an end. Now you come and make me whole and well again. You stand between me and the fools and monsters. Come closer. (*[Barrie gazes into fireplace. Lights in Adelphi out].*)

Notes

1. Joseph Grimaldi (1778–1837) was a famous clown in the London theater. In his honor all later clowns were called "Joey." These days a more fitting "Grimaldi of the boneyard" than Barrie would be Samuel Beckett.

2. This exaggerates, for Shaw's mother seems to have passed some of her dreams of being a professional singer on to her daughter Lucy.

3. Oscar Wilde's favorite London restaurant.

4. A literal translation might be, "Let's go, children of the blue theater!" But "blue" in this context probably means "off-color" or "bawdy," referring to the acting style of Mrs. Lennox.

5. The remotest island Mrs. Lennox can think of to exile her son is Tristan de Cunha, a tiny island in the southern mid-Atlantic between Buenos Aires and Cape Town.

Bernard Shaw

BARRIE:
"THE MAN WITH HELL
IN HIS SOUL"

[*The following obituary article appeared on 20 June 1937, one day after J. M. Barrie's death, in the* Sunday Graphic. *It is one of Shaw's written "interviews" given to the veteran journalist W. R. Titterton and is republished here for the first time*—*J.A.B.*]

You couldn't help liking Barrie, and you couldn't help liking his work. He was a most affectionate creature, and his work is full of affection.

Yet his plays are terrifying. Behind all the tenderness and the playfulness there is the sense of inexorable destiny. For, though in his sentiments Barrie was a most humane person, he was a Calvinist to the marrow.

That is the keynote of the Barrie drama—a profound compassion for these poor human things caught in the cogs of an inexorable destiny.

I am fairly certain that during the last years of his life he was an unhappy man. He gave you the impression that for all his playfulness he had hell in his soul.

Certainly he regretted that he had no children. Perhaps he ought to have had children, though he might not have been easy for the children to get on with. For I do not think he understood them.

Well, that was natural, since he was childless. He belonged to a generation of childless authors. I remember saying to Sidney Webb: "Here have you and I been talking for years about marriage and we know nothing about it."

If he had understood children Barrie would not have written down to them. Parents know better than that. They know they can safely be childish with other grown-ups, but never with their own children.

Barrie was a shy fellow, perhaps even secretive. You know with what

success he evaded pressmen, and in consequence how eagerly the slightest anecdote about him was printed.

But in his private life it was the same. We were near neighbours in the
Adelphi—so near that the tale went (quite untruly) that we could throw
things into each other's windows.

Yet, though we were on the best of terms, I did not see him once in
seven years.

There was, it is true, another reason for this apart from his shyness.
He was inseparable from his large pipe, and a large dose of strong
tobacco gives my wife asthma.

But he hugged seclusion. When we did visit him we would find him in
a room of his flat very like a kitchen sitting silently over the fire and
smoking his big pipe.

It would seem that he craved affection and shunned society. Yet when
you did meet him he was charming. That was the strength and weakness
of his work.

When you review his series of plays—all charming—you can't with
justice say that there is any strong purpose behind the charm.

Perhaps that is why for 14 years he found nothing to write about until
not long ago he tried to make a better story of the Boy David than there
is in the Bible.

Only two of his dramas were failures. One was "Leonora," which he
wrote for that very charming woman and actress, Mrs. Patrick Campbell.
He wrote it first of all as a one-act play, and then expanded it into three
acts.

It was one of the pieces put on by Charles Frohman when he discovered
the intellectual drama, and determined to make it a paying proposition.

The other failure was a film which never was shown. Chesterton and I
and other notorious persons were in it as cowboys. We went down to
Elstree. I had to ride a motor-cycle and fall over a precipice—about
three feet deep, but it looked deeper.

Granville Barker read the scenario and told Barrie that it wouldn't do.
It was a family joke—all right for a Christmas party, but all wrong for a
cinema theatre. So the idea was abandoned, though I have an idea that
some bits of it were used when Gaby Deslys came over to play in "Rosy
Rapture."

You find Barrie's compassion for human beings caught by destiny in
"Mary Rose," which I liked very much, and in "Dear Brutus," which I did
not appreciate until I saw the first act done by the young people of the
Gower-street Academy of Dramatic Art.

They grasped the idea so much better than did Gerald du Maurier and
the other professionals whom first I saw play it.

You find that hint of doom even in such an apparently happy piece as

"A Kiss for Cinderella," and I am reminded that you find it dominating the action in "The Will."

In the "Admirable Crichton" there is the same theme, but it is treated there with common-sense and good-humour.

I know that the common idea of Barrie is that he is the children's playwright. I venture to suggest that this estimate may be altogether wrong.

"Peter Pan" is the play people are thinking of when they say that sort of thing, and I am not at all sure that children really like it. They are taken to see it by grown-ups, who tell them that they will simply love it. The grown-ups certainly do love it.

I had not seen "Peter Pan" for very many years until two years ago in Bournemouth I heard that Jean Forbes Robertson was playing in it. That drew me to the theatre, and I did not like the play very much. I thought it did not ring true.

It is I think quite wrong to imagine Barrie himself as a child who never grew up. He was a charming fellow, but he was not in the least child-like—as, for example, Gilbert Chesterton was.

In fact, I think that he never had been a child. It has been said with some truth that he was born a thousand years old.

For the essential Barrie was a Puckish fairy—very whimsical, very playful, but ancient and, I think, sad.

Though, well-disposed as we were to each other, I saw so little of him, I shall miss Barrie. He was such a friendly fellow. But even playwrights cannot live for ever.

Dan H. Laurence

AS HE LIKED IT: BERNARD SHAW'S PRONOUNCING GUIDE TO HIS STAGE CHARACTERS

As his own director Shaw had only to communicate to actors at first rehearsal his wishes as to pronunciation of the names of characters they were creating. In the years since Shaw's death, especially in American and Canadian productions, mispronunciations of names have become commonplace. Dolly in *Major Barbara,* for example, is almost invariably addressed as "Cousins," and Alderman Brollikins of *On the Rocks* is often introduced by the Mayor of the Isle of Cats as "Allo-WISH-a," as if she were Irish!

The list that follows provides the prescribed Shavian pronunciation of the more difficult names of characters in Shaw's plays, ascertained through examination of his correspondence, rehearsal notes, and recorded voice, as well as from interviews with performers like Ellen O'Malley, Esmé Percy, Ellen Pollock, Sir Ralph Richardson, Dame Wendy Hiller, and Sir Cedric Hardwicke, who had been directed by G.B.S.

THE ADMIRABLE BASHVILLE:	(Adelaide) Gisborne: JIZ-boorn.
THE APPLE CART:	Boanerges: Bo-an-URJ-ees.
ARMS AND THE MAN:	Nicola: rhymes with *tickle-a.*
	Raina: Rah-EE-na, almost rhymes with *farina.*
CAESAR AND CLEOPATRA:	Britannus: BRITAIN-iss.

Cleopatra: CLAY-o-pah-tra (the *pah* as in *oom-pah*).

CANDIDA:

The Rev. (James) Morrell: More-ELL, to rhyme with *compel,* not *quarrel.*

Prosperpine (Garnett): Anglicized as PROSS-ur-pine, to sound like *turpentine.*

CAPTAIN BRASSBOUND'S CONVERSION:

(Lady Cicely) Wayneflete: WAIN-fleet.

Marzo: MAR-tso.

The Cadi: KAH-dee (not KAY-dye)

FANNY'S FIRST PLAY:

Cecil (Savoyard): SEE-s'l.

GETTING MARRIED:

Cecil (Sykes): SESS-s'l, to rhyme with *vessel.*

MAJOR BARBARA:

(Adolphus) Cusins: CU-zins (pronounce the "Cu" as in the first syllable of *cushions*).

MAN AND SUPERMAN:

Don Juan: rhymes with *ruin,* as in Byron's poem. Shaw tended to anglicize foreign names. Thus, to Shaw, Don Quixote was pronounced KWIK-sit.

Dona Ana: DOH-nya AH-na (the "Do" as in *doughnut*).

Octavius (Robinson): Long "a"— his nickname is TAY-vee, not TAH-vee, although the latter is correct for Kipling's Rikki-Tikki-Tavi, misspelled in Act I.

THE MILLIONAIRESS:	Epifania (Ognisanti di Parerga): Shaw noted that the correct pronunciation would be APE-ee-fah-NEE-ya; but he preferred, and called for, Ape-i-FAHN-ya (second syllable short, as in *piffle*).
MRS WARREN'S PROFESSION:	Praed: Although Kitty Warren nicknames him "Praddie," his name rhymes with *trade*.
ON THE ROCKS:	Aloysia (Brollikins): A-LOY-sha (like the Jewish name *Moishe*).
SHAKES VERSUS SHAV:	The latter name rhymes with *cave*. Ditto for *Shavian*. Shaw plays on this in the title of one of his collections: *Short Stories, Scraps and Shavings*.
WIDOWERS' HOUSES:	Cokane: COCK-ayn, like the French name Cockaigne, of which it is probably a corruption.
YOU NEVER CAN TELL:	(Walter) Bohun: BOON. (Finch) M'Comas: Muh-COAM-is (not Mc-COAM-is).

John R. Pfeiffer

SHAW AND OTHER PLAYWRIGHTS: A BIBLIOGRAPHY OF SECONDARY WRITINGS

This list includes books, articles, dissertations, and reviews that connect Bernard Shaw in any way with other playwrights of whatever status, including pieces written by other playwrights about G.B.S. It does not usually include pieces on Shaw and the opera. A very few entries are provided without complete bibliographical data. Many of the works listed I have not seen. Annotations are limited to the language of the work and the names of the other playwrights when they are known but not obvious from the title or authorship of the work.

Entries listed in "General Works" are numbered. An alphabetical list of playwrights and works about them follows. Numbers after the names of the playwrights refer to entries in the "General Works" list.

I. General Works

1. Adams, Elsie B. *Bernard Shaw and the Aesthetes*. Columbus: Ohio State University Press, 1971.
2. Al-Abdullah, Mufeed Faleh. *The Legacy of Prospero in Twentieth Century British and American Drama* (Indiana University, 1981). *DAI* 43 (July 1982), 172-A. Shakespeare, Philip Barry, T. S. Eliot, Saroyan, O'Neill.
3. Amico, Silvio d'. "Shaw e i 'grotteschi' " (Shaw and the Grotesques). *L'Idea Nazionale* (Rome) (5 February 1919). [Italian] Pirandello, Scribe.
4. Anderson, Jarvis Lynn. *The Artist-Figure in Modern Drama* (University of Minnesota, 1971). *DAI* 32 (May 1972), 6594-A. Ibsen, Strindberg, O'Neill, Pirandello, Ionesco, Beckett, Brecht.
5. Archer, William. "Extracts from a Lecture by William Archer on Galsworthy, Barrie and Shaw, Delivered to the College Club, New York, in 1921." *Drama* 42 (Fall 1956): 29–36.

6. ———. *"The Quintessence of Ibsen:* An Open Letter to George Bernard Shaw." *New Review* 5 (November 1891): 463–69.

7. ———. "Shaw v. Shakespeare and Others." *World* (27 May 1896).

8. Bader, Earl D. *The Self-Reflexive Language: Uses of Paradox in Wilde, Shaw, and Chesterton* (Indiana University, 1970). *DAI* 30 (1970), 4934-A.

9. Baxter, Kay M. *Speak What We Feel.* London: SCM Press, 1964. Ibsen, Claudel.

10. Bentley, Eric. *Theatre of War: Comments on 32 Occasions.* New York: Viking, 1972. Ibsen, Brecht.

11. Bermel, Albert. *Farce: A History from Aristophanes to Woody Allen.* New York: Simon & Schuster, 1982. Wilde, Chekhov.

12. Bertolini, John A. *The Playwrighting Self of Bernard Shaw.* Carbondale: Southern Illinois University Press, 1991. Shakespeare, Sheridan, Molière.

13. Boas, Frederick S. "Joan of Arc in Shakespeare, Schiller, and Shaw." *Shakespeare Quarterly* 2 (January 1951): 35–45.

14. Brustein, Robert. *The Theatre of Revolt: An Approach to Modern Drama.* Boston: Little, Brown, 1962, 1964. Brecht, Pirandello, O'Neill.

15. Bühler, Renate. "Drei Lustspiele im Unterricht: Aristophanes, *Die Fröshce,* Plautus, *Amphytrion,* Shaw, *Pygmalion"* (Teaching Three Comedies: Aristophanes, *The Frogs;* Plautus, *Amphytrion;* Shaw, *Pygmalion*). *Der Deutschunterricht* 18 (June 1966): 88–106. [German]

16. ———. "Thoughts on Shaw's Centenary." *Shavian* 7 (1956): 10–12. Sheridan, Shakespeare, Molière.

17. Chesterton, G. K. "Shakespeare and Shaw." *Shakespeare Review* 1 (May 1928): 10–13.

18. Chute, Edward Joseph. *Comic Wrestling: A Comparative Analysis of the Comic Agon and Its Dramatic Idea and Form in Selected Comedies of Aristophanes, Shakespeare, Jonson, Shaw, and Calderon* (University of Minnesota, 1977). *DAI* 38 (1977), 1367-A.

19. Cosgrove, James Daniel. *The Rebel in Modern Drama* (St. John's University, 1988). *DAI* 49 (April 1989), 2864-A. Ionesco, Anouilh, T. S. Eliot, Osborne, Brecht, Ibsen.

20. Denninghaus, Friedhelm. *Die Dramatische Konzeption George Bernard Shaws: Untersuchungen zur Struktur der Bühnengesellschaft und zum Aufbau der Figuren in den Stücken Shaws* (George Bernard Shaw's Dramatic Concept: Studies in the Structure of Stage Society and Construction of Characters in Shaw's Plays). Stuttgart, Berlin, Köln, Mainz: Kohlhammer, 1971. [German] Ibsen, Shakespeare.

21. De Selincourt, Aubrey. *Six Great Playwrights.* London: Hamish Hamilton, 1960. Sophocles, Shakespeare, Molière, Sheridan, Ibsen.

22. Dietrich, Richard F. *British Drama 1890 to 1950: A Critical History.* Boston: Twayne Publishers, 1989.

23. Dukore, Bernard F. *Money and Politics in Ibsen, Shaw, and Brecht.* Columbia: University of Missouri Press, 1980.

24. Ellehauge, Martin. *The Position of Bernard Shaw in European Drama and Philosophy.* Copenhagen: Levin & Munksgaard, 1931.

25. Elliott, Robert Frederick. *Shadows of the Shaughraun: Reflections on the Use of the Stage Irishman Tradition in Plays by Boucicault, Shaw, Synge and O'Casey* (Cornell University, 1983). *DAI* 44 (December 1983), 1627-A.

26. Fan, Ada Mei. *In and Out of Bounds: Marriage, Adultery, and Women in the Plays of Henry Arthur Jones, Arthur Wing Pinero, Harley Granville-Barker, John Galsworthy, and Somerset Maugham* (University of Rochester, 1988). *DAI* 49 (January 1989), 1808-A.

27. Finney, Gail. *Women in Modern Drama: Freud, Feminism, and European Theatre at the Turn of the Century.* Ithaca, N.Y.: Cornell University Press, 1990. Strindberg.

28. Ganz, Arthur. *George Bernard Shaw.* London: Macmillan; New York: Grove, 1983. Shakespeare, Ibsen.

29. ———. *Realms of the Self: Variations on a Theme in Modern Drama*. New York: Columbia University Press, 1981.
30. Ganz, Margaret. "Humor's Devaluations in a Modern Idiom: The Don Juan Plays of Shaw, Frisch, and Montherlant." *Comedy: New Perspectives* 1 (Spring 1978): 117–36.
31. Gassner, John. "Bernard Shaw and the Making of the Modern Mind." *College English* 23 (April 1962): 517–25. Pinero, O'Casey, Pirandello, Giraudoux, Brecht.
32. ———. "Shaw as Drama Critic." *Theatre Arts Monthly* 36 (May 1951): 26–29, 91–95. Pinero, Shakespeare, Ibsen.
33. ———. *Theatre and Drama in the Making*. Boston: Houghton Mifflin, 1964. William Archer, Shakespeare, Ibsen, T. S. Eliot, Coward.
34. Hale, Edward Everett, Jr. *Dramatists of Today: Rostand, Hauptmann, Sudermann, Pinero, Shaw, Phillips, Maeterlinck: Being an Informal Discussion of Their Significant Work*, 6th ed. New York: Holt, 1911.
35. Hamilton, Clayton. *Problems of the Playwright*. New York: Holt, 1917. Pinero, Jones.
36. Hatcher, Joe Branch. *G.B.S. on the Minor Dramatists of the Nineties* (University of Kansas, 1968). *DAI* 29 (January 1969), 2212-A–2213-A. Jones, Pinero.
37. Henríquez Ureña, Pedro. "Tres escritores ingleses: Oscar Wilde, Pinero, Bernard Shaw" (Three English Writers: Oscar Wilde, Pinero, Bernard Shaw). *Obra Crítica* (Mexico) (1959): 7–16. [Spanish]
38. Herzog, Callie Jeanne. *Nora's Sisters: Female Characters in the Plays of Ibsen, Strindberg, Shaw and O'Neill* (University of Illinois, 1982). *DAI* 43 (March 1983), 2988-A.
39. Hill, John Edward. *Dialectical Aestheticism: Essays on the Criticism of Swinburne, Pater, Wilde, James, Shaw, and Yeats* (University of Virginia, 1972). *DAI* 33 (1973), 3648-A–3649-A.
40. Hirata, Tokuboku. "Bernard Shaw no Akugeki" (Bernard Shaw's Unpleasant Plays). *Tokyo Niroku Shinbun* (October 1908): 19–29. [Japanese] Ibsen, Pinero.
41. Hirsch, Foster Lance. *The Edwardian Drama of Ideas* (Columbia University, 1971). *DAI* 32 (December 1971), 3306-A. Granville Barker, Hankin, Houghton, Galsworthy.
42. Hornby, Richard. "The Symbolic Action of *Heartbreak House*." *Drama Survey* 7 (Winter 1968/69): 5–24. Ionesco, Pinter, Beckett, Tolstoy.
43. Huneker, James. *Iconoclasts: A Book of Dramatists*. New York: Scribner's, 1905. Gilbert, Ibsen.
44. James, Eugene Nelson. "The Critic as Dramatist: George Bernard Shaw, 1895–1898." *Shaw Review* 5 (September 1962): 97–108. Wilde, Jones, Pinero, Barrie.
45. Kaul, A. N. *The Action of English Comedy: Studies in the Encounter of Abstraction and Experience from Shakespeare to Shaw*. New Haven, Conn.: Yale University Press, 1970.
46. Kennedy, Andrew. *Six Dramatists in Search of a Language: Studies in Dramatic Language*. New York: Cambridge University Press, 1974. T. S. Eliot, Beckett, Pinter, Osborne, Arden.
47. Kleinhaus, Charles Nelson. *Toward a Generic Definition of Late Nineteenth-Century Farce: Courteline, Feydeau, Pinero, Wilde, Shaw and Jarry* (Indiana University, 1973). *DAI* 34 (February 1974), 5180-A.
48. Koritz, Amy E. *Gendering Bodies, Performing Art: Theatrical Dancing and the Performance Aesthetics of Wilde, Shaw and Yeats* (University of North Carolina at Chapel Hill, 1988). *DAI* 50 (September 1989), 691-A.
49. Kornbluth, Martin L. "Shaw and Restoration Comedy." *Shaw Bulletin* 2 (January 1958): 9–17.
50. Kosok, Heinz. "John Bull's Other Ego: Reactions to the Stage Irishman in Anglo-Irish Drama." In *Medieval and Modern Ireland*, ed. Richard Wall. Gerrards Cross: Colin Smythe, 1988; pp. 19–33, 138–39. Louis D'Alton.

51. Kuehne, A. de. "El mito de Pigmalión en Shaw, Pirandello y Solana" (The Myth of Pygmalion in Shaw, Pirandello, and Solana). *Latin American Theater Review* 2 (1969): 31–40. [Spanish]
52. Liebman, Arthur M. *The Works of W. S. Gilbert: A Study of Their Aristophanic Elements and Their Relationships to the Development of Nineteenth and Twentieth Century British Theatre* (New York University, 1971). *DAI* 32 (November 1971), 2834-A.
53. McDonald, Jan. *The "New Drama" 1900–1914: Harley Granville-Barker, John Galsworthy, St. John Hankin, John Masefield.* New York: Grove Press, 1986.
54. McIlwaine, Robert Shields. *The Intellectual Farce of Bernard Shaw* (Duke University, 1971). *DAI* 32 (February 1972), 4761-A. Beckett, Ionesco.
55. Meisel, Martin. *Shaw and the Nineteenth-Century Theater.* Princeton, N.J.: Princeton University Press, 1963.
56. Metwally, A. A. *Studies in Modern Drama.* Beirut: Beirut Arab University, 1971. Ibsen, Synge, T. S. Eliot, O'Neill.
57. Morgan, A. E. *Tendencies of Modern English Drama.* New York: Scribner's, 1924. Pinero, Jones.
58. Morgan, Margery M. "Bernard Shaw on the Tightrope." *Modern Drama* 4 (February 1962): 343–54. Granville Barker, Euripides.
59. Mouton, Janice Malmsten. *Joan of Arc on the Twentieth-Century Stage: Dramatic Treatments of the Joan of Arc Story by Bertolt Brecht, George Bernard Shaw, Jean Anouilh, Georg Kaiser, Paul Claudel, and Maxwell Anderson* (Northwestern University, 1974). *DAI* 35 (December 1974), 3693-A–3694-A.
60. Mulliken, Clara. "Reading List on Modern Dramatists: D'Annunzio, Hauptmann, Ibsen, Maeterlinck, Phillips, Rostand, Shaw and Sudermann." *Bulletin of Bibliography* 5 (October 1907): 52–53. Revised as Clara Norton Mulliken, Frank K. Walter, and Fanny Elsie Marquand, *Modern Drama and Opera: A Reading List on the Works of D'Annunzio, Hauptmann, Ibsen, Jones, Maeterlinck, Phillips, Pinero, Rostand, Shaw, Sudermann, and of Debussy, Puccini, Richard Strauss.* Boston: Boston Book Co., 1911; pp. 61–66.
61. Munitz, Barry. *Joan of Arc and Modern Drama* (Princeton University, 1968). *DAI* 29 (1969), 2720-A.
62. Nicoll, Allardyce. *British Drama,* 4th ed. London: Harrap, 1947. Ibsen, Wycherley.
63. Osborn, Margaret E. *The Concept of Imagination in Edwardian Drama* (University of Pennsylvania, 1967). *DAI* 28 (October 1967), 1443-A. Granville Barker, Synge.
64. Prang, Helmut. *Geschichte Des Lustspiels: Von der Antike bis zur Gegenwart* (A History of Comedy: From Classical Antiquity to the Present Time). Stuttgart: Alfred Kröner, 1968. [German] Carl Sternheim, Walter Hasenclever, Ferdinand Bruckner.
65. Rodgers, W. R. *Irish Literary Portraits: W. B. Yeats, James Joyce, George Moore, George Bernard Shaw, Oliver St. John Gogarty, F. R. Higgins, AE.* London: British Broadcasting Corporation, 1972; New York: Taplinger, 1975. O'Casey, Denis Johnston.
66. Rodríguez-Seda, Asela C. *George Bernard Shaw in the Hispanic World: His Reception and Influence* (University of Illinois, 1973). *DAI* 34 (1974), 7779-A.
67. Roy, Emil. *British Drama Since Shaw.* Carbondale: Southern Illinois University Press, 1972. O'Casey, Wilde.
68. Schroeder, J. G. "Brecht, Büchner y Shaw." *Primer Acto* (Spain) 47 (1963): 50–51. [Spanish]
69. Schwarz, Alfred. *From Büchner to Beckett, Dramatic Theory and the Modes of Tragic Drama.* Athens: Ohio University Press, 1978.
70. Shatzky, Joel Lawrence. *Shaw, Barker and Galsworthy: The Development of the Drama of Ideas* (New York University, 1970). *DAI* 31 (1971), 4180-A.

71. "Shaw and His Contemporaries," "The Theater of Social Problems," *History of the Drama*, Unit 7. Films for the Humanities, P.O. Box 2053, Princeton, N.J. 08540. No date [1980s].

72. Spenker, Lenyth. "The Dramatic Criteria of George Bernard Shaw." *Speech Monographs* 17 (1950): 24–36. Shakespeare, Beaumont and Fletcher, Pinero.

73. Spong, Hilda. "Working with Pinero, Barrie and Shaw." *Theatre* (New York) 32 (July/August 1920): 32, 34.

74. Stein, Rita Louise. *The Serious Comedy of St. John Hankin and Harley Granville-Barker: A Study of Two Edwardian Contemporaries of Shaw* (Columbia University, 1972). *DAI* 33 (April 1973), 5750-A.

75. Stokes, John. *Resistible Theatres: Enterprise and Experiment in the Late Nineteenth Century.* London: Paul Elek Books; New York: Barnes & Noble, 1972. Ibsen, Pinero, Jones.

76. Sühnel, Rudolf. "Eine Betrachtung über die englischen Klassiker der Moderne" (A View of the English Classical Writers of the Modern Age). In *Englische Dichter Der Moderne: Ihr Leben und Werk* (Modern English Writers: Their Lives and Work), ed. Rudolf Sühnel and Dieter Riesner. Berlin: Erich Schmidt, 1971; pp. 1–15. [German] Jonson, Molière, Ibsen, Congreve, Wilde.

77. Taylor, Thomas J. "Cumberland, Kotzebue, Scribe, Simon: Are We Teaching the Wrong Playwrights?" *College English* 43 (January 1981): 45–50.

78. Thaler, Estelle Manette. *Major Strategies in Twentieth-Century Drama: Apocalyptic Vision, Allegory and Open Form* (St. John's University, 1983). *DAI* 44 (July 1983), 163-A. Chekhov, Pinter, Shepard, Witkiewicz, Beckett.

79. Turner, W. J. "Drama." *London Mercury* 1 (1919–20): 111–14. Ibsen, Chekhov.

80. Valency, Maurice. *The End of the World: An Introduction to Contemporary Drama.* New York: Oxford University Press, 1980. Beckett, Giraudoux, Pirandello.

81. Watt, Stephen M. "Boucicault and Whitbread: The Dublin Stage at the End of the Nineteenth Century." *Eire-Ireland* 18 (Fall 1983): 25–53. Yeats, Synge, O'Casey.

82. ———. *The Making of the Modern History Play* (University of Illinois, 1982). *DAI* 43 (March 1983), 2991-A. Tom Taylor, W. G. Wills, Augustus Harris, Tennyson, Dion Boucicault, Whitbread, O'Casey.

83. Weales, Gerald. "The Edwardian Theater and the Shadow of Shaw." In *Edwardians and Late Victorians, English Institute Essays, 1959*, ed. Richard Ellmann. New York: Columbia University Press, 1960; pp. 160–87.

84. Weinreb, Ruth Plaut. "In Defense of Don Juan: Deceit and Hypocrisy in Tirso De Molina, Molière, Mozart, and G. B. Shaw." *Romanic Review* 74 (November 1983): 425–35.

85. Weintraub, Stanley. "Bernard Shaw and the American Theatre." *UNISA English Studies* 29 (September 1991): 36–41.

86. ———. "Shaw in Fiction" and "Influence and Reputation," in *Bernard Shaw: A Guide to Research.* University Park: Penn State University Press, 1992; pp. 124–41.

87. Whitaker, Thomas R. *Fields of Play in Modern Drama.* Princeton, N.J.: Princeton University Press, 1977. Chekhov, Claudel.

88. Wilhelmsen, Leif J. "Fortalens Betydning I Bernard Shaws Produksjon" (The Significance of the Preface in Bernard Shaw's Production). *Edda* 38 (1938): 449–56. [Norwegian] Dryden, Synge, Dumas *père*.

89. Withington, Robert. "The Sage of Dubdon: A Critical Note on G. B. Shaw." *Sewanee Review* 43 (April/June 1935): 224–29. Shakespeare, Jonson.

90. Worthen, William Blake. *The Idea of the Actor: Dramatic Style and Histrionic Meaning* (Princeton University, 1981). *DAI* 42 (October 1981), 1652-A. Stanislavsky, Artaud, Brecht, Grotowski.

II. Works on Authors

AKUTAGAWA, RYUNOSUKE (1892–1927)

Shimada, Kinji. "Akutagawa Ryunosuke to Eibungaku—Hikakubungaku Koen' " (Ryuno-suke Akutagawa and English Literature—Lecture in Comparative Literature). In *Nihonbungaku to Eibungaku* (Japanese Literature and English Literature), ed. Yoshie Okazaki and Kinji Shimada. Tokyo: Kyoiku Shuppan Center, 1973; pp. 42–74. [Japanese]

ANDERSON, MAXWELL (1888–1959): 59.

ANOUILH, JEAN (1910–): 19, 59. *See also* Jewkes and Landfield under SCHILLER, below.

ARCHER, WILLIAM (1856–1924)

Archer, Charles. *William Archer: His Life, Work and Friendships.* New Haven, Conn.: Yale University Press, 1931.

Gassner, John. Introduction to William Archer, *Play-Making: A Manual of Craftsmanship.* New York: Dover, 1960; pp. v–xxxi.

Also: 33, 70.

ARDEN, JOHN (1930–): 46.

ARISTOPHANES (ca. 450–385 B.C.)

Kárpáti, Aurél. "Bernard Shaw: A modern Arisztofanész" (Bernard Shaw: The Modern Aristophanes) (1956). In *Tegnaptól Máig: Valogatt Irodalmi Tanulmányok* (From Yesterday to Today: Selected Literary Essays). Budapest: Szépirodalmi Könyvkiadó, 1961; pp. 400–404. [Hungarian]

Speckhard, Robert R. "Shaw and Aristophanes: How the Comedy of Ideas Works." *Shaw Review* 8 (September 1965): 82–92.

Williams, Katherine Gamewell. *Heroic Archetypes in the Comedies of Aristophanes and Later Playwrights* (Florida State University, 1983). *DAI* 44 (December 1983), 1785-A–1786-A.

Also: 15, 18, 52.

ARTAUD, ANTONIN (1896–1948): 90.

AYCKBOURN, ALAN (1939–)

Dukore, Bernard F. *Alan Ayckbourn: A Casebook.* New York: Garland, 1991.

———. "Alan Ayckbourn's Liza Doolittle." *Modern Drama* 32 (September 1989): 425–39.

BAHR, HERMANN (1863–1934)

Reid, Louis R. "Shaw and Bahr Compared." *New York Dramatic Mirror* 76 (23 December 1916): 4.

Rubinstein, H. F. "The German Bernard Shaw." *Forum* (New York) 53 (March 1915): 375–79.

BARKER, HARLEY GRANVILLE: *See* GRANVILLE BARKER, HARLEY, below.

BARNES, PETER (1931–)

Dukore, Bernard F. "Plays and Playing: Conversations at Leeds." *Theatre Topics* 1 (September 1991): 99–116.

———. "*Red Noses* and *Saint Joan.*" *Modern Drama* 30 (September 1987): 340–51.

BARRIE, J. M. (1860–1937)

Beerbohm, Max. "Little Mary." *Saturday Review* 96 (1903): 423–24.

Birkin, Andrew. *J. M. Barrie and the Lost Boys.* New York: Clarkson N. Potter, 1979.

Hamilton, Clayton. "Criticism and Creation in the Drama of Bernard Shaw and J. M. Barrie." *Bookman* (New York) 44 (February 1917): 628–32.

Hugo, Leon H. "*PUNCH:* J. M. Barrie's Gentle Swipe at 'Supershaw'." *SHAW: The Annual of Bernard Shaw Studies* 10 (1990): 60–72.

Thomas, Gwyn. "Mr. Barrie and Mr. Shaw." *Listener* (14 August 1975), pp. 218–19.

Also: 5, 44, 73.

BARRY, PHILIP (1896–1949): 2.

BEAUMARCHAIS, PIERRE AUGUSTIN (1732–1799)
Varona, Enrique José. "Una Transfiguración de Rosina y Querubín" (A Transfiguration of Rosina and Cherubin) (1904). In *Desde Me Belvedere* (From My Viewpoint). Havana: Papeleria de Rambla y Bouza, 1907; pp. 253–58. [Spanish]
BEAUMONT (1586–1615) and FLETCHER (1576–1625): 72.
BECKETT, SAMUEL (1906–1991)
Collar, Georges. "Beckett, Shaw y dos actores ingleses" (Beckett, Shaw, and Two English Actors). *Cuadernos del Sur* 13 (August 1963): 738–39.
Also: 4, 42, 46, 54, 69, 78, 80.
BLACKMUR, R. P. (1904–1965)
Fraser, Russell. *A Mingled Yarn: The Life of R. P. Blackmur.* New York and London: Harcourt, Brace, Jovanovich, 1979, 1981.
BOUCICAULT, DION (1820–1890)
Fawkes, Richard. *Dion Boucicault: A Biography.* London, Melbourne, and New York: Quartet Books, 1979.
Also: 25.
BRADBURY, RAY (1920–)
Bradbury, Ray. Introduction to *The Wonderful Ice Cream Suit and Other Plays.* New York, Toronto, and London: Bantam Pathfinder Editions, 1972.
BRECHT, BERTOLT (1898–1956)
Abel, Lionel. *Metatheatre: A New View of Dramatic Form.* New York: Hill & Wang, 1963; pp. 106–7.
Adler, Henry. "Bertolt Brecht's Contribution to Epic Drama." *Listener* 55 (12 January 1956): 309–17.
———. "Brecht and After." *Drama* 63 (Winter 1961): 29–31.
Brecht, Bertolt. *Arbeitsjournal: Erster Band 1938–1942* (Working Diary: First Volume, 1938–1942). Frankfurt: Suhrkamp, 1973; pp. 189, 199.
———. "Ovation for Shaw" [from "Ovation für Shaw," 1926], translated from German by Gerhard H. W. Zuther. *Modern Drama* 2 (September 1959): 184–87.
Bryden, Ronald. "Brecht and Shaw." *New Statesman* 67 (19 June 1964): 966–67.
Dobrev, Shadar. "Geroika i ironiîa" (Heroics and Irony). *Teatŭr* (Sofia) 7 (1968): 30–34. [Bulgarian]
Dukore, Bernard F. "Brecht's Shavian Saint." *Quarterly Journal of Speech* 50 (April 1964): 136–39.
G., F. "Bernard Shaw und die junge Dichtergeneration" (Bernard Shaw and the Generation of Young Authors). *Die Volksbühne* 3 (February 1929): 44–45. [German]
Hunningher, B. "Shaw en Brecht: Wegen en grenzen van socialistisch theater" (Shaw and Brecht: Ways and Limits of Socialist Theater). *Forum Der Letteren* 12 (1971): 173–90. [Dutch]
Luck, Georg. "Didaktische Poesie" (Didactic Literature). In *Das Fischer Lexikon: Literatur II/1* (The Fischer Encyclopedia: Literature II/1), ed. Wolf-Harmut Friedrich and Walther Killy. Frankfurt: Fischer, 1965; pp. 151–62. [German]
Sauvageau, David Ronald. *Shaw, Brecht and Evolution: The Early Plays* (University of Minnesota, 1977). *DAI* 38 (1977), 1383-A.
Scheops, Karl-Heinz. *Bertolt Brecht und Bernard Shaw: Studien zur Germanistik, Anglistik und Komparatistik, 26.* Bonn: Bouvier, 1974. [German]
Schuler, Catherine Ann. *Bernard Shaw and Bertolt Brecht: A Comparative Study Utilizing Methods of Feminist Criticism* (Florida State University, 1984). *DAI* 45 (March 1985), 2698-A.
Williams, Arthur Ernest. *Comparative Dramaturgical Structure in Selected Plays of Bernard Shaw and Bertolt Brecht* (Ohio State University, 1984). *DAI* 45 (December 1984), 1574-A–1575-A.

Also: 4, 10, 14, 18, 23, 31, 59, 68, 90.
BRIEUX, EUGÈNE (1858–1932)
Fyfe, H. Hamilton. "Brieux and Bernard Shaw." *Independent Shavian* 13 (Winter 1975): 24–25.
Klein, John W. "Shaw and Brieux—An Enigma." *Drama* 67 (Winter 1962): 33–35.
Mundell, Richard Frederick. *Shaw and Brieux: A Literary Relationship* (University of Michigan, 1971). *DAI* 32 (September 1971), 1522-A.
BRUCKNER, FERDINAND (1891–1958): 64.
BÜCHNER, GEORG (1813–1837): 68, 69.
CALDERON, PEDRO (1600–1681): 18.
CANNAN, GILBERT (1884–1955)
Farr, Diana. *Gilbert Cannan: A Georgian Prodigy.* London: Chatto & Windus, 1978.
ČAPEK, KAREL (1890–1938)
Bradbrook, B. R. "Letters to England from Karel Čapek." *Slavonic and East European Review* 39 (December 1960): 61–72.
CHEKHOV, ANTON (1860–1904)
Harris, Harold J. "Shaw, Chekhov, and Two Great Ladies of the Theatre." *Shaw Review* 6 (September 1963): 96–99.
Iijima, Kohei. "Shaw to Chekhov—Shoshin no Ie to Sakura no Sono tono Kankei nitsuite—" (Shaw and Chekhov—The Relationship between *Heartbreak House* and *The Cherry Orchard*). *Eibungaku, Kenkyu to Kansho* (Waseda University, Tokyo) 2 (June 1951): 27–38. [Japanese]
Kirillova, L. Iâ. "B. Shou i A. Chekhov: o zhanrovo-kompozitsíonnykh osobennostiâkh" (B. Shaw and A. Chekhov: Genre and Compositional Peculiarities). *Sbornik Nauchnykh Trudov Tashkentskogo Universiteta* 577 (1977): 34–45. [Russian]
Meister, Charles W. "Chekhov's Reception in England and America." *American Slavic and East European Review* 12 (1953): 109–21.
Mendelsohn, Michael J. "The Heartbreak Houses of Shaw and Chekhov." *Shaw Review* 6 (September 1963): 89–95.
Valency, Maurice. *The Breaking String: The Plays of Anton Chekhov.* New York: Oxford University Press, 1966.
Also: 11, 78, 79, 87.
CLAUDEL, PAUL (1868–1955): 9, 59, 87.
CONGREVE, WILLIAM (1670–1729): 76.
COURTELINE, GEORGES (1858–1929): 47.
COWARD, NOËL. (1899–1973)
Coward, Noël. *The Noël Coward Diaries,* ed. Graham Payn and Sheridan Morley. Boston: Little, Brown, 1982.
Fisher, Clive. *Noël Coward.* New York: St. Martin's Press, 1992.
Lahr, John. *Coward the Playwright.* London: Methuen, 1982.
Walker, Roy. "Theatre Royal." *Twentieth Century* 153 (June 1953): 466–70.
Also: 33.
CUMBERLAND, RICHARD (1732–1811): 77.
D'ALTON, LOUIS (1900–1951): 50.
D'ANNUNZIO, GABRIELE (1863–1938): 60.
DE MOLINA, TIRSO (1571?–1648): 84.
DRYDEN, JOHN (1631–1700): 88.
DUMAS, ALEXANDRE (1802–1870): 88.
ELIOT, T. S. (1888–1965)
Galinsky, Hans. "G. B. Shaw als Gegenstand der Kritik und Quelle dramatischer Anregung für T. S. Eliot" (G. B. Shaw as Object of Criticism and Source of Dramatic Inspiration

for T. S. Eliot). *Germanisch-Romanische Monatsschrift Neue Folge* 7 (April 1957): 146–64. [German]

Martz, Louis L. "The Saint as Tragic Hero: *Saint Joan* and *Murder in the Cathedral.*" In *George Bernard Shaw's Saint Joan,* ed. Harold Bloom. New York, New Haven, and Philadelphia: Chelsea House, 1987.

Also: 2, 19, 33, 46, 56.

EURIPIDES (480–406 B.C.)

Norwood, Gilbert. *Euripides and Shaw.* London: Methuen, 1921.

Also: 58.

FEYDEAU, GEORGES (1862–1921): 47.

FLECKER, JAMES ELROY (1884–1915)

Kidd, Timothy J. "James Elroy Flecker and Bernard Shaw." *Shaw Review* 21 (September 1978): 124–35.

FRISCH, MAX (1911–): 30.

GALSWORTHY, JOHN (1867–1933)

Galsworthy, John. *Another Sheaf.* London: Heinemann, 1919; pp. 88–109.

———. "The New Spirit in the Drama." *Living Age* 277 (1913): 259–66.

Gindin, James. "The Belated Shavian Influence: Wartime Disillusion and Galsworthy's *The Foundations.*" *SHAW: The Annual of Bernard Shaw Studies* 10 (1990): 73–84.

"J'accuse: The Dramatists v. Civilization." *English Review* 38 (April 1924): 599–602.

Takenaka, Toshikazu. "Shaw to Galsworthy" (Shaw and Galsworthy). *Corona Australis* (Hiroshima) 6 (June 1932): 1–3. [Japanese]

Vidmar, Josip. "Drama na raskršču" (Drama at the Crossroads). *Izraz* (Sarajevo) 24 (1968): 288–92. [Serbo-Croatian]

Also: 5, 26, 41, 70.

GATTIE, ALFRED WARWICK (1856–1925)

Wellwarth, George E. "Gattie's Glass of Water; or, the Origin of Breakages, Ltd." *Shaw Review* 11 (September 1968): 99–103.

———. " 'Gattie's Glass of Water': Addendum." *Shaw Review* 12 (January 1969): 28–29.

GILBERT, W. S. (1836–1911)

Moulan, Frank. "The Humor of Gilbert and Shaw." *Theatre* (New York) 31 (1920): 158–60.

Also: 43, 52.

GIRAUDOUX, JEAN (1882–1944): 31, 74.

GOLDING, WILLIAM (1911–)

Oldsey, Bernard S., and Stanley Weintraub. "Ambassadors at Large: Other Writings." In *The Art of William Golding.* New York: Harcourt, Brace & World, 1965; pp. 147–58.

GORKY, MAXIM (1868–1936)

Michailowski, Boris. "Gorki und Shaw." In *Maxim Gorki: Drama und Theater,* ed. Ilse Stauche. Berlin: Henschel, 1968; pp. 34–47. [German]

Pravdev, Nikolar. "Shou i Gorki v Burgaskiîa teatŭr" (Shaw and Gorky at the Burgaski Theater). *Teatŭr* (Sofia) 5 (1971): 38–43. [Bulgarian]

GRANVILLE BARKER, HARLEY (1877–1946)

Casson, Lewis. "G.B.S. and the Court Theatre." *Listener* 46 (12 July 1951): 53–54.

Dukore, Bernard F. "*The Madras House* Prefinished." *Educational Theatre Journal* 24 (May 1972): 135–38.

Dymkowski, Christine. *Harley Granville-Barker: A Preface to Modern Shakespeare.* Washington, D.C.: Folger Shakespeare Library, 1986.

Evans, T. F. "Granville-Barker: Shavian Disciple." *Shaw Bulletin* 2 (May 1958): 1–19.

F. "Granville Barker, Shaw and Anatole France at Wallack's." *Nation* 100 (1915): 150.

Kennedy, Dennis. *Granville Barker and the Dream of Theatre.* Cambridge: Cambridge University Press, 1985.

Kershner, William Robert. *The Theatre as a Social Institution: A Study of Harley Granville-Barker's Theories of Theatrical Art* (University of Southern California, 1981). *DAI* 42 (April 1982), 4203-A.

Morgan, Margery M. *A Drama of Political Man: A Study in the Plays of Harley Granville Barker.* London: Sidgwick & Jackson, 1961.

———. "Two Varieties of Political Drama: *The Apple Cart* and Granville Barker's *His Majesty.*" *Shavian* 2 (April 1962): 9–16.

Nickson, Richard. "Using Words on the Stage: Shaw and Granville-Barker." *Modern Drama* 27 (September 1984): 409–19.

Salenius, Elmer W. "Harley Granville Barker and the Modern English Theater" (Boston University, 1951). Unpublished dissertation.

Shrive, Norman. "Granville-Barker and Edwardian Theatre." *Waterloo Review* 1 (Winter 1959): 34–46.

Stier, Theodore. "Barker and Shaw at the Court Theatre: A View from the Pit." *Shaw Review* 10 (January 1967): 18–33.

Whitaker, Thomas R. "Granville Barker's Answer to *Heartbreak.*" *SHAW: The Annual of Bernard Shaw Studies* 10 (1990): 85–95.

Also: 26, 41, 53, 58, 63, 70, 74.

GROTOWSKI, JERZY (1933–): 90.

HACKS, PETER (1928–)

Theater in de Zeitenwende: Zur Geschichte des Dramas und des Schauspieltheaters in der Deutschen Demokratischen Republik 1945–1968 (Theater in an Age of Transition: On the History of the Drama and the Stage in the German Democratic Republic, 1945–1968), ed. Werner Mittenzwei. Berlin: Henschelverlag Kunst und Gesellschaft, 1972. [German]

HAN-CHING, KUAN (1210–1298)

Hung, Josephine Huang. "The Candida Character in Kuan Han-ching's *The Riverside Pavilion.*" In *Proceedings from the International Comparative Literature Conference Held 18–24 July at Tamkang College of Arts and Sciences, Taipei, Taiwan, Republic of China. Tamkang Review* 2–3 (October 1971/April 1972): 295–308.

HANKIN, ST. JOHN (1869–1909)

Beerbohm, Max. "The Return of the Prodigal." *Saturday Review* 100 (1905): 463–64.

Hankin, St. John. "Dramatic Sequels: *Octavian and Cleopatra.*" *Shaw Review* 22 (September 1979): 142–46.

———. "Mr. Bernard Shaw as Critic." *Fortnightly Review* (New York) 87 (June 1907): 1961–66.

Phillips, William H. *St. John Hankin: Edwardian Mephistopheles.* Cranbury, N.J.: Associated University Presses, 1979.

Also: 41, 53, 74.

HARRIS, AUGUSTUS (1851–1896): 82.

HASENCLEVER, WALTER (1890–1940): 64.

HAUPTMANN, GERHART (1862–1946): 60.

HOUGHTON, STANLEY (1881–1913): 41.

IBSEN, HENRIK (1828–1906)

Adler, Jacob H. "Ibsen, Shaw and *Candida.*" *Journal of English and Germanic Philology* 59 (1960): 50–58.

Astafeeva, M. "Ibsen kak sozdatel' sotŝial'noĭ dramy: Shou ob Ibsene" (Ibsen as Founder of Social Drama: Shaw on Ibsen). In *Problemy Zarubezhnogo Teatra I Teatrovedeniia* (Problems of Foreign Theater and Theater Criticism). Moscow: n.p., 1977). [Russian]

Britain, I. M. "Bernard Shaw, Ibsen and the Ethics of English Socialism." *Victorian Studies* 21 (Spring 1978): 381–401.

Brooks, Harold F. "*Pygmalion* and *When We Dead Awaken.*" *Notes and Queries* 7 (December 1960): 469–71.

Cocco, Maria Rosaria. " 'Malodorous Ibsen'." *Annali Instituto Universitario Orientale, Napoli, Sezione Germanica* 11 (1968): 171–93.

Durbach, Errol. "Pygmalion: Myth and Anti-Myth in the Plays of Ibsen and Shaw." *English Studies in Africa* 21 (March 1978): 23–31.

Fischer, Friedrich. *George Bernard Shaw als Dramatiker und sein Verhaltnis zu Henrik Ibsen* (George Bernard Shaw as Dramatist and His Relationship to Henrik Ibsen). Published Ph.D. dissertation, University of Dusseldorf, 1917. [German]

Fisher, F. G. "Ibsen and His Background." *Anglo-Welsh Review* 10 (1959): 42–47.

Franc, Miriam Alice. *Ibsen in England.* Boston: Four Seas, 1919.

Gassner, John, and Norbert O'Donnell. "Shaw on Ibsen and the Drama of Ideas." In *Ideas and the Drama: Selected Papers from the English Institute*, ed. John Gassner. New York and London: Columbia University Press, 1964; pp. 71–100.

Gerould, Daniel Charles. "George Bernard Shaw's Criticism of Ibsen." *Comparative Literature* 15 (1963): 130–45.

Irvine, William. "Shaw's *Quintessence of Ibsenism.*" *South Atlantic Quarterly* 46 (April 1947): 252–62.

Irving, John Douglas. *Mary Shaw, Actress, Suffragist, Activist* (Columbia University, 1978). *DAI* 39 (October 1978), 1932-A–1933-A.

Lamm, Martin. "Ibsen och Shaw" (Ibsen and Shaw). *Edda* (Oslo) 47 (1947): 130–40. [Swedish]

Lavrin, Janko. *Studies in European Literature.* New York: Richard R. Smith, 1930; pp. 80–89.

Leland, Charles. "Ibsen, Chesterton and Shaw: A Misunderstanding All Around: A Response to Vincent Balice." *Chesterton Review* 3 (Fall/Winter 1976–77): 35–42.

May, Keith M. *Ibsen and Shaw.* London: Macmillan, 1985.

McDowell, Frederick P. W. "Fountainhead and Fountain: Ibsen and Shaw." *Shaw Review* 23 (September 1980): 139–47.

Metwally, A. A. "The Influences of Ibsen on Shaw" (Trinity College, Dublin, 1960). Unpublished dissertation.

Munzar, Jiří. "Shaw und Ibsen." *Brunner Beiträge zur Germanistik und Nordistik* (Brno) 1 (1977): 137–51. [German]

O'Donnell, Norbert F. "Ibsen and Shaw: The Tragic and the Tragic-Comic." *Theatre Annual* 15 (1957–58): 15–27.

Rodenbeck, John. "*The Irrational Knot:* Shaw and the Uses of Ibsen." *Shaw Review* 12 (May 1969): 66–76.

Schlauch, Margaret. "Postacie Symboliczne i Technika Symboliki u Shawa" (Symbolic Form and Symbolic Technique in Shaw). *Kwartalnik Neofilologiczny* 4 (1957): 30–40. [Polish]

Stümcke, Heinrich. "Von den Berliner Theatern 1903/04" (About the Berlin Theaters 1903/04). *Bühne und Welt* 6.1 (1903–4): 471–74, 520–23. [German]

Turco, Alfred, Jr. *Shaw's Moral Vision.* Ithaca, N.Y.: Cornell University Press, 1976.

Weintraub, Stanley. "Ibsen's *Doll's House:* Metaphor Foreshadowed in Victorian Fiction." *Nineteenth Century Fiction* 13 (June 1958): 67–69.

West, E. J. "Shaw's Criticism of Ibsen: A Reconsideration." *University of Colorado Studies, Series in Language and Literature* 4 (July 1953): 101–27.

Wiedner, Elsie M. "Shaw's Transformation of Ibsen in *The Devil's Disciple.*" *Shaw Review* 22 (January 1979): 23–28.

Wisenthal, J. L. "Introductory Essay." In *Shaw and Ibsen: Bernard Shaw's* The Quintessence of Ibsenism *and Related Writings*, ed. J. L. Wisenthal. Toronto: University of Toronto Press, 1979.

Wood, Frederick T. "Individualism in Religious Thought in the Plays of Ibsen and Bernard Shaw." *Calcutta Review* (June 1935): 243–55.
Also: 4, 6, 9, 10, 19, 20, 21, 23, 28, 32, 33, 38, 40, 43, 56, 60, 62, 75, 76, 79.
INGE, W. R. (1913–)
Armstrong, Martin. "Who Wrote Shaw?" *Week-End Review* 6 (20 August 1932): 203–4.
IONESCO, EUGÈNE (1912–): 4, 19, 42, 54.
JAMES, HENRY (1843–1916)
Edel, Leon. *Henry James, the Master: 1901–1916*. Philadelphia and New York: J. B. Lippincott, 1972.
Hatcher, Joe Branch. "Shaw the Reviewer and James's *Guy Domville*." *Modern Drama* 14 (December 1971): 331–34.
Swartz, David L., Jr. "Bernard Shaw and Henry James." *Shaw Review* 10 (May 1967): 50–59.
Also: 39.
JARRY, ALFRED (1873–1907): 47.
JOHNSTON, DENIS (1901–)
Johnston, Denis. Preface to *Collected Plays*. London: Jonathan Cape, 1960; 1:7–9.
Kilroy, Thomas. "*The Moon in the Yellow River*: Denis Johnston's Shavianism." In *Denis Johnston: A Retrospective*, ed. Joseph Ronsley. Gerrards Cross: Colin Smythe, 1981; Totowa, N.J.: Barnes & Noble, 1982.
JONES, HENRY ARTHUR (1851–1929)
Brome, Vincent. *Six Studies in Quarrelling*. London: Cresset Press, 1958.
Cordell, Richard A. *Henry Arthur Jones and the Modern Drama*. New York: Long & Smith, 1932.
Also: 26, 35, 44, 57, 75.
JONSON, BEN (1572/73–1637)
Armand, I. L. "Kharakternye cherti angliiskogo iumora v p'esakh Bernarda Shou" (Characteristic Features of English Humor in Bernard Shaw's Plays). *Trudy Tbliskogo Pedagogicheskogo Instituta Inostrannykh Iazikov* (Tiflis) 4 (1961): 51–56. [Russian]
Garner, Stanton B. "Shaw's Comedy of Disillusionment." *Modern Drama* 28 (December 1985): 639–58.
Stokes, E. E., Jr. "Jonson's 'Humour' Plays and Some Later Plays of Bernard Shaw." *Shavian* 2 (October 1964): 13–18.
KAISER, GEORG (1878–1945): 59.
KOTZEBUE, AUGUST VON (1761–1819): 77.
KUAN, HAN CHING. *See* HAN-CHING, KUAN, above.
LANGNER, LAWRENCE (1890–1962)
Langner, Lawrence. "Saint Bernard and Saint Joan." *Shaw Review* 17 (September 1974): 114–23.
LERNER, ALAN JAY (1918–)
Lerner, Alan Jay. "*Pygmalion* and *My Fair Lady*." *Shaw Bulletin* 1 (November 1956): 4–7.
———. *The Street Where I Live*. New York and London: Norton, 1978.
MAETERLINCK, MAURICE (1862–1949): 34, 60.
MASEFIELD, JOHN (1878–1967)
Smith, Constance Babington. *John Masefield: A Life*. New York: Macmillan, 1978.
Also: 53.
MAUGHAM, W. SOMERSET (1874–1965)
Parker, R. B. "*The Circle* of Somerset Maugham." In *Shaw: Seven Critical Essays*, ed. Norman Rosenblood. Toronto: University of Toronto Press, 1971; pp. 36–50.
Also: 26.
MILLER, ARTHUR (1915–)

Miller, Arthur, interviewed by Phillip Gelb. "Morality and Modern Drama." *Educational Theatre Journal* 10 (October 1958): 190–202.

MOLIÈRE (1622–1673)

Dalmasso, Osvaldo de. "Molière, George Bernard Shaw y los médicos" (Molière, George Bernard Shaw, and the Doctors). *Lyra* (Argentina) 2 (September/December 1965): n.p. [Spanish]

Hamon, Augustin. *Le Molière du XXe Siecle: Bernard Shaw* (The Twentieth-Century Molière: Bernard Shaw). Paris: Figuière, 1913. [French]

———. "Un Nouveau Molière: A French View of Bernard Shaw." *Nineteenth Century* 64 (July 1908): 48–63.

Also: 12, 16, 21, 76, 84.

MONTHERLANT, HENRY DE (1896–1972): 33.

O'CASEY, SEAN (1880–1964)

Darin, Doris de Podesta. *Influences on the Dramas of Sean O'Casey: "Past Experiences—The Molds in Which Myself Was Made"* (New York University, 1968). *DAI* 30 (December 1969), 2523-A.

Hogan, Robert Goode. *The Experiments of Sean O'Casey.* New York: St. Martin's Press, 1960.

Krause, David. *Sean O'Casey: The Man and His Works.* New York: Macmillan, 1960.

Mikhail, E. H. "Bernard Shaw and Sean O'Casey: An Unrecorded Friendship." In *Essays on Sean O'Casey's Autobiographies,* ed. Robert G. Lowery. Totowa, N.J.: Barnes & Noble, 1981; pp. 123–46.

O'Casey, Eileen. *Cheerio, Titan: The Friendship between George Bernard Shaw and Eileen and Sean O'Casey.* New York: Scribner's, 1989.

———. *Sean,* ed. Jonathan Courtney Trewin. London: Macmillan, 1971.

O'Casey, Sean. *The Green Crow.* New York: George Braziller, 1956.

———. *The Letters of Sean O'Casey,* ed. David Krause. New York: Macmillan, 1975.

———. *The Letters of Sean O'Casey, 1942–54,* ed. David Krause. New York: Macmillan, 1980.

Rabey, David Ian. *British and Irish Political Drama in the Twentieth Century: Implicating the Audience.* New York: St. Martin's Press, 1986.

Turner, Tramble Thomas. *Bernard Shaw's Influence on Sean O'Casey's Later Plays* (University of North Carolina at Chapel Hill, 1987). *DAI* 48 (March 1988), 2347-A.

Weintraub, Stanley. "Shaw's Other Keegan: O'Casey and G.B.S." In *Sean O'Casey: Centenary Essays,* ed. David Krause and Robert G. Lowery. Totowa, N.J.: Barnes & Noble, 1980; pp. 212–27.

Worth, Katharine J. "A Horn of Plenty." *Shavian* 3 (Spring/Summer 1967): 25–27.

Also: 25, 31, 67, 81, 82.

O'NEILL, EUGENE (1888–1953)

Brashear, W. R. "O'Neill and Shaw: The Play as Will and Idea." *Criticism* 8 (Spring 1966): 155–69.

Shaeffer, Louis. *O'Neill: Son and Artist.* Boston: Little, Brown, 1973.

Also: 2, 4, 14, 38, 56.

OSBORNE, JOHN (1929–)

Cohn, Ruby, and Bernard F. Dukore, eds. *Twentieth Century Drama: England, Ireland, the United States.* New York: Random House, 1966; pp. 542–43.

Worth, Katharine J. *Revolutions in Modern English Drama.* London: Bell, 1973.

———. "Shaw and John Osborne." *Shavian* 2 (October 1964): 29–35.

Also: 19, 46.

PHILLIPS, STEPHEN (1864–1915): 34, 60.

PINERO, ARTHUR (1855–1934)

Kornbluth, Martin L. "Two Fallen Women: Paula Tanqueray and Kitty Warren." *Shavian* 14 (February 1959): 14–15.

Nethercot, Arthur H. "*Mrs Warren's Profession* and *The Second Mrs. Tanqueray.*" *Shaw Review* 13 (January 1970): 26–28.

Okumura, Saburo. "Pinero no Tanqueray no Gosai—Igirisukindaigeki no Ichi Keitai" (Pinero's *The Second Mrs. Tanqueray*—A Type of Modern English Drama). *Jinbun Kenkyu* (Osaka Municipal University, Osaka) 26 (October 1974): 268–86. [Japanese]

Ronning, Robert Thomas. *The Development of English Comic Farce in the Plays of Sir Arthur Pinero* (Wayne State University, 1972). *DAI* 33 (May 1973), 6494-A.

Wearing, J. P. *The Collected Letters of Sir Arthur Pinero*. Minneapolis: University of Minnesota Press, 1974.

Also: 26, 31, 32, 34, 35, 37, 40, 44, 47, 57, 72, 73, 75.

PINTER, HAROLD (1930–): 42, 78.

PIRANDELLO, LUIGI (1867–1936)

Boza, Masvidal Aurelio. "La dramática de Shaw y Pirandello" (The Dramatic Art of Shaw and Pirandello). *Estudios de Literatura Italiana* (Havana) (1934): 7–36. [Spanish]

Fergusson, Francis. "The Theatricality of Shaw and Pirandello." *Partisan Review* 16 (June 1949): 589–603.

Girosi, Pablo. "Pirandello y Shaw" (Pirandello and Shaw). *Revista de Literaturas Modernes* (Argentina) 1 (1956): 47–72. [Spanish]

Lux, George L. "His Excellency, Luigi Pirandello: Random Comparisons with Other Writers." *South Atlantic Quarterly* 37 (January 1938): 67–72.

Pettinati, Mario. "A Colazione fra Pirandello e G. B. Shaw" (At Lunch between Pirandello and G. B. Shaw). *Eloquenza Siciliana* (Rome) 9 (1969): 262–66. [Italian]

Pirandello, Luigi. "Pirandello Distills Shaw." *New York Times* (13 January 1924), part IV, pp. 1, 14.

Rebora, Piero. "Ricordi Culturali Italiani di Bernard Shaw" (Italian Cultural Memories of Bernard Shaw). *English Miscellany* 4 (1953): 179–86. [Italian]

Also: 3, 4, 14, 31, 51, 80.

PLAUTUS (ca. 224–184 B.C.): 15.

RATTIGAN, TERENCE (1911–1977)

Darlow, Michael, and Gillian Hodson. *Terence Rattigan: The Man and His Work*. New York: Horizon Press, 1979.

Rusinko, Susan. *Terence Rattigan*. Boston: G. K. Hall, 1983.

ROSTAND, EDMOND (1868–1918): 60.

SAROYAN, WILLIAM (1908–1981): 2.

SCHILLER, FREDERICK (1759–1805)

Biasio, Laura del Giudice. "Giovanna d'Arco nel Dramma di Schiller ed in Quello di Shaw: Crisi Individuale e Crisi Sociale" (Joan of Arc in the Plays of Schiller and Shaw: Personal Crisis and Societal Crisis). *Annuario* (Yearbook) (Liceo-Ginnasio Statale "G. Palmieri," Lecce) (1960–61): 59–79. [Italian]

Blankenagel, John C. "Shaw's *Saint Joan* and Schiller's *Jungfrau von Orleans.*" *Journal of English and Germanic Philology* 25 (1926): 379–92.

Jewkes, William T., and Jerome B. Landfield. *Joan of Arc: Fact, Legend, and Literature*. New York: Harcourt, Brace & World, 1964.

Also: 13.

SCRIBE, EUGÈNE (1791–1861)

Stanton, Stephen S. "Shaw's Debt to Scribe." *PMLA* 76 (December 1961): 575–85.

Also: 3, 77.

SHAKESPEARE, WILLIAM (1564–1616)

Almási, Miklós. *A Modern Dráma Útjain: Az Újabb Drámatörténet És Shakespeare—I Hagyományok* (Along the Byways of Modern Drama: The More Recent History of Drama and the Shakespearean Tradition). Budapest: Gondolat, 1961; pp. 166–201. [Hungarian]

Armstrong, Cecil Ferard. *Shakespeare to Shaw: Studies in the Life's Work of Six Dramatists of the English Stage*. London: Mills & Boon, 1913.

Breïtburg, S. "Bernard Shou v spore s Tolstym o Shekspire" (Bernard Shaw's Quarrel with Tolstoy over Shakespeare). *Literaturnoe Nasledstvo* (Moscow) 37/38 (1939): 617–32. [Russian]

Cohn, Ruby. *Modern Shakespeare Offshoots*. Princeton, N.J.: Princeton University Press, 1976.

Collins, P.A.W. "Shaw on Shakespeare." *Shakespeare Quarterly* 7 (Winter 1957): 1–13.

Couchman, Gordon W. "*Antony and Cleopatra* and the Subjective Convention." *PMLA* 76 (September 1961): 420–25.

Crompton, Louis, and Hilayne Cavanaugh, eds. "Shaw's 1884 Lecture on 'Troilus and Cressida'." *Shaw Review* 14 (May 1971): 48–67.

Dukore, Bernard F. "Shaw on *Hamlet*." *Educational Theatre Journal* 23 (May 1971): 152–59.

Eastman, Arthur. *A Short History of Shakespearean Criticism*. New York: Random House, 1968.

Edwards, Anne. *Vivien Leigh, A Biography*. New York: Simon & Schuster, 1977.

Fagan, J. B. "Shakespear v. Shaw," ed. Leon H. Hugo. *Shaw Review* 13 (September 1970): 105–31.

Gassner, John. "Shaw on Shakespeare." *Independent Shavian* 2 (Fall 1963): 1, 3–5; (Winter 1963/64): 13, 15, 23–24.

Harrison, G. B., ed. *Julius Caesar in Shakespeare, Shaw and the Ancients*. New York: Harcourt Brace, 1960.

Haywood, Charles. "George Bernard Shaw on Shakespearean Music and the Actor." *Shakespeare Quarterly* 20 (Autumn 1969): 417–26.

Henderson, Archibald. "Shaw and Shakespeare." *Shaw Bulletin* 1 (September 1954): 1–6.

[Howells, W. D.]. "Editor's Easy Chair." *Harper's Monthly* 111 (September 1905): 633–35.

Jaffé, Gerhard. "Shaws Oppfatning Av Dramatisk Diktkunst Sammenlignet Med Shakespeares" (Shaw's Concept of Dramatic Art Compared with Shakespeare's). *Edda* 50 (1950): 56–92. [Norwegian]

Kantorovich, I. "Na zare i no zakte (Shekspir i Shou)" (At Dawn and Dusk: Shakespeare and Shaw). *Ural* 4 (1964): 159–63. [Russian]

Larson, Gale K. *Bernard Shaw's Caesar and Cleopatra as History* (University of Nebraska, 1968). *DAI* 29 (June 1969), 4495-A.

———. " 'Caesar and Cleopatra': The Making of a History Play." *Shaw Review* 14 (May 1971): 73–89.

Leary, Daniel J. "Shaw Versus Shakespeare: The Refinishing of *Cymbeline*." *Educational Theatre Journal* 30 (March 1978): 5–25.

Lecky, Eleazar. "Lecky on Shaw on Shakespeare." *California Shavian* 3 (July/August 1962): n.p.

Leech, Clifford. "Shaw and Shakespeare." In *Shaw: Seven Critical Essays*, ed. Norman Rosenblood. Toronto: University of Toronto Press, 1971; pp. 84–105.

Lutz, Jerry Wayne. *Pitchman's Melody: Shaw about "Shakespeare."* Lewisburg, Pa.: Bucknell University Press, 1974.

Mason, Michael. "Mr. Shaw, Shakespeare, and the Secondary Schoolboy." *Nineteenth Century* (London) 103 (1928): 525–36.

Matoba, Junko. "Shaw Versus Shakespeare." *Seishin Joshidaigaku Ronso* (Tokyo) 41 (December 1972): 1–14.

McInerney, John M. " 'Shakespearean' Word-Music as a Dramatic Resource in Shaw." *Shaw Review* 14 (May 1971): 90–94.

Pedersen, Lise. "Shakespeare's *The Taming of the Shrew* vs. Shaw's *Pygmalion*: Male Chauvinism vs. Women's Lib." *Shaw Review* 17 (January 1974): 32–39.

———. *Shavian Shakespeare: Shaw's Use and Transformation of Shakespearean Materials in His Dramas* (Louisiana State University, 1971). *DAI* 32 (May 1972), 6998-A.

Price, Joseph G. "The Mirror to Nature: Shaw's 'Troilus and Cressida' Lecture." *Shaw Review* 14 (May 1971): 68–72.

Rodenbeck, John. "A Shaw/Shakespeare Checklist." *Shaw Review* 14 (May 1971): 95–99.

Silverman, Albert H. "Bernard Shaw's Shakespeare Criticism." *PMLA* 72 (September 1957): 722–36.

Smith, J. Percy. "Superman Versus Man: Bernard Shaw on Shakespeare." *Yale Review* 42 (1952): 67–82.

Speaight, Robert. *Shakespeare on the Stage*. Boston: Little, Brown, 1973.

Stamm, Rudolf. "Shaw und Shakespeare." *Shakespeare Jahrbuch* 94 (1958): 9–28. [German]

Stone-Blackburn, Susan. "Shaw on Cutting Shakespeare." *Shaw Review* 22 (January 1979): 46–49.

Weintraub, Stanley. *"Heartbreak House:* Shaw's *Lear." Modern Drama* 15 (December 1972): 255–65.

———. "Shaw's *Lear." Ariel: A Review of International English Literature* 1 (1970): 59–68.

West, E. J. "G.B.S. on Shakespearean Production." *Studies in Philology* 45 (1948): 216–35.

———. "Shaw, Shakespeare, and *Cymbeline." Theatre Annual* 8 (1950): 7–24.

White, David Allen. *"Amaz'd with Matter"*: *A Study of Shakespeare's Innovative Techniques in Cymbeline via Mozart, Dickens and Shaw* (Indiana University, 1981). *DAI* 42 (January 1982), 3170-A.

Wilson, Donal Stuart. *Shaw on the Production of Shakespeare* (UCLA, 1972). *DAI* 33 (October 1972), 1880-A.

Wilson, Edwin. Introduction and Headnotes to *Shaw on Shakespeare: An Anthology of Bernard Shaw's Writings on the Plays and Production of Shakespeare*. New York: E. P. Dutton, 1961.

———. "Shaw's Shakespearean Criticism" (Yale University, 1958). Unpublished dissertation.

Also: 2, 7, 12, 13, 16, 17, 18, 20, 21, 28, 32, 33, 45, 72, 89.

SHELLEY, PERCY BYSSHE (1792–1822)

Johnson, Betty Freeman. "Shelley's *Cenci* and *Mrs Warren's Profession." Shaw Review* 15 (January 1972): 26–34.

SHEPARD, SAM (1943–): 78.

SHERIDAN, RICHARD BRINSLEY (1751–1816)

Beers, Henry A. "The English Drama of To-Day." *North American Review* 158 (May 1905): 746–57.

Street, G. S. "Sheridan and Mr. Shaw." *Blackwood's Magazine* 167 (June 1900): 832–36.

Also: 12, 16, 21.

SHERWOOD, ROBERT (1896–1955)

Lausch, Anne N. "Robert Sherwood's *Heartbreak House." Shaw Review* 6 (May 1963): 42–50.

SIMON, NEIL (1927–): 77.

SOPHOCLES (495–405 B.C.): 21.

STANISLAVSKY, KONSTANTIN (1863–1930): 90.

STERNHEIM, CARL (1878–1942)

Winkgens, Meinhard. "Shaw und Sternheim: Der Individualismus als Privatmythologie" (Shaw and Sternheim: Individuality as Private Mythology). *Arcadia* 12 (1977): 31–46. [German]

Also: 64.

STRINDBERG, AUGUST (1849–1912)

Meyer, Michael. *Strindberg*. London: Secker & Warburg, 1985.

Morgan, Margery M. "Strindberg and the English Theatre." *Modern Drama* 7 (September 1964): 161–73.

Wilson, Colin. "Shaw and Strindberg." *Shavian* 15 (June 1959): 22–24.

Also: 4, 38.
SUDERMANN, HERMANN (1857–1928): 34, 60.
SYNGE, JOHN MILLINGTON (1871–1909): 25, 60, 63, 81, 88.
TAYLOR, TOM (1817–1880): 82.
TENNYSON, ALFRED (1809–1892): 82.
TOLSTOY, LEO (1828–1910): 42.
TREBITSCH, SIEGFRIED (1869–1956)
Matlaw, Myron. *Jitta's Atonement: Shaw's Adaptation and the Translation of Trebitsch's Original.* Ann Arbor, Mich.: Monograph Publishing, 1979.
TURNER, W. J. (1889–1946)
Häusermann, H. W. "W. J. Turner and Bernard Shaw: A Disagreement." *English Miscellany* 10 (1959): 293–327.
WELLS, H. G. (1866–1946) (adapted for radio by Orson Welles)
Timko, Michael. *"Entente Cordiale:* The Dramatic Criticism of Shaw and Wells." *Modern Drama* 8 (May 1965): 39–46.
WHITBREAD, J. W. (1848–1916): 82.
WHITING, JOHN (1917–1963)
Robinson, Gabrielle Scott. "Beyond the Waste Land: An Interpretation of John Whiting's *Saint's Day.*" *Modern Drama* 14 (February 1972): 463–77.
WILDE, OSCAR (1854–1900)
Ellman, Richard. *Oscar Wilde.* New York: Knopf, 1988.
Hark, Ina Rae. *Bernard Shaw and Victorian Satiric Inversion* (UCLA, 1975). *DAI* 36 (January 1976), 4509-A.
Hyde, H. Montgomery. *Oscar Wilde.* New York: Farrar, Straus & Giroux, 1975.
Kimura, Masami. "Shaw, Wilde, Webbfusai—Rekishi Ishiki omegutte" (Shaw, Wilde and the Webbs—On Their Sense of History). *Kenkyunenpo* (Department of Economics, Kagawa University, Takamatsu) 18 (March 1979): 1–61. [Japanese]
Miserocchi, Manlio. "Attraverso il Centenario di G.B. Shaw Quello di O. Wilde" (The Centennial of O. Wilde through that of G. B. Shaw). *Nuova Antologia* 92 (1957): 377–86. [Italian]
Ohmann, Richard. "Studies in Prose Style: Arnold, Shaw, Wilde" (Harvard University, 1960). Dissertation. Published partly as *Shaw: The Style and the Man.* Middletown, Conn.: Wesleyan University Press, 1962.
Pearson, Hesketh. *The Life of Oscar Wilde.* London: Methuen; Toronto: S.J.R. Saunders, 1946. Alternate title: *Oscar Wilde: His Life and Wit.* New York and London: Harper, 1946.
Van Doren, Carl, and Mark van Doren. *American and British Literature since 1890.* New York and London: Century, 1925.
Also: 8, 11, 37, 39, 44, 47, 48, 67, 76.
WILLIAMS, TENNESSEE (1911–1983)
Weales, Gerald. "Tennessee Williams Borrows a Little Shaw." *Shaw Review* 8 (May 1965): 63–64.
Williams, Tennessee. " 'Candida': A College Essay." *Shaw Review* 20 (May 1977): 60–62.
WILLS, W. G. (1828–1891): 82.
WITKIEWICZ, STANISLAW IGNACY (1885–1939): 78.
WYCHERLEY, WILLIAM (1640/41–1715): 62.
YEATS, W. B. (1865–1939)
Cary, Elisabeth Luther. "Apostles of the New Drama." *Lamp* (New York) 27 (January 1904): 593–98.
Also: 39, 48, 65, 81.

REVIEWS AND CHECKLIST

Reviews

The New Woman Versus the Old Adam

J. Ellen Gainor. *Shaw's Daughters: Dramatic and Narrative Constructions of Gender.* Ann Arbor: University of Michigan Press, 1991. 296 pp. Illustrated. $32.50.

Shaw's reputation as a feminist is now more than a century old. However, it was not until some time after Shaw's death that full-scale studies of his relations to women appeared. They were launched with *A Shavian Guide to the Intelligent Woman* (1964), Barbara Bellow Watson's ground-breaking exploration of Shaw's views of women as depicted in the drama and selected prose works. The following decade added cultural and historical depth with Sonja Lorichs's *The Unwomanly Woman in Bernard Shaw's Drama and Her Social and Political Background* (1973). Then *Fabian Feminist* (1977), the frequently cited essay collection edited by Rodelle Weintraub, directly addressed the artistic, social, and political issues generated by Shaw's particular form of feminism. Much of the continuing importance of that collection lies in the wisdom of including a range of assessments and a variety of approaches. Soon after, Margot Peters's literary biography *Bernard Shaw and the Actresses* (1980) offered a richly textured view of Shaw's personal relationships with women, one that suggested a more complex and, at times, less admirable man than previously assumed.

Identifying herself as a member of "the current generation of feminist critics," J. Ellen Gainor asserts that "feminist criticism of Shaw has not progressed significantly over the past twenty years." By this she turns out to mean that Shaw's female critics do not subscribe to her critical formulas. Gainor—who admits to being "haunted" throughout her research by the question, "Is there really anything left to be said about Shaw?"—justifies her study of a male author not because of his importance as either dramatist or social thinker, but because of Shaw's "literary and social impact in part through [his] creation of women's speech." She declares her intention to "move beyond" what she calls the " 'representations of women' approach and engage with subtler textual issues of language and structure." Unfortunately, this worthwhile intention is never fulfilled.

At the outset, Gainor cites J. L. Wisenthal's judgment that Shaw is "an essentially Victorian writer" (*Shaw's Sense of History*, 1988). However, she ignores the main thrust of Wisenthal's study, which shows Shaw moving between "antithetical Victorian traditions" which he transforms into his own visionary alternative. This significant omission is a harbinger of things to come, for Gainor seeks only to show Shaw's "adherence to Victorian concepts throughout his career" in order to "question the view of him as remarkably progressive that some scholars propound." With the question settled before she begins, Gainor assumes the role of prosecuting attorney, determined to prove Shaw's "latent prejudice, regressive values, and even hostility" toward advancing the cause of women.

A number of Shaw's female contemporaries are represented to "demonstrate significant early twentieth-century feminist concern with Shaw's work" (elsewhere cited as "deprecating views of Shaw"). Anarchist Emma Goldman, for instance, had "nothing to say about Shaw as feminist or as concerned with women's roles or issues." Gainor admits that Goldman "praises Shaw," but "only for his socialist dramas, such as *Mrs Warren's Profession* and *Major Barbara*"—apparently an inadequate position since Goldman is thereby reduced to discussing "only their political, economic, and moral import." Rather remarkably, Constance Barnicoat, author of the 1906 article "Mr. Bernard Shaw's Counterfeit Presentment of Women," is transformed by Gainor from an offended proper lady into a feminist prototype (and rescued from Barbara Bellow Watson in the process). Never mind that Barnicoat insists on the term "lady" for herself and that she feels shamed by Shaw's "hard as nails" women. Gainor would have it that "Barnicoat looked to Shaw for an image of what women could be. . . . That his plays did not correspond to her sense of what types of characters would be fitting assets to the woman's movement gives early evidence of women questioning the views of Shaw."

In her eagerness to expose Shaw's thinking as derivative, Gainor disregards chronology. The initially plausible suggestion that "part of Shaw's thinking" about women "may have come from his close association" with Beatrice Webb cannot be supported by the single example Gainor supplies—Webb's movement from advocating celibacy for professional women in 1887 to her position quoted in an 1894 diary entry: "the vastly more important question of the breeding" of the next generation.

Gainor cites this as evidence of Webb's influence on Shaw, since it "coincides so clearly with much of Shaw's thinking about the eugenic need for women to return to their childbearing function." Gainor thus moves directly from supposition to quotation to assertion, a technique she favors. But she never considers the possibility that the reverse process might have occurred—that is, Beatrice Webb might have been influenced by Shaw. Yet the then Beatrice Potter did not meet Shaw until 1890—and he had been a eugenicist since at least 1882, the year the bulk of *Cashel Byron's Profession* was written. This was a full twelve years earlier than the date Gainor assigns to Webb's embrace of eugenics.

Viewing these earlier writings by women as important documents, Gainor suggests that their absence in recent studies raises "provocative questions about the differing agendas" of early and later female critics, the latter purportedly intent on presenting an idealized view of Shaw. However, much of this early material has already appeared and been assessed—especially, but not exclusively, in Watson, whom Gainor admittedly uses throughout as her "touchstone." That Gainor raises the specter of "agenda" reveals more about her than about those whose motives she questions.

Gainor discusses Shaw's assumptions about gender in the drama and selected prose works, basing her study on the theory that gender is "socially formulated" and that the meanings of terms like "masculine" and "feminine" vary according to time and place (as Shaw himself would agree). Certainly, this is a potentially rich lode to mine since issues revolving around gender identity are present in Shaw from first to last. Instead of the method she attributes to feminist critics of the 1960s who "sorted through texts by men to see which presented women in a positive light" and merely classified the women into categories of Bitch, Witch, Vamp, and Virgin/Goddess, Gainor classifies Shaw's women under the rubrics of the New Woman, the Androgyne, and Daughters in order to traverse the oeuvre pointing out Shaw's lapses from feminism.

Shaw's art has been linked from its inception with the image of the New Woman—that figure of independent spirit who refused to conform to male-determined rules of conduct, avoiding domestic roles like motherhood in the pursuit of professional self-realization. Gainor's strategy is to begin with the five novels of Shaw's apprenticeship. She contends that these conform to the tenets of male-authored New Woman novels identified by feminist critics "in which the New Woman, independent at the opening of the work, is reinscribed in a conventional emotional or domestic role by its conclusion," indicating "the anxiety surrounding the independence and strength of these female figures, and their potential threat to traditionally patriarchal society." Therefore, in the space of two clauses devoted to each novel, we learn that Shaw "compromises" and "punish[es]" the progressive women he portrays. For example, Gainor asserts that in *Immaturity*, Harriet Russell, despite "financial success," sells her dressmaking shop "to marry and have children"; that in *The Irrational Knot*, the actress Susanna Conolly, who gives birth to an illegitimate child, "dies alone and destitute in New York City (surely the punishment for her unconventional lifestyle)"; that in *Love Among the Artists*, Letitia Cairns "holds a college degree and supports the suffrage movement," yet she is a "spinster" who "longs hopelessly for love affairs and gossip (her fate for having chosen celibacy earlier)"; that in *Cashel Byron's Profession*, Lydia Carew "abandons plans as a writer to marry Cashel and raise a family, while he enjoys no fewer than four additional professions in which he is highly successful"; and that in *An Unsocial Socialist*, the outspoken Agatha Wylie "subjects herself to . . . misogyny" by marrying the eponymous Sidney Trefusis. Gainor concludes, "Independent women either ultimately conform to the Victorian patriarchal view of home as the proper feminine sphere, or suffer greatly for straying from its prescribed code of feminine behavior."

Gainor's handling of the novels ignores a mountain of contravening evidence, hardly showing "the close engagement with the text" she previously invoked. Since this approach is symptomatic of her critical method throughout her book, a review of what actually occurs in the novels is warranted. More accurately than Gainor, we recall that in the final pages of *Immaturity* Harriet Russell advises Shaw's hero, Robert Smith, that marriage is the only way "to have a decent home," but that "it is not fit for some people; and some people are not fit for it." Similarly, the irrational knot of Shaw's second novel specifically refers to the institution of marriage; Susanna Conolly dies from the ravages of alcohol, not poverty (a genderless attribution, given Shaw's association of drink with his father); moreover, Susanna was not alone, but was comforted in her last days by Marian Conolly, her sister-in-law, and mourned on her deathbed by her brother. Far from punishment for Susanna, her death reinforces the pregnant Marian's sense of independence: "That unfortunate woman did me good." Marian has had a romance, has left her husband, and refuses to return even after he tells her that "you may have ten love romances every year with other men, if you like. Be anything rather than a ladylike slave and liar." (Years later Shaw would suggest the novel was "an early attempt on the part of the Life Force to write A Doll's House in English.")

Additionally, in *Love Among the Artists*, Letitia (a mere cameo character) was no intellectual, nor did she long hopelessly for love affairs. Having "read much for the purpose of remembering it at examinations," she "tir[ed] of books, lectures, and university examinations of women" and then "addicted herself with some zest to advising and gossiping on the subject of [her friends'] love affairs." Her fate results from not daring to be as unconventional as the novel's Madge Brailsford, the unmarried actress who stands unpunished "on her own honor according to her own instinct," while Aurélie Szczympliça, the Polish concert pianist who insists she never was of a nature to fall in love, agrees to marry, only to leave husband and child to tour in America at novel's end, her spouse waiting hopefully and nonjudgmentally for her return. Just as both women place their professional identities first, Owen Jack, Shaw's unmarried hero, insists that marriage "kills the heart," making a trio of the novel's major characters singing the same tune. As to Cashel's "four additional [and] highly successful" professions, Gainor misses Shaw's satiric edge in the final pages of the novel, where we learn that Cashel "farmed, and lost six thousand pounds by it; tried gardening with better success; began to meddle in commercial enterprise," finally becoming an independent politician thanks to "the extent of his wife's information." Moreover, Gainor never mentions that Cashel, boxing champion supreme, gave up *his* career to marry. Indeed, Cashel is Shaw's first vital genius, and the marriage to Lydia, a eugenicist, symbolizes the joining of superior intellect (hers) and godlike physique (his)—an *overturning* of cultural stereotypes. Finally, in *An Unsocial Socialist,* the strong-minded Agatha's realistic attitude suggests that Sidney, political firebrand and would-be world savior, has met his match in this practical woman who will bring him down to earth, and once again Shavian barbs are aimed at Victorian hypocrisy surrounding romance and marriage.

Having misrepresented all five novels, Gainor then proclaims a pattern in which Shaw is said to emphasize the "affectional lives" of women over their professional identities. Allegedly this pattern—which also "reveals the priority he places on the institution of marriage"—is carried over into the drama. Acknowledging that Shaw saw "problems" with marriage, Gainor nevertheless insists that he preferred it to alternate life-styles. In support, she quotes a brief passage from the Preface to *Getting Married,* her commentary consisting entirely of italicizing certain words or phrases. Although they are crucial to her argument, she does not probe Shaw's extensive views on marriage any further. Yet as early as 1891, in two chapters from *The Quintessence of Ibsenism*—"Ideals and Idealists" and "The Unwomanly Woman"—Shaw offered a searching critique of both marriage and gender stereotypes in late-Victorian England. There the intellectual position of the paradigmatic Shavian "realist" is defined specifically in opposition to the "British family arrangement" of monogamous marriage, Shaw's main example of a reactionary ideal.

For Gainor, Shaw paralleled many other male authors of the period by using the figure of the New Woman through the *Plays Pleasant and Un-*

pleasant "for other dramatic ends, not presented in her right or focused on as the product of a burgeoning struggle over the status of women in society"—in short, Shaw's failing was to be a dramatic artist. This stricture reverses her criticism throughout the book of Shaw's supposed didacticism. Not even the portrait of the role-breaking Vivie Warren in *Mrs Warren's Profession* can measure up to Gainor's standard since Vivie is marked by a "lack of overt feminist concern for her fellow women." Viewing Sylvia Craven in *The Philanderer* solely as a "caricature" of the New Woman, Gainor misses Shaw's real target—ideological excess, which is satirized in Dr. Percy Paramore's scientism as well. By dubiously proclaiming Proserpine in *Candida* to be a New Woman, Gainor can then decry Shaw's treatment as another caricature he "replicates" from the pages of *Punch*. In the "mythological significance" of her name, Gainor sees Shaw "twist[ing] rape and the forced imprisonment of a woman into voluntary self-victimization." Gainor has no interest in Candida herself, a character whose conflict she calls "personal" rather than "universal"; for Shaw in *Candida* "safeguards the larger, extant patriarchal order," since the "struggle over women's independence never extends beyond the confines of the home." Are we then to believe that elucidating the source of a secondary character's name can replace the need to explain the dynamics of how Shaw's play actually *works*—culminating in the heroine's pointed exposure of the underlying egotism of male assumptions surrounding female roles and marriage?

What Watson called Shaw's belief "in the androgynous nature of personality" receives somewhat different treatment from Gainor, who sees Shaw as influenced by sex theorists like Richard von Krafft-Ebing and Havelock Ellis. Thus, "Shaw finds his own revolutionary example of 'the third sex' in the artist Marie Bashkirtseff," who "stands for both the unwomanliness associated with sexual inversion and the masculinity of a 'real' man. She positively embodies a male essence at the same time her masculine identification makes her a threatening image of female inversion." From this, Gainor argues that "Shaw's assumption of a male center, as he feels Marie has, for his strong women . . . conform[s] to his theory of essentially unisexual humanity." However, Gainor misses that Shaw's point in *The Quintessence of Ibsenism* is exactly the opposite: he refutes the notion of a "third sex" as an illusion of conventional idealists. Here in its entirety is the relevant passage, quoted by Gainor without the last two sentences:

> Hence arises the idealist illusion that a vocation for domestic management and the care of children is natural to women, and that women who lack them are not women at all, but members of the third, or Bashkirtseff, sex. Even if this were true, it is obvious that

if the Bashkirtseffs are to be allowed to live, they have a right to suitable institutions just as much as men and women. But it is not true. The domestic career is no more natural to all women than the military career is natural to all men. . . .

The omitted lines do more than *reinforce* Shaw's position on the third sex (Gainor has misread even what she includes), for he also directly addresses the question of women's social roles. Significantly, the final clause, clearly progressive for 1891, turns up out of context later in Gainor's book as support *for* Shaw's Victorianism as she writes— reversing Shaw's emphasis—that "male professional capacities are always contrasted to female biological function."

Of Shaw's most famous women in male garb, Gainor sees Joan as "a character of both androgynous personality and masculine action," a "Shavian superwoman," Gainor consistently emphasizing the woman to the exclusion of the saint. Lina Szczepanowska, the strong, courageous aviator in *Misalliance,* "appear[s] an ideal woman," on the basis of the "stirring speech" she makes in the final moments of the play. Nevertheless, there is a "pairing off" with the weak, fearful Bentley Summerhays. The "need for Lina . . . to mate with anyone," if she is "already an androgynous whole," is "puzzling" and "strange" to Gainor. Only by overstating this final tenuous "alliance" can Gainor fault Shaw for "another misalliance." Moreover, Gainor's passing mention of Lina's triumphant affirmation of her independent womanhood, often hailed as one of the finest bravura pieces in Shaw, omits any reference to her scathing denunciation of bourgeois marriage. This elliptical tendency is characteristic of a critical method that appears to treat—while actually dismissing—any material damaging to the thesis that Shaw was "still a Victorian in the mid-twentieth century." For Gainor, both Joan and Lina represent "the mixed natures . . . described by the sexual theorists"; their masculine dress "coincides with the essential gender orientation they feel."

In Shaw's theatrical use of androgynous figures, Gainor sees "female identity privileged through male costume." Additionally, since the one-act *Press Cuttings* contains the only example of a man in drag, Shaw is said to practice a "biased androgyny." Even in *Press Cuttings,* Shaw is faulted because Gainor finds that "serious issues" are discussed only after female attire is discarded. This objection obscures a theatrical reality—the man in petticoats always elicited a howl of laughter from audiences, assuring mockery of any attempt at thoughtful discussion. In contrast, the woman in breeches was established within a venerable stage tradition that included Shakespeare as well as popular theater—and her costume was designed to enhance mystery and allure.

Further clouding her argument, Gainor blurs the line between two separate issues—cross-dressing and homosexuality. She criticizes Shaw because *Press Cuttings* contains "no sexuality associated with the temporary male transvestism," nor any "discussion of its wearer's gender identity." This criticism does not take into account another factor—one strikingly absent from a study seeking to "further [the] contextualization" of Shaw. Specifically, the licensing laws prohibited "indecency" on stage. Even without laughter-prone audiences, after Oscar Wilde's sensational 1895 trial, having men in skirts seriously probe their "personal goals" or gender identity on stage, as Gainor wants, would have been impossible. The taboo against homosexuality was so tenacious that it lasted until the 1968 revocation of stage censorship, preventing the appearance on the English stage of plays by such important dramatists as Arthur Miller, Lillian Hellman, and Jean-Paul Sartre. Shaw himself had run afoul of the Lord Chamberlain for violating lesser taboos. Out of eight thousand plays submitted for licensing between 1895 and 1909, only thirty were completely banned. Of that total, 10 percent were by Shaw—a surprising accomplishment for a man Gainor accuses of adhering to "Victorian concepts." The banned plays were *Mrs Warren's Profession* (deemed "immoral and otherwise improper for the stage"), *The Shewing-up of Blanco Posnet* (considered blasphemous), and *Press Cuttings* (labeled an "offensive" representation of a living person). After the banning of *Blanco Posnet,* Shaw wrote a statement that the parliamentary committee on censorship tried to suppress. In it he identified himself as "a specialist in immoral and heretical plays. My reputation has been gained by my persistent struggle to force the public to reconsider its morals. In particular, I regard much current morality as to economic and sexual relations as disastrously wrong." Clearly, Shaw was not an advocate of lingering Victorianism, but its critic.

Gainor finds a lesbian subtext in several of the plays—in *Widowers' Houses* between Blanche and her maid, in *Heartbreak House* between Hesione and Ellie, and especially in *Pygmalion* in the bath scene between Eliza and Mrs. Pearce, which escalates into "lesbian 'rape.' " Mrs. Pearce, "a parallel character to Higgins's mother, . . . a domineering, scolding, condescending woman," is also "a female surrogate for the male rapist," that is, for Higgins. This interpretation, corresponding to what no audience in the world has ever felt, proves difficult to support within the confines of the play. Therefore, Gainor turns to the action and sound track from the film version, where Shaw allegedly "implicates" himself. As Gainor describes the film, Mrs. Pearce, "almost like the witch" with her "broomstick," mixes bath salts in the tub, her "bubbling cauldron." Eliza is seen in the tub "screaming and struggling." Then the camera "cuts to a shot of Higgins and Pickering. . . . Higgins shrugs and turns back to his study, while Pickering remains, smirking." The camera "cuts back to Eliza, still screaming. . . . Her hand grasps hold of a handle and suddenly the shower head explodes with a cascade of shooting water." According to Gainor, this "ejaculatory conclusion to the scene clearly literalizes the subtextually heterosexual paradigm controlling the attack on Eliza." But unmentioned by Gainor is Eliza's reaction after her "rape": "I tell you, it's easy to clean up here. . . . Woolly towels. . . . Soft brushes . . . soap smelling like primroses. Now I know why ladies is so clean. Washing's a treat for them." This response hardly suggests the victim of sexual assault, but rather reiterates the reason for Eliza's earlier (comic) apprehensiveness—she has never had a bath in her life! Yet via the above interpretation of the bath scene, Gainor reaches her final destination. She can claim the play "exposes and exploits the subgenre" of "father/daughter, teacher/pupil/lover," and end her study with her view of Shaw untainted by contact with his actual writings.

Certainly, the belief of contemporary feminist critics in the primacy of culture in forming and shaping views of self and world, and their untiring efforts to reconstruct historical periods so as to give voice to the silent and oppressed woman, stand out as major contributions to late twentieth-century social and political thought. Indeed, such a sense of mission can itself be termed Shavian. Therefore, Gainor's goal of contextualizing Shaw must be seen as admirable, whatever reservations one may have about its implementation. Moreover, Gainor has gathered selections from the writings of important feminists like Hélène Cixous (on male-authored myths), Sandra Gilbert (on the male author's interest in costume), Susan Gubar (on female cross-dressers), Carolyn Heilbrun (on Shaw's Joan), and Catherine R. Stimpson (on androgyne)—quoted comments that are of substantial interest in themselves. Yet despite the impressive array of scholars and the intriguing documents, Gainor never comes near the "deeper analysis and more thorough investigation" she claims for herself on the crucial issue of Shaw's attitudes toward women.

Neither praise nor blame is of much use in understanding Shaw's feminism. Where Shaw is a mouthpiece for patriarchy, either overtly or covertly, consciously or unconsciously, he should be exposed. But where Shaw is a progressive champion of women's rights, he should be applauded. Moreover, the tangled strands of patriarchy and progressivism need to be traced to their roots. Eric Bentley is surely on the mark in suggesting that a large part of the vitality of Shavian drama stems from Shaw's self-identification with exemplars of rebellious young womanhood. Gainor's slippery use of selective evidence in the attempt to turn this truth into its opposite results in a travesty of Shaw. The polarized views that Gainor attacks and which she herself embodies issue from

unresolved tensions in Shaw's intellectual and emotional responses to
women, the clash of the old drama with the new, the opposition of the
visionary's hope with the satirist's indignation—most of all, perhaps,
from his own peculiar nature, part saint, part Mephistopheles. To do less
than plumb the mysteries of that nature is ultimately a disservice both to
feminism and to Shaw.

Sally Peters

The Reviewer in Spite of Himself

Bernard Shaw's Book Reviews Originally Published in the Pall Mall Gazette
from 1885 to 1888, edited with an introduction by Brian Tyson. University
Park: Penn State University Press, 1991. 511 pp. $65.00.

In his *Lectures on Shakespeare and Milton* (1811–12), Coleridge confidently
proclaims that "Reviewers are usually people who would have been poets, historians, biographers, etc., if they could; they have tried their
talents at one or the other, and have failed; therefore they turn critics."
Shelley's *Fragments of Adonais* (1821) presents the same view more em-
phatically: "Reviewers, with some rare exceptions, are a most stupid and
malignant race. As a bankrupt thief turns thief-taker in despair, so an
unsuccessful author turns critic." Disraeli's *Lothair* (1870) follows suit:
"You know who the critics are? The men who have failed in literature
and art." Shaw might have agreed with Mark Twain that criticism of
books was "the most degraded of all trades," but he would have rejected
the notion that he had failed in literature and had therefore turned his
hand to criticism. During his stint of reviewing books for the *Pall Mall
Gazette,* three of his own novels were serialized in other periodicals, and
Cashel Byron's Profession and *An Unsocial Socialist* were published as books.
When he realized that the novel was not his genre, his response was not
to forgo literature "in despair" but to turn to another genre, which he
made his own.

Readers of Shaw's 111 *Pall Mall Gazette* book reviews, collected and
excellently annotated by Brian Tyson, will find the reviews far from
"malignant" even in their treatment of absolutely dreadful novels and
verse, while the young reviewer's deft handling of a wide variety of
subjects shows him as being far from "stupid." As Professor Tyson notes
in his Introduction, "About half of Shaw's book reviews are of nonfiction: volumes of biography, musical history, spiritualism, and ghost sto-

ries (the Society for Psychic Research had made its popular appearance in 1882), plus sundry volumes on ethics, economics, folklore, physiognomy, travel, and Socialism." Many of the books Shaw had to read were uninspiring, but he enlivened his reviews with a combination of humor, irony, and sardonicism that makes his criticism readable long after the works under his scrutiny have been forgotten. Frequently Shaw uses a review as an occasion for advancing his own opinions on music, economics, and the like, as when he objects to the practice of publishing novels by women under male pseudonyms, or when he refuses to support Walter Besant's scheme to enrich authors through international copyrights on the grounds that this would simply enable an author "to do unto others that which he complains of others doing to him." He starts one review, "An autobiography is usually begun with interest by writer and reader alike, and seldom finished by either." The first sentence of his review of Fayr Madoc's novel *Thereby* is, " 'Thereby' hangs a tale."

In many reviews previously accessible only from back numbers of the *PMG*, Shaw is genial in his treatment of popular works despite their failings. He does not apply the standard of literary immortality to books destined for Mudie's but recognizes that an ephemeral work has a value of its own. He says of Mrs. Henry Wood's fiction that "If her novels will not survive her long it is not because they are worthless, but because each generation can manufacture such work for itself with the advantage of the newest fashions. Shakspere himself would have been discarded long ago could we have produced an equally clever man every half-century or so." Of Blanche Roosevelt's novel he wrote, "It is difficult to describe 'The Copper Queen.' To praise it would be treason to Literature; to condemn it would belie the sensation of reading it." After enumerating several instances of blundering and bungling by Fitzgerald Molloy, Shaw's summation is ironically favorable: "It only remains to draw the unexpected conclusion that a man may be a tolerable novelist without knowing how to write. Shocking as some of the above examples of Mr. Molloy's workmanship may be to experts, the people whom he calls 'the bran-brained crowd' will find 'A Modern Magician' quite readable." In another review he remarks that "It would be ungrateful to Mr. Grant Allen to enjoy so good a story as 'The Devil's Die' and then say nothing for it except that its philosophy is hopelessly inadequate," and he accepts the validity of an earlier complaint by Allen that "competitive bookmaking leads to the survival of the fastest rather than of the fittest." Despite the opportunities for biting sarcasm, Shaw preferred to take the more charitable view.

This does not mean that Shaw compromised his standards. He frequently ridiculed machine-made plots and various departures from realism. On facetiously humane grounds, he deplored such devices as staging a timely train wreck simply to eliminate an undesirable character: "Why should a number of innocent passengers be maimed, slain, or delayed in their travels merely to kill a man who might have been removed without any such sacrifice of life or rolling-stock? Could he not have been run over, or struck by lightning, or rent by an unmuzzled dog?" In his review of Hall Caine's *Son of Hagar* (part of which was published in the first volume of Michael Holroyd's *Bernard Shaw*), Shaw enumerates sixteen requirements for realistic and readable fiction, anticipating Mark Twain's "Fenimore Cooper's Literary Offenses" by almost a decade (Shaw's sixth rule, for example, demands that characters "shall bear their disappointments in love with reasonable fortitude, and find something else to talk and think about after the lapse of a week"). When W. E. Norris expresses "heresies" through his narrator, Shaw objects to allowing an author to hide behind one of his characters, arguing "the supreme importance of having some responsible person to hang in case of national disaster traceable to the teaching of the volume."

Some of Shaw's reviewing techniques reveal a budding dramatist. On four occasions Shaw adopts a persona for his review. The piece on "Mr. Proctor's *Chance and Luck*" is ostensibly by "An Inveterate Gambler," and "A Firm Believer" is the alleged reviewer of two works regarding spiritualism. Shaw frequently criticizes dialogue in novels as being unrealistic, and on some occasions he inserts mock dialogue into his review. In his brief dismissal of Julian Hawthorne's *David Poindextre's Disappearance* on 26 July 1888, Shaw resorts to a dramatic approach:

> the unfortunate reviewer is tempted to turn to the publishers who have submitted David for rational criticism, and address them, with laboured politeness, in these terms: "Pray, gentlemen, what—as between man and man, and bearing in mind that I have no right to waste the public time and attention—do you expect me to say about these inventions?" To which it is conceivable that Messrs. Chatto and Windus might reply: "Sir, so clever a person as you cannot be at a loss for an entertaining remark, were it but that, unpretentious as our author's tales are, it is not every one could have written them." Which the reviewer hastily admits, and passes on.

Without pause, he turns to the fifth work reviewed in "A Batch of Books."

Professor Tyson comments in his Introduction that "while it is true to say that Shaw made short work of these romances, it might be truer to say that they made short work of him." On 14 September 1888, Shaw wrote a letter to *PMG* subeditor C. Kinloch-Cooke to complain about "the slow murder of the cursed parcels of rubbish with which you blast my prime" and to ask for more readable fare. The subeditor's response was to print an extract from the letter in the *PMG* on 17 September, and Shaw continued as he had until his final *PMG* book review appeared on 26 December 1888. What seems to have done in Shaw was not the reviewing itself as much as the time that it took from his other pursuits. He was speaking frequently for the Fabian Society, he began a sixth novel (unfinished) on 14 May 1887, and he was devoting more time to art and music criticism. As Professor Tyson observes, "of the more than four hundred Shavian articles published between 1885 and 1888, 65 percent were submitted to journals other than the *Pall Mall Gazette!*" Shaw could write about art after a brief visit to a gallery or about music after attending an afternoon or evening concert, but he had to spend two or three days wading through triple-deckers and lengthy nonfiction works before he could write his review. The most tedious and time-consuming of his activities was book reviewing, and it was the logical activity for him to jettison.

More than a century after their initial publication, the reviews are less important for their own sake than for what they can tell us about Shaw the dramatist. Professor Tyson's thorough annotations point to many connections between the reviews and the later plays. Shaw's review of a book on physiognomy suggests much about his approach to stage directions. The review of "Memoirs of an Old-Fashioned Physician" includes a sentence readily suggestive of sources for statements by Sir Patrick Cullen in *The Doctor's Dilemma*: "Even when modern scientists rediscovered old discoveries of his, and blew the trumpet over them a little, he was not stung with jealousy or provoked to self-assertion, although he did not deny himself the pleasure of referring the discoverers, with a quiet chuckle, to some forgotten paper of his in which he had anticipated them." In 1886, Shaw reviewed Thomas Tyler's facsimile edition *Shakespeare's Sonnets*, which claimed that one Mary Fitton was the "dark lady." Professor Tyson comments,

> Shaw abandoned Tyler's theory when a portrait of Mary Fitton came to light that indicated that she was not a dark lady but a fair one. Nevertheless, when he came to write *The Dark Lady of the Sonnets* in 1910 to raise funds for establishing a National Theatre as a memorial to Shakespeare, Shaw resurrected Tyler's notion, mainly because it presented the possibility of a "scene of jealousy between Queen Elizabeth and the Dark Lady at the expense of the unfortunate Bard."

In a review of Louis Engel's *From Mozart to Mario*, Shaw quotes the phrase "worse than two fathers," and Professor Tyson finds this "the source of one of [Shaw's] witticisms" in *Pygmalion*: "HIGGINS: If I decide to teach you, I'll be worse than two fathers to you." Similar indications of sources abound in the reviews.

Professor Tyson's annotations are remarkably thorough and illuminating, and they reflect an impressive amount of hard work. The annotations include the complete textual history of each review, background information on the authors of the works being reviewed (including personal associations, if any, with the reviewer), and a wealth of detail about various allusions that would otherwise be unintelligible, as when Shaw's obscure allusion to "Sir Boyle Roche's bird" results in an annotation explaining that this Irish politician had once actually stated, "Mr. Speaker, how could I be in two places at once unless I were a bird?" When Shaw uses "takes the cake" within quotation marks, the annotation indicates that this was the first instance of the phrase in print according to the *OED*. When G.B.S. misquotes a line from Tennyson or mangles the spelling of a name or title, an annotation provides the correct version. When information is virtually impossible to trace, an annotation indicates that as well (Shaw's reference to "a celebrated line about a certain place being full of such Cliffords" is hopelessly obscure, but an annotation informs us that the line does *not* refer to the Cliffords of the *Henry VI* cycle).

One change in approach would have improved this excellent edition. It would have been helpful to indicate which of the 111 reviews are appearing for the first time since their original publication in *PMG*. According to those sources available on my shelves, including Dan H. Laurence's *Bibliography*, twenty-nine of these reviews have appeared in book form and therefore are already familiar: one in *Shaw on Vivisection*, ed. G. H. Bowker (1949), three in Shaw's *How to Become a Musical Critic*, ed. Dan H. Laurence (1961), two in *The Matter with Ireland*, ed. Dan H. Laurence and David H. Greene (1962), seven in *Bernard Shaw's Nondramatic Literary Criticism*, ed. Stanley Weintraub (1972), eleven in *Shaw's Music*, ed. Dan H. Laurence (1981), one in *Shaw on Dickens*, ed. Dan H. Laurence and Martin Quinn (1985), one in *SHAW* 7, ed. Alfred Turco, Jr. (1987), one in *SHAW* 8, ed. Stanley Weintraub (1988), and two in *SHAW* 10, ed. Stanley Weintraub and Fred D. Crawford (1990). Such information was necessary simply to enable me to confine my remarks and quotations to the reviews that had not appeared outside the backfiles of the *PMG,* but perhaps the main reason for including this minor cavil is an echo of Shaw's desire in one review to avoid being "monotonously eulogistic."

                                                         Fred D. Crawford

Old Age Shavian Style

Michael Holroyd. *Bernard Shaw.* Vol. 3, *1918–1950: The Lure of Fantasy.*
New York: Random House, 1991. 544 pp. + ix. Illustrated. $30.00.

Mr. Shaw is so vast a subject that none will envy the ultimate biographer.

—*The Times,* 26 July 1946

It is an axiom that Shaw would use in arguing his place in the evolution of mind that we stand on the shoulders of our predecessors. The common or garden word for this is "tradition," but Shaw preferred "apostolic succession," at least when placing himself in the line that included such apostles of progress as Bunyan, Shelley, and Ibsen. Is there a similar succession of criticism—not apostolic so much as, shall we say, investigative? Is there an investigative succession of Shavian criticism? There surely is, and now that Michael Holroyd has completed his three-volume account of Shaw's lifetime with *The Lure of Fantasy,* this succession, and the role it has played in underpinning Holroyd's account of Shaw's life and work, is plain to see. It is an entertaining and harmless exercise to go through the biography playing "spot-the-source"; it is sometimes a teasing exercise as well because, as readers will know, Holroyd's policy has been to dispense with footnotes, references, sources—all the paraphernalia of scholarship—the better to render, in his words, "a less-expensive non-fiction story in line with Shavian principles of publishing." Consequently, not a single source has been placed, and at most occasional biographers, critics, and commentators will be named in the text and index when Holroyd quotes from them or acknowledges a point of view.

So one plays "spot-the-source," and, to resist the temptation to indulge in retrospective spotting, one sees that the volume under present review has a veritable queue of predecessors: Blanche Patch's *Thirty Years with G.B.S.,* Rodelle Weintraub's *Shaw Abroad* (*SHAW* 5), Stanley Weintraub's *Private Shaw and Public Shaw,* Vivian Elliot's *Dear Mr. Shaw,* to name four that come immediately to mind; also of course the even more submerged contribution of Dan H. Laurence's *Bernard Shaw: A Bibliography,* without which no Shavian researcher can afford to move an inch these days, and the same editor's third and fourth volumes of the Shaw letters, without which no researcher can begin to work. This is not to say that Holroyd has not gone beyond these sources; of course he has. But the contribution of these scholars is both a tribute to the work they have done and a reminder that no one, least of all the author of the authorized biography, can work in isolation.

Holroyd's use of this investigative succession is, then, not a negative

factor. Far from it. This is what scholarship is—the building up of knowledge from both primary and secondary sources, bit by bit over generations of research. But such use raises the question of proper and improper
practice. Scholarship has evolved an ethic around itself; and so far, simply
because Holroyd's policy has been not to cite chapter and verse for his
sources, the fear is that he has been inclined to flout this ethic. There was
consternation when the first volume appeared without references, resig-
nation when the second volume appeared, and now, with the third volume, acquiescence. Not acceptance, however. That will be accorded only
when the sources are made available for scrutiny and found to answer all
questions. Report has it that Holroyd is working on these, which will
constitute the promised volume of sources "for the specialist." It will contain more than ten thousand references, Holroyd says. It sounds impressive. To say that its appearance is awaited with keen-eyed anticipation is to
put it mildly. Scholarship exercises a jealous—sometimes too jealous—
guardianship over its domain.

Meanwhile there is *The Lure of Fantasy* to consider. Like its two predecessors, it reads remarkably well. In the previous volumes Holroyd
employed Shaw as chief assistant scribe, so to speak, using his subject's
wit and high-velocity prose to keep the narrative rattling along. There
is less of this here, partly no doubt because the Shaw of the later years
had less to say about himself than the Shaw of the earlier periods, but
also because it seems that Holroyd has gained in assurance: he has
taken more complete control of his subject and seems more ready than
before to capture it on his own terms. At all events, the "non-fiction
story" is told with great urbanity and geniality and an unerring sense of
appropriate tone. Coupled with this is the admirable ordering of what
in its raw state can only be described as an utterly disordered, not to say
chaotic, life—disordered in its prodigality, chaotic in the way Shaw jam-
packed a hundred and one different interests and activities into his
working day. Holroyd's answer to this has been to package segments of
the life in sequences of themes. On the whole this works although
chronology tends to suffer, and it is occasionally not altogether clear
whether one is in the 1920s or the 1930s or the 1940s; but the problem
is not nearly as acute as it was in the previous volumes. Perhaps because
this was recognized as a problem, Holroyd has added a year-by-year
chronology of Shaw's major undertakings to the index of this volume.
It is a help.

What, now, about the thesis implicit in the title? After the frankly
reductive portraits of Sonny in the search for love in volume 1 and of
G.B.S. in the pursuit of power in volume 2, the idea of the aging Shaw
being lured by fantasy in the present volume seems, on the face of it, to

promise a geriatric fading away into cloud-cuckoo-land. Nothing of the kind happens. Holroyd applies his thesis with so light a hand that it amounts in the end to little more than an occasionally informing theme, the gist of which is that Shaw, confronted by the realities of the 1914–1918 war and the aftermath but refusing to succumb to the Giant Despair, invested his hopes in futuristic scenarios—utopian fantasies of worlds beyond the spiritually and morally bankrupt present—the better to preach his gospel of Shavian salvation. This has a good deal to commend it. Not all, but nearly all, the plays from 1920 onward find their dramatic impetus in the exploration of present realities in future or otherworldly contexts. The questions that the trauma of those years brought starkly to the fore—the incorrigibility or otherwise of human beings, the nature of effective leadership, the all-too-palpable threat of extinction facing Western civilization and all of humankind—these questions are Shaw's, and his plays are variations on the theme of survival. Similarly, the major prose works—*The Intelligent Woman's Guide* and *Everybody's Political What's What?*—argue the same cause in terms that strenuously deny man's "natural depravity" and point instead to a future Shavian dispensation where most noble elements of the human psyche have assumed government of individuals and nations.

This theme also goes a long way to explain, if it does not exonerate, Shaw's misadventures among the despots of the 1920s and the 1930s. We are inclined to forget just how appalling conditions were in Britain in those years. Shaw's hope for good navigation, the Labour party, so far from saving the ship of state, helped steer it to shipwreck as efficiently as its rival for power, the Conservatives. The country was on the rocks, and not only Shaw turned away in frustration and disgust to cast hopeful eyes on the strongmen of Europe and Soviet Russia. He was wrong about them, and he was seen even then to be wrong in the excess of his praise of, particularly, Soviet communism, but this wrongness was clearly the product of reaction against the temporizing and extemporizing that passed for political and economic policy in Britain. Wishful thinking, the creation of a communist utopia where none existed, was the next, almost inevitable step. Shaw said this in a letter to *The Times* many years before:

> And by Socialism I mean . . . the complete acceptance of Equality as the condition of human association, and Communism as the condition of human industry. This conviction . . . has grown with my growth, and become strong enough to keep me rigidly to its point whilst the general Socialist movement has been swaying and wavering and wobbling and splitting in all directions before the transient gusts . . . of party politics.

Holroyd does not quote this, and there is no reason that he should, but it does anticipate by some thirty years the gradual turn of events that drove Shaw into the beguiling arms of the Bolsheviks.

There is a corollary to this, and it is implicit in the much-quoted passage from the Preface to *Immaturity* in which Shaw refers to "a deeper strangeness" within himself which made him all his life "a sojourner on this planet rather than a native of it"; where he knows that his "kingdom is not of this world." The point about these lines is that Shaw wrote them in 1921, immediately after the war, and published them in 1930, which is to say they testify to his profound sense of alienation from the ignominy that did service for the "real world" of the time and, more, his awareness of his isolation from this world. The paradox is striking: one of the most "involved" and famous men of the day was also the most lonely. There is something poignant—and epic—about the image that emerges, the more poignant and the more epic as Shaw aged and the world continued to ignore his counsels of perfection, hell-bent on proving its chronic imperfection.

Holroyd has seen this, and the fact that he has indicates a marked change of stance. He said this about his task at the beginning of *The Search for Love:* "The line [the biographer] tries to follow points towards empathy without veering off into sentimentality and maintains a detachment that stops short of incompatibility." The reaction among many Shavians to the first two volumes was that Holroyd had fallen short on empathy and allowed his detachment to veer toward displays of not incompatibility so much as disconsonance, as though the key he had selected was in the minor mode when the subject demanded a major. This is not the case here. There is no sentimentality, still less hagiography, but the empathy and detachment are underscored by understanding and appreciation—appreciation above all that the Shaw of these years was a major figure.

This brings us to the comment from *The Times* at the head of this review and quoted tongue-in-cheek by Holroyd. Shaw was, and remains, a "vast" subject, too vast to be dealt with exhaustively in a biography of a mere sixteen hundred pages. Holroyd has had to cut his subject down to manageable and apprehensible size, while recognizing (in this volume) that he had to do justice to at least three constituent parts of the multiple personality: the political Shaw, the playwriting Shaw, and the private Shaw. This is an oversimplification, but Holroyd does not make these three categories all-inclusive; he finds space, as he must, for a spiritual Shaw in, for example, his account of the writing of *The Adventures of the Black Girl* and Shaw's consequent estrangement from Dame Laurentia McLachlan; and he finds plenty of time, again as he must, to write about the playwriting Shaw, at age eighty, turning with most marvelous agility into a screenwriter and the extraordinary association that developed with that prince of cheeky opportunism, Gabriel Pascal. Equally, the "missionary Shaw" of the world tours of the 1930s is fairly fully reported, with the address to the American Academy of Political Science in New York a minor tour de force of descriptive rhetoric. But the main thrust of Shaw's public campaigns in these years was political, and Holroyd is quite correct to emphasize this.

The political Shaw, to the extent that it was the Shaw of public pronouncements in the press, was of course the most controversial of the three personalities. Hindsight makes clear what was apparent even at the time, that Shaw's lifelong penchant for overstating a case resulted in many dizzying flights from reality. Stalin did not preside over a communist utopia; Mussolini was not "the right sort of tyrant" for Italy or any other country; the "political sagacity and courage" with which Shaw credited Hitler were not borne out by Nazi policy. The cause of such violently antiliberal statements has already been suggested; even so, the intellectual stance Shaw adopted, and the unfeelingness which resulted, remain hard to swallow. This was the Shaw of newspaper headlines, and Holroyd records him in this vein; he also records him in a less publicized vein, showing him to be far less outrageously perverse than popular opinion allowed—to be, in fact, extraordinarily acute in his reading of the European situation and the probable course that events would take. He does not label Shaw a "prophet," but he allows his political prescience to emerge time and again. He seems to me to miss a trick in not emphasizing that Shaw praised the European dictators for getting the things done that mumbling, fumbling democracy seemed unable to get done; that nevertheless, in spite of his contempt for the way the democratic system was being made not to work, he supported it as the best system available. There is also some thinness of background knowledge, particularly in regard to Shaw's involvement with Irish and British politics, where Holroyd seems happy to skip the details and go for a broad account of the political infighting of the time.

The political Shaw of the two major prose works of the period—*The Intelligent Woman's Guide* and *Everybody's Political What's What?*—is dealt with very fairly. *The Intelligent Woman's Guide* earns a ten-page essay, a tribute in itself, more of a tribute in that Holroyd applies his highly effective brand of understated rhetoric to his appraisal, producing one of the highlights of his book. The Shaw that emerges is, for all the shakiness of his economic arguments, an heroic figure achieving greatness by the eloquence of his language—the poetry in the dogma, as Holroyd puts it. If it is a lesser, and much older, Shaw one sees in *Everybody's Political What's What?*, Holroyd still acknowledges the "prophet of change conjuring his powers of transcendental reasonableness and compelling us to remake society in the image he has divined." One would like to think that he doffs his cap to the master of "simple rhetoric" who at the age of eighty-nine could still make "passions stir and the embers glow." It is in these two books rather than in the newspaper controversies of the 1930s that Shaw's political testament resides. All credit to Holroyd for reminding one that this is so.

As for the other, and greater, testament, the plays, Holroyd probably pays more attention to them than academic critics have. *Saint Joan* is comparatively scamped, which is not surprising considering the amount of critical work that has been done on it, but most of the other plays, including such traditionally "neglected" ones as *The Simpleton of the Unexpected Isles* and "*In Good King Charles's Golden Days*" are discussed at some length and implicitly granted recognition as the works of a major dramatist who, even if his powers are not as incandescent as before, demands to be taken seriously. Holroyd contents himself by and large with providing plot summaries, which Shavians will think are too long, and then appraising the abstract issues and reviewing the plays in their biographical and theatrical contexts: Malvern is prominently featured, for example. Although he is not a drama critic and does not set himself up as one, he allows himself an occasional personal assessment, and these are generally favorable, particularly regarding the enduring theatrical and intellectual qualities of the plays. He regularly invokes contemporary theatrical-critical opinions which usually reveal the traditional response to Shaw's plays—some unfavorable, some favorable—but it is the favorable response (MacCarthy praising *Methuselah*, Tynan enthusing over *The Millionairess*, Agate dewy-eyed about "*In Good King Charles's Golden Days*") that is given the conclusive word. Holroyd has done his duty by the plays and perhaps reminded scholars that a good number of these texts deserve more detailed exploration than they have enjoyed in the past.

This said, one has also to report that there is very little about Shaw's plays in translation. Holroyd continues his account of the long association with Trebitsch, as he should, while Hamon is mentioned; but the story of the plays in translation into other languages, that is to say the story of Shaw's impact worldwide, is overlooked. The exigency of space may have dictated this, but one feels the omission. Shaw's plays on BBC radio (and, later, television), which became a constant of these years and an important component of the career, are also neglected in that Holroyd gives only a couple of paragraphs to BBC productions.

The Molly Tomkins affair was the highlight of Shaw's private life in the 1920s. Holroyd handles it well. He does not try to establish whether Shaw and Molly consummated their relationship or whether Shaw fathered the child she aborted. This is as it should be since the evidence is inconclusive and speculation would be idle. The other important relationships of these years, with T. E. Lawrence (to whom Shaw *did* write a tribute for a South African newspaper), the Webbs, Barry Jackson, Elgar, Blanche Patch, Lady Astor, and, most important, Charlotte, are woven into the life. Perhaps the most memorable and moving picture is of Charlotte in stricken old age, with Shaw in loving attendance; then dying and leaving Shaw bereft, weeping openly in the streets of London. As for two leeches who attached themselves to Shaw after Charlotte's death— Winsten and Loewenstein—Holroyd pins them down with nicely judged irony. There is no information about Shaw's earnings, which is a pity; it is not enough having to infer that he became affluent. The old man's last years and death are handled with great sensitivity. There is no fanfare after the death (readers will remember that a fanfare began the first volume) and no attempt to assign stature to Shaw in his time or since, but he tries to indicate that Shaw lives on in his recently released fourth volume, *The Last Laugh*. The monument, if one needs such a thing, is the biography; the tribute in Holroyd's text is considerable.

Leon H. Hugo

Bernard Shaw Research: Is It Only Just Begun?

Stanley Weintraub. *Bernard Shaw: A Guide to Research*. University Park: Penn State University Press, 1992. 154 pp. $35.00.

After forty years of distinguished contributions to Shavian studies, Stanley Weintraub is singularly well qualified to provide an update and summary of Shaw scholarship. He edited the *Shaw Review* and the *SHAW* for some thirty-five years, prepared bibliographical essays on Shaw studies for *Anglo-Irish Literature: A Review of Research* (1976) and *Recent Research on Anglo-Irish Writers* (1983)—upon which the present *Guide* is based—and has been the author or editor of some twenty books devoted to G.B.S. "Much remains to be done in Shaw studies," Weintraub announces in the transcription of the 1975 MLA session on the status of Shavian research, and while much has appeared in print since then, his statement still applies. *Bernard Shaw: A Guide to Research* is a bibliographical monograph on works by and about Bernard Shaw that picks out the significant published material on G.B.S. By rough count it names more than four hundred scholar/critics who have published to date some eight hundred works related to Shaw. The *Guide* will make it easier for Shaw scholars to contribute significantly to the field, for it not only points out what we have done but also indicates several directions for future research.

The *Guide's* twelve sections begin with "Provenance and Copyright," providing locations of the substantial collections of Shaw manuscripts, letters, and printed materials. There is also an explanation of the copyright calendar on Shaw works, noting that all manuscripts will be in the public domain by 31 December 2027. Section 2, "Bibliographies," notes the fundamental importance to Shaw studies of Dan H. Laurence's *Bernard Shaw: A Bibliography* (1983); the three-volume *G. B. Shaw: An Annotated Bibliography of Writings about Him* (to 1980), edited by J. P. Wearing, Elsie B. Adams, and Donald C. Haberman; and the *SHAW's* "Continuing Checklist of Shaviana."

Section 3, "Editions," describes the considerable achievement of those in charge of the Shaw corpus. I mention here only the most important and most recent undertakings. The plays (to date) and the five G.B.S. novels were published in the Ayot St. Lawrence (American edition) and Constable Standard (British edition) in the early 1930s, adding titles through *Sixteen Self Sketches* in 1949. *The Bodley Head Edition of Collected Plays with Their Prefaces* (1970–74), edited by Dan H. Laurence, provides the finally revised versions of each of the plays. Laurence also edited four volumes of *Collected Letters* (1965–88; which includes fewer than three thousand of the many thousands that exist) and was general editor of the twelve-volume *Early Play Manuscripts in Facsimile* (1980–81). E. Dean Bevan made a *Concordance* to the plays (in the Constable Edition) in 1971. Publication of Shaw's book reviews has begun with Brian Tyson's 1991 volume, which Tyson will complete in another; and a new *Complete Prefaces,* edited by Laurence and Daniel J. Leary, is scheduled for 1992. The section also notes studies by Donald P. Costello and Marjorie Dean of Shaw as a writer for the cinema and devotes a paragraph to Bernard Dukore's publication of the screenplay scripts of several of the plays.

Section 4, "Biographies and Autobiographies," mentions three biographies by Archibald Henderson (1911, 1932, 1956)—indispensable, but unreliable, ironically, because G.B.S. had so much to do with their writing. Most noteworthy among about forty others listed are by Frank Harris (1931), Hesketh Pearson (1942), William Irvine (1949), Audrey Williamson (1963), Stanley Weintraub (1963, 1969–70, 1971), B. C. Rosset (1964), *Bernard Shaw: The Diaries, 1885–1897,* edited by Weintraub (1986), and Michael Holroyd's four-volume *Bernard Shaw* (1988–92), with one volume of sources still to come. Other major material and interpretations are in A. M. Gibbs's *Shaw: Interviews and Recollections* (1990), Rodelle Weintraub's *Shaw Abroad* (*SHAW* 5, 1985), Norman and Jeanne MacKenzie's edition of *The Diary of Beatrice Webb* (1982–86), and Eric Salmon's edition of *Granville Barker and His Correspondents* (1986), these last two volumes publishing many letters from Webb and Barker to G.B.S.

Section 5 notices "Early Criticism" by H. L. Mencken (1905), Holbrook Jackson (1907), Desmond MacCarthy (1907), G. K. Chesterton (1909; 1935), Augustin Hamon (1913; 1916), and samples of much more in the Critical Heritage volume edited by T. F. Evans (1976). Section 6, "General Critical Evaluations," calls attention to a long list of important works, including ones by Julian B. Kaye (1958), Martin Meisel (1963), Arthur Nethercot (1954, 1966), Charles A. Carpenter (1969), J. L. Wisenthal (1974, 1988), Charles A. Berst (1973), Louis Crompton (1969), Bernard F. Dukore (1973), Leon H. Hugo (1971), Maurice Valency (1973), Elsie Adams (1971), Richard Whitman (1977), Alfred Turco (1976, 1987), Colin Wilson (1969), Warren Smith (1982), Samuel Yorks (1981), Arthur Ganz (1983), Nicholas Grene (1984), and John A. Bertolini (1991).

Section 7, "The Novels and Other Fiction," notes immediately that Shaw's criticism of his own fiction is best—in *The Novel Review* (February 1892). Other important accounts of Shaw's fiction are by Maurice Holmes (1928), Richard F. Dietrich (1959), E. Nageswara Rao (1959), Weintraub (1959), and Robert Hogan (1965). Section 8, "Early Musical, Dramatic, and Literary Journalism," tells us that Laurence's introductions to Shaw's *How to Become a Musical Critic* (1961) and *Shaw's Music* (1981) are the most thorough analyses of G.B.S. as a music reviewer. Very recent are two essays on Shaw's music criticism in *SHAW* 12 (1992) by Richard Corballis and Josephine Lee. Weintraub's edition of *Bernard Shaw on the London Art Scene* (1989) locates all Shaw's writing on art. There are also recent studies on G.B.S. and photography by Bill Jay and Margaret Moore (1987), Gerald Weales (1990), and Melinda Boyd Parsons (1989). Daniel C. Gerould (1963) and John Gassner (1964) provide some of the better analyses of G.B.S. on Ibsen. On Wagner some good accounts are by William Blissett (1957–58) and Arthur Ganz (1979).

Section 9, "Criticism of Individual Plays," with thirty-four subsections, includes entries for *Passion Play, Widower's Houses, Philanderer, Mrs Warren, Arms, Candida, Man of Destiny, Devil's Disciple, You Never Can Tell, Caesar, Brassbound, Superman, John Bull, Major Barbara, Doctor's Dilemma, Getting Married, Misalliance, Androcles, Blanco Posnet, Fanny's First Play,* "Tomfooleries" (including *Dark Lady, Bashville, Passion, Poison, Foundling, Press Cuttings, How He Lied, Overruled, Jitta,* and *Annajanska*), *Pygmalion, Heartbreak, Methuselah, Joan, Apple Cart, Too True, Village* and *Calais, Rocks, Simpleton, Millionairess,* "Shakespearean Plays" (including *Cymbeline, Dark Lady* [again], and *Shakes v. Shav*), *Geneva, King Charles, Bouyant Billions,* and the "Last Plays." The eight top page-getters are *Saint Joan* (6), *Heartbreak House* (5), *Major Barbara* (3½), *Pygmalion* (3), *Man and Superman* (2¾), *Back to Methuselah* (2¾), *Doctor's Dilemma* (2⅛), and *Caesar and Cleopatra* (2). By page count the greatest increase in useful new studies during the past decade is for *Heartbreak* and *Joan.* Using 61 of the volume's 154 pages, the "Individual Plays" section is impossible to digest usefully here. Weintraub's opinion is that "the quantity and range of criticism of individual Shavian plays seem to be a reflection of the depths that critics feel can be sounded rather than an index to their popularity in performance, although in a few cases—*Candida, Pygmalion,* and *Man and Superman,* for example—critics and audiences seem equally bemused. More and more research and criticism are being directed toward the less produced plays, partly because the soil is less tilled but partly, too, because their political, philosophical, and technical complexities were in advance of their time and can now be better understood."

The final three sections suggest where a great deal of useful work might be done. Section 10, "Criticism in Languages Other Than English," notes Julius Bab's *George Bernard Shaw* (1909; 1926) as still one of the most perceptive works. Various quantities of commentary exist for G.B.S. in Finland, Russia, Germany, France, and Spanish America. There are also *Research Essays on Bernard Shaw* (1986) by members of the Shaw Society of Japan and Florence Chien's translations of prewar China's "Lu Xun's Six Essays in Defense of Bernard Shaw" (*SHAW* 12, 1992). Section 11, "Shaw in Fiction," names a few of the many novels, stories, verses, and plays that present Shaw as a character or evoke his works in their plots. Weintraub mentions the significant Ray Bradbury/ G.B.S. connection. The last section, "Influence and Reputation," notes immediately that studies of Shaw's influence "remain insubstantial," which sounds a most significant and appropriate note in this account. A list of subjects needing major study includes Shaw's influence in Ireland, England, and America; his influence on the generation of writers and playwrights that followed him; his influence upon the BBC in its formative years; and his role in practical politics and other areas not literary or theatrical. It is worth adding here that a G.B.S. influence on the increasingly respectable, important, and perhaps most commercially robust literary genre of the late twentieth century, science fiction, is substantial, but study of this influence has merely begun.

Much more needs to be done. Thousands of Shaw's letters remain unpublished. Some of Shaw's writing on Ibsen is not collected. The other polemical writing—articles, treatises, and books on politics, philosophy, economics, and society in general—has been largely neglected. In another certainly fascinating category of study are the several forms of Shaw's presence in fiction (as himself, his works, or references to him and his works), much multiplied but not yet sufficiently identified.

Meanwhile, some suggestions for the inevitable next transmutation of this *Guide* are for a more analyzed index of subjects. There is, for example, no entry for "screenplays," so we must know that Bernard F. Dukore edited them to find Weintraub's discussion of them on page 10. "Screenplays," moreover, came to mind as I reflected that this *Guide* could appropriately include a section on G.B.S. in recorded forms, listing the films and video versions that exist for a number of the plays, as well as movie newsreels and radio recordings of Shaw himself. Could there be, as well, a catalogue of photos of Shaviana?

In any event, the most remarkable suggestion for Shaw studies is provided in the *Guide* itself—Weintraub's renewal of Frederick P. W. McDowell's call for a variorum edition of the plays. This proposal is bold, ambitious, and wise. One has only to examine the variorum volumes of the Shakespearean corpus to be reminded of the awesome scale of research endeavor required for volumes that draw together manuscripts, text, sources, stage history, and literary history and criticism. Here it is worth remembering that a variorum edition implies all that is presented in critical and definitive editions of literary works, and transcends these to combine in a single format information that is disparate, fugitive, fundamentally important, and often unpublished anywhere because the economics of all but the variorum catalogue are prohibitive. The prospect of a variorum Shaw is wonderful.

John R. Pfeiffer

John R. Pfeiffer*

A CONTINUING CHECKLIST
OF SHAVIANA

I. Works by Shaw

Shaw, Bernard. *Androcles and the Lion,* edited with an introduction by William-Alan Landes. Studio City, Calif.: Players Press, Inc., 1992. Not seen. This "playscript," along with the plays named at the end of this annotation, are listed as published in the OLUC network. Sources of these editions are not provided in the network information. Entries are for *Arms and the Man, Caesar, Candida, Captain Brassbound, Devil's Disciple, Man of Destiny, Mrs Warren, Overruled, Philanderer, Pygmalion, Widowers' Houses,* and *You Never Can Tell.*

————. *Arms and the Man.* White Plains, N.Y.: Longman, 1991. Not seen.

————. *Buoyant Billions.* See Joyce, Steven, in Books and Pamphlets, below.

————. "Duse and Bernhardt" (*Saturday Review,* 15 June 1895). See Gold, Arthur, in Books and Pamphlets, below.

————. "Early Journalism in the *Pall Mall Gazette.*" *SHAW: The Annual of Bernard Shaw Studies,* Volume Twelve. University Park: Penn State University Press, 1992; pp. 287–96.

————. Excerpt from *"In Good King Charles's Golden Days".* In *A Literary Companion to Science,* ed. Walter Gratzer. New York and London: W. W. Norton, 1990; pp. 128–29.

————. Excerpt from the Preface to *The Simpleton of the Unexpected Isles,* collected in "Plays Extravagant" (Penguin), in "Noted with Pleasure." *New York Times Book Review* (3 May 1992), p. 39.

————. Excerpts from *Doctor's Dilemma* and the Preface to *Doctor's Dilemma.* In *A Literary Companion to Science,* ed. Walter Gratzer. New York and London: W. W. Norton, 1990. From the play, speeches between Sir Patrick and Ridgeon (230–31; 475–77). From the Preface (228–30).

————. "George Bernard Shaw v. English Spelling." In *Spelling, A Compendium of Tests, Super Tests and Killer Bees,* ed. David Grambs. New York: Harper & Row, 1989. The

*Thanks to Richard E. Winslow III for discovering and supplying copies for a number of entries in this list. Professor Pfeiffer, *SHAW* Bibliographer, welcomes information about new or forthcoming Shaviana: books, articles, pamphlets, monographs, dissertations, films, videos, reprints, and the like, all of which may be sent to him at the Department of English, Central Michigan University, Mount Pleasant, MI 48859.

selection begins "The English language cannot be spelt . . ." and ends ". . . so the language gets senselessly altered." Source not reported.

————. Letter to the Editor of *The London Mercury and Bookman*. "From *The London Mercury*," Arthur Sherbo, *Studies in Bibliography* 45 (1992): 299. The letter follows Sherbo's explanation: "Max Kenyon, musicologist, author of *Harpsichord Music* (1905) and the later *Mozart in Salzburg* (1959), wrote 'To the Editor of *The London Mercury and Bookman*' to protest Shaw's statement that Mozart had written the conclusion to Gluck's overture to *Iphigenia in Aulis* and to clear up the matter. Shaw's letter of gratitude was printed below Kenyon's." Excerpt from Shaw's letter: ". . . *Don Giovanni?* It is also provided with a very similar finish, no doubt by the same Johann Schmidt. This was considered necessary in the days when overtures as concert pieces had to end, in the key in which they began, with the usual tonic and dominant rum-tum-bang burlesqued by Beethoven and finally relegated to the dustbin by Wagner." Sherbo says he has not located the source of Shaw's pronouncement on Gluck's overture: "it is not in his 'Gluck in Glastonbury' in the May 6, 1916, *Nation*."

————. Letters previously unpublished and unrecorded, both early and late, in Edward McNulty's "Memoirs of G.B.S.," edited and annotated by Dan H. Laurence. *SHAW: The Annual of Bernard Shaw Studies*, Volume Twelve. University Park: Penn State University Press, 1992; pp. 1–46.

————. Letters to Margaret Wheeler. In *Letters from Margaret: Correspondence between Bernard Shaw and Margaret Wheeler, 1944–1950*, ed. Rebecca Swift. Chatto & Windus, November 1992?. Not seen. From the advertisement: "In 1936, Margaret Wheeler, apparently an ordinary mother and housewife, found herself in the bizarre situation of suspecting that her child had been swapped with another at birth. The search for the truth led her finally, in 1944, to write to the one man she thought might help—a 'latter-day Solomon'—Bernard Shaw. The enchanting correspondence which ensued reveals the irrepressible Margaret as 'a natural born writer,' and 'woman of genius,' as Shaw called her. Here, she challenges him, disagrees with, rebukes, intrigues, charms and even flirts with him." For details, see *Collected Letters 1926–1950*, in which Dan Laurence, editor, published several of the Shaw letters, with headnote biography on page 699.

————. *Major Barbara*. In *Stages of Drama: Classical to Contemporary Masterpieces of the Theater*, ed. Carl H. Klaus, Miriam Gilbert, and Bradford S. Field, Jr. 2d ed. New York: St. Martin's Press, 1991. Not seen. Catalogue also notes that the text is accompanied by photographs of the Royal Shakespeare Company production of the play and by Stanley Price's review of this production.

————. *Major Barbara*. See *Pygmalion and Major Barbara*, below.

————. *Monologues from George Bernard Shaw*, ed. Ian Michaels. Toluca Lake, Calif.: Dramaline Publications, 1991. Not seen.

————. "My Memories of Oscar Wilde." In Frank Harris, *Oscar Wilde, Including My Memories of Oscar Wilde by George Bernard Shaw and an Introductory Note by Lyle Blair*. New York: Carroll & Graf, 1992 (ca. 1958). Not seen.

————. *Pygmalion*, ed. Jacqueline Fisher. New York: Longman, 1991. Not seen.

————. *Pygmalion and Major Barbara*. Introduction by Michael Holroyd. New York: Bantam Books, 1992. Set from the texts of the first published editions—*Major Barbara*, Brentano (1907), and *Pygmalion*, Constable (1916). Holroyd finds *Barbara* the most "unpleasant," and *Pygmalion* the most "pleasant," of all Shaw's plays.

————. Quotation from *Blanco Posnet*, wherein G.B.S. asserts the similarity between himself and a dentist in the necessity to give pain, in David B. Morris, *The Culture of Pain*. Berkeley and Los Angeles: University of California Press, 1991.

————. Quotation of Michael Holroyd's 1989 quotation of G.B.S. from the *Pall Mall Ga-*

zette, in N. John Hall, *Trollope: A Biography*. Oxford: Clarendon Press, 1991. " 'He delivered us from the marvels, senseless accidents, cat's cradle plots of old romance, and gave us, to the best of his ability, a faithful picture of the daily life of the upper and middle classes.' " This is the only reference to Shaw, but it is, significantly, in the chapter where Hall is looking for a way to measure Trollope's achievement.

————. Quotations from "Herr Richter and His Blue Ribbon" (1885), *Music in London* (1931), and "Wagner in Bayreuth" (1889) in Christopher Fifield's "Conducting Wagner: The Search for Melos," *Wagner in Performance*. Edited by Barry Millington and Stewart Spencer. New Haven and London: Yale University Press, 1992; pp. 1–14.

————. *Saint Joan*. New York: Longman, 1992. Not seen.

————. *Selected Plays of George Bernard Shaw*. Introduction by Alfred Kazin. New York: Vintage Books, 1991. Specific plays not identified. Not seen.

————. *Shaw on Women*. Edited by Mary Chenoweth Stratton. Foreword by Margot Peters. Illustrated by Linda Holmes. Ellen Clarke Bertrand Library Limited Edition. Lewisburg, Pa.: Bucknell University and The Press of Appletree Alley, 1992. 68 pages. Includes "My Dear Dorothea" (based on the 1956 first edition, not the 1878 ms.); a 25 October 1930 letter to Murray Feder (owned by Bucknell and printed here for the first time); letters of 10, 14, and 23 January 1923 to Georgina Rogers (from the *Collected Letters*); and "Women as Councillors" (first edition in 1900, ms. owned by Bucknell). See Peters, Margot, in Books and Pamphlets, below.

————. *Shengnu Zhende* [*Saint Joan*]. Guilin, Guangxi: Lijiang Chubanshe [Li River Publishing House], 1987. This single title actually includes the Chinese translation of six Shaw plays, some previously published, others recent translations: *Mrs Warren's Profession* by Pan Jiaxun, *Candida* by Chen Shouzhu, *Man and Superman* by Zhang Quanquan, *Pygmalion* by Yang Xianyi, and *Arms and the Man* and *Saint Joan* by Shen Huihui. In addition, Shen wrote the thirty-page introduction and appended a speech on Shaw by the chairman of the Nobel Prize Committee, as well as a chronological table and a list of productions. The publication of this book, one of a ten-volume set entitled "Nobel Literary Prize Winners: Series Four," has been described as representing "a new stage of Shaw study in China." Entry provided and translated by Florence Chien.

————. *Three Plays for Puritans*. New York: Viking-Penguin, 1991. Not seen.

————. An unnamed fantastic tale by G.B. Shaw. In *Black Water 2: More Tales of the Fantastic*, ed. Alberto Manguel. Toronto: Lester & Orpen Dennys, 1990. Not seen. Information from Linda Avril Burnett's review in *Dalhousie Review* 71 (Spring 1991): 131–34. "This huge eclectic anthology contains 68 fantastic tales by 68 writers."

————. *An Unsocial Socialist*. Introduction by Michael Holroyd. New York: Penguin Books–Virago Press, 1991. Not seen.

————. Works and excerpts in *The Field Day Anthology of Irish Writing*, ed. Seamus Deane. 3 vols. Derry: Field Day Publications, 1991. Included are *John Bull's Other Island*, *O'Flaherty V.C.*, "The Protestants of Ireland," "A Note on Aggressive Nationalism," "How to Settle the Irish Question," "War Issues for Irishmen," "Composite Autobiography," "The Censorship," and "Preface to *Immaturity*." Also included are "The London Exiles: Wilde and Shaw" and an introduction by Declan Kiberd to the selections by Shaw. The text is from the Bodley Head edition.

See also Recordings, below.

II. Books and Pamphlets

Amalric, Jean-Claude. *Studies in Bernard Shaw. Cahiers Victoriens et Edouardiens, Documents 7*. Montpellier: Université Paul Valéry, 1992. Amalric's Shaw articles and unpublished papers. The table of contents describes the book's four parts: (1) Shaw as literary critic, drama critic, and critic of Dickens; (2) Shaw as dramatist, with major attention to *Mrs Warren, Arms,* and *Superman;* (3) Shaw as thinker, with emphases on Victorian morals and the Shavian hero; and (4) Shaw on France, discussing "Shaw, Hamon and Rémy de Gourmont," Shaw's visits to France, and Shaw's plays in France. Nine of the essays have been revised and updated from earlier printings, while three, including "The Production of Shaw's Plays in France," appear for the first time.

Ashton, Rosemary. *G. H. Lewes: A Life.* New York: Clarendon Press, 1991. Ruth Bernard Yeazell's review in the *New York Times Book Review* (15 March 1992, p. 12) reminds us that Lewes's theater criticism delighted and inspired G.B.S.

Behan, Brendan. *The Letters of Brendan Behan,* ed. E. H. Mikhail. Montreal and Kingston: McGill-Queens University Press, 1992. One interesting reference: From a letter to Sinbad Vail, Dublin, October 1952: "There is of course no such thing as an Anglo-Irishman, as Shaw pointed out in the preface to *John Bull's Other Island,* except as a class distinction."

"Bernard Shaw, Volume III: 1918–1950, The Lure of Fantasy," a review. *Magill's Literary Annual 1992.* Pasadena: Salem Press, 1992.

Bitonti, Tracy Simmons. "Shaw's Offstage Characters." *SHAW: The Annual of Bernard Shaw Studies,* Volume Twelve. University Park: Penn State University Press, 1992.

Bloom, Lynn Z. "Shaw, George Bernard." *St. James Guide to Biography,* ed. Paul E. Schellinger. Chicago and London: St. James Press, 1991; pp. 712–14. A much too glib survey of thirty-two biographical treatments of G.B.S. by twenty biographers, including Ivor Brown, Chappelow, Maurice Colbourne, Daniel Dervin, Charles DuCann, Ervine, Harris, Henderson, Holroyd, Irvine, R. J. Minney, John O'Donovan, Patch, Pearson, Margot Peters, Rattray, Rosset, Charles Shaw, Weintraub, and Winsten.

Boller, Paul F., Jr. *Congressional Anecdotes.* New York and Oxford: Oxford University Press, 1991. One reference to G.B.S.: The reporters teased Robert F. Kennedy about his propensity for ending a speech with a favorite quotation: "As George Bernard Shaw once said. . . ." After twenty or thirty instances, this became the signal to head for the bus, train, or plane scheduled to take them to the next place. Once RFK forgot to quote Shaw, and the campaign train started off, leaving all the reporters stranded. When they caught up with RFK, they asked him always to use the Shaw cue afterward. At the next stop Kennedy ended his speech, "As George Bernard Shaw once said, 'Run for the bus!' "

Bradbury, Ray. *Green Shadows, White Whale.* Drawings by Edward Sorel. New York: Alfred A. Knopf, 1992; pp. 183–200. Autobiographical elements of Bradbury's sojourn in 1953 in Ireland combine with whimsy in this "novel," which includes a chapter (26) wherein Shaw is remembered to have stopped at Heeber Finn's pub, the result of car problems his drunken chauffeur cannot immediately fix. At the pub Shaw accepts and "swigs" a shot of brandy, and engages in a Bradburyian/Shavian legerdemain involving four fired-clay signs featuring the words "Stop," "Think," "Consider," and "Do." Shaw briefly resurrects his dart-throwing expertise, explicitly credited to his childhood experience in pubs with his alcoholic father. There are skewed references to *Saint Joan, Devil's Disciple,* and G. K. Chesterton. Shaw leaves when the car is fixed.

Brustein, Robert. *Reimagining American Theatre.* New York: Hill & Wang, 1991. In a chapter on "Polemics" are the following remarks on Shaw and Brecht:

> The advent of aestheticism was bound to stimulate an adversary reaction from playwrights with a strong political conscience. And, sure enough, the drama of the twentieth century became dominated by two figures—Bernard Shaw and Bertolt Brecht—who not only held a more or less Platonic view of the stage but often scourged the Aristotelian tendencies of past and present writers. . . . Platonist

though he was, however, Shaw continually tried to find ways to *include* the artist in his ideal Republic, if only by proving that the artist had utilitarian value.... And though Shaw tried to justify Wagner's aestheticism by interpreting *The Ring* as an allegory of the Industrial Revolution, the split in his own nature between the ethical and aesthetic ideals of art was never fully healed.... Brecht couldn't heal that split either.... Shaw's politics were always modified by the kindness of his own nature and the gradualism of his Fabian beliefs; Brecht's are intensified by his savage indignation and his harrowing vision of life. Shaw was a suppressed poet who rarely broke the skin of the unconscious, and while he called himself a puritan, he kept an abiding faith in human goodness and decency; Brecht was a lyric and dramatic poet of fierce intensity, and few Calvinist theologians have been more obsessed with the brutal, the satanic, the irrational side of behavior. Brecht's concern with the darker aspects of human nature grows out of his struggles with himself, but also characterizes his relationship to Communism. Shaw's Fabianism reflects his own genial personality; Brecht's Communism is a strict discipline imposed on an essentially morbid and sensual character.... In short, while Shaw was able to imagine utopias, Brecht was too honest to do more than suggest why they were necessary.

Byrd, Rudolph. *Jean Toomer's Years with Gurdjieff: Portrait of an Artist, 1923–1936.* Athens: University of Georgia Press, 1990. Byrd contends strongly that the works of G.B.S. were a powerful influence upon Toomer, who stated, "Shaw's independence and candor showed me to myself. He as a person struck deep into me, convincing me that it was valuable to be as he was. I felt I could be and should be independent and candid.... Ever since discovering Shaw my taste for the written word had increased." *Man and Superman* was "unquestionably a favorite of Toomer, for John Tanner, a central figure in Shaw's fascinating critique of marriage, bears an uncanny resemblance, in temperament and outlook to Nathan Merilh of [Toomer's play] *Natalie Mann.*"

Cheyette, Bryan. "Superman and Jew: Semitic Representations in the Work of Bernard Shaw." *SHAW: The Annual of Bernard Shaw Studies,* Volume Twelve. University Park: Penn State University Press, 1992.

Chien, Florence. "Lu Xun's Six Essays in Defense of Bernard Shaw." *SHAW: The Annual of Bernard Shaw Studies,* Volume Twelve. University Park: Penn State University Press, 1992.

Clerk, Honor. See Gibson, Robin, below.

Cook, Blanche Wiesen. *Eleanor Roosevelt, Volume I, 1884–1933.* New York: Viking, 1992. "Most significantly, she saw George Bernard Shaw's play *Candida* at least three times.... *Candida* explores many themes that were later to become significant in Eleanor Roosevelt's life: love between people of different generations, unrequited love, loyalty in marriage, a woman's right to her own unfettered spirit, and especially Candida's decision to give her heart to the one who needs her most, the one who cannot function successfully without her."

Corballis, Richard. "Why the Devil Gets all the Good Tunes: Shaw, Wagner, Mozart, Gounod, Bizet, Boito, and Stanford." *SHAW: The Annual of Bernard Shaw Studies,* Volume Twelve. University Park: Penn State University Press, 1992.

Corbett, Mary Jean. *Representing Femininity: Middle-Class Subjectivity in Victorian and Edwardian Women's Autobiographies.* New York: Oxford University Press, 1992. Shaw is mentioned sparingly, but with complete respect, using his opinions of Terry, Duse, and Campbell to characterize the times.

Cronyn, Hume. *A Terrible Liar: A Memoir.* New York: William Morrow, 1991. Cronyn played smaller roles in Shaw plays in his salad days.

Dickstein, Morris. *Double Agent, The Critic and Society.* New York and Oxford: Oxford

University Press, 1992. Mencken's "portrayal of Shaw, supposedly the most intellectual of writers, is simply a piece of Shavian paradox: Just the way Shaw might have eviscerated anyone who dared influence *him*." He summarizes Mencken on Shaw: "In other words, Shaw, like Mencken himself, is a style: a dazzling high-wire act, an endlessly resourceful iconoclasm [*sic*]."

Dietrich, R. F. "Shaw as Dramatic Icon: A Bibliography of Impersonations." *SHAW: The Annual of Bernard Shaw Studies*, Volume Twelve. University Park: Penn State University Press, 1992.

Dukore, Bernard F., ed. *Alan Ayckbourn: A Casebook.* New York and London: Garland, 1991. Several mentions of Shaw, including one by Ayckbourn in Dukore's interview of him, wherein G.B.S. is lumped with Coward and Wilde as among the playwrights that he knew and, by inference, that influenced him. But he does not name Shaw, pointedly, as a major influence. Ayckbourn names Ionesco, Pirandello, and Anouilh as major influences.

Ely, Melvin Patrick. *The Adventures of Amos 'n' Andy: A Social History of an American Phenomenon.* New York: The Free Press, 1991. Not seen. Mel Watkins, in the *New York Times Book Review* (7 July 1991), p. 1, reminds us at the beginning that G.B.S. said, " 'There are three things which I shall never forget about America—the Rocky Mountains, Niagara Falls, and "Amos 'n' Andy".' "

Evans, T. F. "Shaw and Cricket." *SHAW: The Annual of Bernard Shaw Studies*, Volume Twelve. University Park: Penn State University Press, 1992.

Fifield, Christopher. See Quotations from "Herr Richter . . ." in Works by Shaw, above.

Fisher, Clive. *Noel Coward.* New York: St. Martin's Press, 1992. Coward admired and was inspired by G.B.S., whom he came to know. Nothing here about the connection is new.

Foltz, William. Review of Michael Holroyd's *Bernard Shaw: Vol. 3.* In "The Year in Literary Biography," *Dictionary of Literary Biography Yearbook: 1991.* Edited by James W. Hipp. Detroit and London: Gale Research, 1992; pp. 93, 98–99.

Fordyce, William D. T. "The Quasi-Agon in *The Doctor's Dilemma.*" *SHAW: The Annual of Bernard Shaw Studies*, Volume Twelve. University Park: Penn State University Press, 1992.

Gainor, J. Ellen. *Shaw's Daughters: Dramatic and Narrative Constructions of Gender.* Ann Arbor: University of Michigan Press, 1991. Reviewed in this volume of *SHAW*.

Gibson, Robin, and Honor Clerk. *G.B.S.: Bernard Shaw Postcard Pack.* Intro. Michael Holroyd. London: National Portrait Gallery, 1992. This consists of eight beautifully done postcard reproductions of works featured in the NPG's exhibition "G.B.S. In Close Up: Bernard Shaw" (10 April–5 July 1992) with a sixteen-page booklet including Holroyd's introduction, Gibson and Clerk's descriptions of the eight works, and Gibson and Clerk's "Brief Chronology." The NPG produced no exhibition catalogue, feeling that much of the ground had been covered by Michael Holroyd's four-volume biography. The eight reproductions include Sir Emery Walker's 1888 photograph of Shaw, Alvin Langdon Coburn's 1908 photograph of Shaw, John Singer Sargent's 1900 chalk drawing of Harley Granville Barker, Charlotte Fairchild's early 1900s photograph of Mrs. Patrick Campbell, Charles Buchel's 1914 *Pygmalion* poster (lithograph), Bertram Park's 1924 photograph of Dame Sybil Thorndike portraying Saint Joan, Sir Bernard Partridge's ca. 1925 watercolor of Shaw, and Dame Laura Knight's 1932 oil portrait of Shaw.

Gold, Arthur, and Robert Fitzdale. *The Divine Sarah: A Life of Sarah Bernhardt.* New York: Knopf, 1991. Three interesting references to G.B.S.: The book opens by quoting Shaw's famous reduction of Bernhard: "the childishly egotistical character of her acting. . . ." He never approved of her. Second, several pages describe the debate between Beerbohm and Shaw, with Beerbohm defending Bernhardt and Shaw defending Eleanora Duse. These biographers of Bernhardt give Shaw the edge because he made later generations think of Bernhardt as money-grubbing and Duse as otherworldly. Third, there is a long extract from Shaw's "Duse and Bernhardt" (*Saturday Review*, 15 June 1895).

Gonne, Maud, and William Butler Yeats. *The Gonne-Yeats Letters, 1893–1938: Always Your Friend.* Edited by Anna MacBride White and A. Norman Jeffares. London: Hutchinson, 1992. A very few G.B.S. references in these letters, barely a footnote to the Shaw/Yeats relationship.

Gratzer, Walter, ed. *A Literary Companion to Science.* New York and London: W. W. Norton, 1990. Includes an excerpt from Gwyn Macfarlane's biography of Alexander Fleming, who worked in the department at St. Mary's Hospital Medical School where Colonel Sir Almroth Wright was professor and known to Shaw, and from whom G.B.S. took some of the inspiration for *Doctor's Dilemma* (226–28). In addition, there is Martin Gardner's mention of Shaw's clever "flat-earther" from *Everybody's Political What's What?*, from Gardner's *Fads and Fallacies in the Name of Science* (441). Finally, several pages print extracts from the Preface and the script of *Doctor's Dilemma;* see Excerpts from *Doctor's Dilemma* in Works by Shaw, above.

Griffin, Penny. *Arthur Wing Pinero and Henry Arthur Jones.* London: Macmillan, 1991. Primarily concerned to survey the lives and works of the two dramatists, Griffin occasionally is led to see the Shavian reputation as problematic:

His achievement has totally eclipsed that of Pinero, whose contribution to the mainstream of English drama is the greater. Shaw stands on his own—a dramatist of the mind. He is the dramatist of polemic and debate, who writes mainly from an objective, satiric viewpoint, frequently clumsy in his use of theatre. Pinero is a playwright of greater variety: of irony; of subtle psychology and emotion; of comedy; and whose knowledge of theatre is unsurpassed.

Hampton, Aubrey. *GBS & Co., a Full-Length Play about George Bernard Shaw.* Studio City, Calif.: Players Press, Inc., 1992. This is a new edition of Hampton's 1989 play, which has received cordial reviews from Shaw scholars. It includes roles for Houdini, Conan Doyle, Madame Blavatsky, Chesterton, Henry George, the Webbs, Charlotte Shaw, Mrs. Pat, Ellen Terry, Granville Barker, H. G. Wells, and other contemporaries who interact with G.B.S. on stage.

Hearst, William Randolph, Jr. (with Jack Casserly). *The Hearsts: Father and Son.* Niwot, Colo.: Robert Rinehart Publishers, 1991. Reviews several of the well-known G.B.S. effects on the Hearst publications and household—he visited Hearst Castle in the spring of 1933. Marion Davies, the senior Hearst's mistress, wrote to G.B.S. in England afterward as long as Shaw lived.

Himmelfarb, Gertrude. *Poverty and Compassion: The Moral Imagination of the Late Victorians.* New York: Knopf, 1991. A number of references to G.B.S., who is a predictable touchstone in a book with this title.

Holroyd, Michael. *Bernard Shaw.* Vol. 3, *1918–1950: The Lure of Fantasy.* New York: Random House, 1991. See many reviews in Periodicals, below. Reviewed in this volume of *SHAW.*

———. *Bernard Shaw,* Vol. 4, *1950–1991: The Last Laugh.* London: Chatto & Windus, 1992. This slim volume (some 85 pages of text supplemented by the wills of Charlotte and Bernard Shaw) comes as something of a surprise—it is not the long-promised volume of sources. Holroyd presents a lively and entertaining account of Shaw's afterlife, including the (still continuing) wrangling over the terms of Shaw's will, the "alfabet" movement, the attention generated by *My Fair Lady,* and other aspects of Shaw's posthumous presence. Random House plans to release the American edition during winter 1992–93.

————. See Gibson, Robin, above.

————. See *Pygmalion and Major Barbara* in Works by Shaw, above.

Houghton, Norris. *Entrances and Exits: A Life In and Out of the Theatre.* New York: Limelight Editions, 1991. Not seen. John Russell's review in the *New York Times Book Review* (18 August 1991), p. 2, indicates a number of instances where Houghton was connected to G.B.S. plays: *Pygmalion, Candida,* and *Saint Joan* among them.

Huggett, Richard. *Binkie Beaumont.* London: Hodder & Stoughton, 1989. The life story of the man who called himself the "eminence grise" of London West End theater from 1933 to 1973. There are passages of special interest to students of Shaw in connection with the London productions of *Candida* (1937), *Doctor's Dilemma* (1942), and *Heart-break House* (1943).

Hughes, Geoffrey. *Swearing: A Social History of Foul Language, Oaths and Profanity in English.* Oxford, England, and Cambridge, Mass.: Blackwell, 1991. In the book's theme the "Modern Explosion" is bracketed by Eliza Doolittle's scandalous ejaculation, "Not bloody likely," in *Pygmalion* (1914) and the protracted trial to remove the ban of *Lady Chatterley's Lover* in 1960. It excerpts the 11 April 1914 notice of the *Pygmalion* production in the *Daily Sketch:* "Mr. Shaw introduces a certain forbidden word. Will Mrs. Patrick Campbell speak it?" Hughes recounts the huge popular uproar in England over the word, which in America caused no stir.

Hugo, Leon H. "In Search of Shaw: An Interview with Stanley Weintraub." *SHAW: The Annual of Bernard Shaw Studies,* Volume Twelve. University Park: Penn State University Press, 1992.

Humphries, Rolfe. *Poets, Poetics and Politics: America's Literary Community Viewed from the Letters of Rolfe Humphries, 1910–1969,* ed. Richard Gillman and Michael Paul Novak. With a biographical essay by Ruth Limmer. Lawrence: University of Kansas Press, 1992. Humphries, a friend of Louise Bogan, Edmund Wilson, and Theodore Roethke, discovered G.B.S. in his 1912–1913 Stanford year. Most interesting of the eight references here: "I have been reading some of the penultimate Shaw; pretty bad, most of it, though *The Simpleton, The Six of Calais* and *The Millionairess* have some funny roughhouse. At 80, he seems to be working around to the position that sexual intercourse might be fun; there are several references which have nothing to do with the Life Force, and are quite tricksy-pranksy. No critic has noticed this" (12 July 1938). "There are some books that are good to read when you are in the mood; others which can put you in the mood—one of the latter for me, to which I occasionally go when I am inclined to be depressed, is Shaw's book of criticisms of music in the '90's. He's a great old boy, and please don't blaspheme him . . ." (4 December 1946).

Innes, Christopher. *Modern British Drama, 1890–1990.* Cambridge: Cambridge University Press, 1992. Not seen.

Isser, Edward R. "Bernard Shaw and British Holocaust Drama." *SHAW: The Annual of Bernard Shaw Studies,* Volume Twelve. University Park: Penn State University Press, 1992.

Jeffares, A. Norman. See Gonne, above.

Jenkins, Anthony. *The Making of Victorian Drama.* New York: Cambridge University Press, 1991. Not seen. From the review by J. P. Wearing (see Periodicals, below): "Shaw made little impact on the Victorian theatre and yet . . . merits a whole thirty-five page chapter."

Jones, Dorothy Richardson. *"King of Critics": George Saintsbury, 1845–1933. Critic, Journalist, Historian, Professor.* Ann Arbor: University of Michigan Press, 1992. A number of interesting references to G.B.S. As literary editor of the *Saturday Review,* Saintsbury was accused of ignoring Ibsen, Wilde, Shaw, Tolstoy, and Nietzsche, whose works he discounted as "topsiturvification" or "satanic pose," "easy twists of inversion and unexpectedness, . . . or literary pastiche." In his later *Nineteenth Century* Saintsbury included Zola, Ibsen, Nietzsche, and Tolstoy, but omitted Wilde and Shaw. That he ultimately credited G.B.S. with significant literary stature is evident in his letter to Helen Wadell dated 25 September 1932, his last extant, wherein he tells her that she is the equal of any Irish man except Yeats and Shaw.

Joyce, Steven. *Transformations and Texts: G. B. Shaw's Buoyant Billions.* Columbia, S.C.: Camden House, 1991. Not seen. From a Camden House advertisement: A "detailed examination of the typescript of the play in the holdings of the British Library as well as of several rehearsal copies that were issued primarily for the Malvern Festival of 1949. . . . Treats Siegfried Trebitsch's German translation of the play entitled *Zu viel Geld.* It argues that Trebitsch also exerted a shaping influence on the text of *Buoyant Billions.*"

Karl, Frederick. *Franz Kafka: Representative Man.* New York: Ticknor & Fields, 1991. One reference to G.B.S.: Kafka quoted Shaw to his parents to the effect that rather than struggle for a livelihood, G.B.S. let his mother support him and hung on his old father's coattails: "I lead a horribly synthetic life and am cowardly and miserable enough to follow Shaw only to the extent of having read the passage to my parents."

Kiberd, Declan. See "Works and Excerpts . . ." in Works by Shaw, above.

Kirstein, Lincoln. *By With To & From: A Lincoln Kirstein Reader,* ed. Nicholas Jenkins. New York: Farrar, Straus & Giroux, 1991. In these writings on dance, painting, photography, theater, politics, and literature, Kirstein notes "Bernard Shaw, a man almost alone in his position, appealed (naturally in vain) for the exemption of the British male dancer during the last war." Also, "Lacking a Shakespeare, it would have taken a Bernard Shaw—who understood T. E. Lawrence as Private Shaw, Ross, the Bastard, the Poet, the Adventurer, the Failure, the Success—to utilize all of [Marilyn] Monroe's maniacal procrastination, her treacheries to those who 'helped' her—that wolf pack and rat pack, agents and instructors, who of course expected only a kind word for their investment [irony]."

Klaic, Dragan. *The Plot of the Future: Utopia and Dystopia in Modern Drama.* Ann Arbor: University of Michigan Press, 1991. "In the following . . . the subtle interaction of social ideas about the future and the functioning of the future in drama will be considered in its prominent phases—culminating in the full-fledged utopian dramaturgy at the beginning of the twentieth century in the works of G. B. Shaw and Vladimir Mayakovsky, and followed by a crisis in utopian thinking in the prevalence of the dystopian paradigm." Later, in "Shaw's Quest for a Superman," he deals with *Heartbreak House, Man and Superman,* and, especially, *Back to Methuselah.* Shaw's works are disappointing: "The whole predictive and polemical effort is defeated by rhetorical overkill and by its disappointing utopian climax. . . . The sheer optimism of his vision remains unsustained by its content and intellectual infrastructure. Most important, Shaw's enormous prophetic energy lacks a commensurate utopian imagination, one that could titillate, inspire, and mobilize."

Knowles, Pat and Joyce, and Bob Hunt. *Cloud's Hill, Dorset: "An Handful with Quietness."* Weymouth, Dorset: E.V.G. Hunt, 1992. Includes several G.B.S./T.E. Lawrence references, especially one in a letter from Alec Guinness of 19 June 1960? mentioning a robe owned successively by Sir Sydney Cockerell, T.E., and G.B.S.—used as a dressing gown.

Larson, Gale K. "Shaw's Artistic Selves." Review of John A. Bertolini, *The Playwrighting Self of Bernard Shaw* and David Gordon, *Shaw and the Comic Sublime. SHAW: The Annual of Bernard Shaw Studies,* Volume Twelve. University Park: Penn State University Press, 1992.

Laurence, Dan H. "The McNulty 'Memoirs'." *SHAW: The Annual of Bernard Shaw Studies,* Volume Twelve. University Park: Penn State University Press, 1992.
———. See *Widowers' Houses,* below.
Lee, Josephine. "The Skilled Voluptuary: Shaw as Music Critic." *SHAW: The Annual of Bernard Shaw Studies,* Volume Twelve. University Park: Penn State University Press, 1992.
Martin, Timothy. *Joyce and Wagner: A Study of Influence.* Cambridge: Cambridge University Press, 1991. Shaw's role as a Wagnerite is substantially represented, as is the connection between Joyce and Shaw regarding Wagner, especially noticing Joyce's knowledge of *The Perfect Wagnerite.* Moreover, "in his attempt to bring the resources of music to literature Joyce's ability approached that of Shaw and his ambition surpassed even that of George Moore."
May, Rollo. *The Cry for Myth.* New York and London: W. W. Norton, 1991. From this very respected, popular psychotherapist, two references to G.B.S. in this latest book. From *Saint Joan,* "How long, O Lord, how long?" From G.B.S. on Ibsen, "The universality of Ibsen, and his grip upon humanity, makes his plays come home to all nations, and Peer Gynt is as good a Frenchman as a Norwegian."
MacGibbon, James. "Desmond MacCarthy: A Memoir of Affection." In *A Cézanne in the Hedge, and other Memories of Charleston and Bloomsbury.* Edited by Hugh Lee. Foreword by Michael Holroyd. Chicago: University of Chicago Press, 1992; pp. 111–15. MacGibbon tells us that "probably it was MacCarthy's *Shaw,* containing all his reviews of the G.B.S. plays . . . , that show him at his best as a dramatic critic." In his forty years as a critic he had written "more about Shaw than any other writer living or dead."
McNulty, Edward. "Memoirs of G.B.S.," edited and annotated by Dan H. Laurence. *SHAW: The Annual of Bernard Shaw Studies,* Volume Twelve. University Park: Penn State University Press, 1992.
Mezon, Jim. See *Widowers' Houses,* below.
Müller, Ulrich, and Peter Wapnewski, ed. *Wagner Handbook.* Cambridge and London: Harvard University Press, 1992. Includes four articles with Shaw references: Isolde Vetter, "Wagner in the History of Psychology" (118–55); Ernst Hanisch, "The Political Influence and Appropriation of Wagner" (186–201); Erwin Koppen, "Wagnerism as Concept and Phenomenon" (343–53); and Ulrich Müller, "Wagner in Literature and Film" (373–396).
Newton, Christopher. See *Pygmalion,* below.
Nicolson, Harold. See Sackville-West, below.
Nicolson, Nigel. See Sackville-West, below.
Niven, Penelope. *Carl Sandburg: A Biography.* New York: Charles Scribner's Sons, 1991. In the early portion of the book we are told Sandburg "steeped himself" in the work of G.B.S.—in 1907–1908—whom he pronounced the soulmate of Jeremiah, Isaiah, and Mark Twain. There is no further mention in these eight-hundred–odd pages.
O'Hara, Michael M. "*On the Rocks* and the Federal Theatre Project." *SHAW: The Annual of Bernard Shaw Studies,* Volume Twelve. University Park: Penn State University Press, 1992.
Overruled: Shaw Festival 1992 (Shaw Festival production program, 1992). Includes "Director's Notes" by Roy Surette and "Shaw's Sanely Adulterous Farce" by Margot Peters, who sees in *Overruled* at least five meanings for G.B.S.: his alternative to the boring, hypocritical Victorian drama of infidelity; a statement against the patriarchal proprietorship of marriage; a "forum for airing the truths two married couples are forced to tell each other when they face their infidelities without excuses"; an expression of his love for Mrs. Patrick Campbell; and, finally, the "real theme . . . is less the attractions

of adultery than the irresistability of romance which, after all, is based on expectation rather than fulfillment."

Peters, Margot. "Foreword" to *Shaw on Women*. Lewisburg, Penna.: Bucknell University & The Press of Appletree Alley, 1992; pp. 9–17. Peters, re-examining the pieces collected here—*My Dear Dorothea, Women as Councillors*, and letters to Georgina Rogers (10, 14, 23 January 1923) and Murray Feder (25 October 1930)—notes Shaw's identity as a "born teacher" and his commitment to the equality of women: "Although some women have accused Shaw of evasion, subterfuge, and even treachery, his stand on women's rights, on the contrary, was remarkably consistent. The young man who advises Dorothea to be selfish and the septuagenarian who sets Mr. Murray Feder straight on woman's work are one and the same."

————. See *Overruled*, above.

Peters, Sally. "The Noble Art: Shaw and Boxing." *Rackham Journal of the Arts and Humanities, 1991* (1991–92), pp. 2–14. Explores the meaning of Shaw's attraction to boxing and suggests a line of influence flowing from his comments on that sport to Hemingway's comments on bullfighting.

Pfeiffer, John R. "Colin Wilson." In *Twentieth Century Science Fiction Writers*, ed. Noelle Watson and Paul E. Schellinger. 3d ed. Chicago and London: St. James Press, 1991; pp. 874–75. This updated article on Wilson provides the following new information on Wilson, a long-standing admirer of G.B.S.: "In the four books of the Spider World series, *The Desert* (1988), *The Tower* (1987), *The Fortress* (1987), and *The Delta* (1987), Wilson . . . [has written a work of children's science fiction], and thanks his three children for helping to form the guidelines. . . . It imagines, as in earlier works, a universe imbued with [an explicitly] Shavian life force engaged in creative evolution. In the not-too-distant future, a vegetable embodiment of the life force comes to earth, and causes a riot in the evolution of earth's flora and fauna." There is a way to adapt to this symbolic problem. "Humanity has another chance to solve what Wilson contends is its abiding problem: Man must learn to control his own mind so that the control he so easily exerts over the material world can avoid yet another catastrophe like those that fill human history." Another part of the entry reprints Wilson's comment in reference to one of his earlier works of science fiction: "In *The Philosopher's Stone*, I was again concerned with the problem of the invisible blocks to human evolution, but this time I accepted Shaw's challenge to write a parable about longevity—his belief that, if we could simply be galvanized by a sense of necessity, we would find it perfectly natural to live to be at least 300."

Poitou, Marc. *Bernard Shaw and the Comedy of Approval: A Lecture Given at the Princess Grace Irish Library on Friday 9 December 1988*. Printed with Monique Gallagher, *Flann O'Brien: Myles from Dublin*, as no. 7 in The Princess Grace Irish Library Lectures. Gerrards Cross: Colin Smythe, 1991. Referring to characters and situations in *Joan, Arms, Superman, Major Barbara, Caesar*, and *Brassbound*, Poitou explains three methods by which Shaw achieves "comedy of approval": "The first method by which Shaw makes you laugh and admire a character is by showing him, or her, overcoming an obstacle, triumphing over somebody, outwitting an enemy, in an unexpectedly clever, and therefore humorous, manner. This is not Shaw's invention: his originality consists in having introduced it into serious literature" (33). "Method number two begins with a display of human foibles, which are slightly ludicrous, and, shifting the angle of vision, turns them into something we are called upon to admire. The most striking example of this is Lady Cicely" (42). "Method number three relies, not on the kinship between a character and an idea, but on their opposition. Laughing at the character's weakness helps us to accept the idea. This is what we find in *Man and Superman* [John Tanner]" (43).

Porter, Stephen. "Discovering Shaw by Directing Shaw." *SHAW: The Annual of Bernard Shaw Studies*, Volume Twelve. University Park: Penn State University Press, 1992.

Pygmalion: Shaw Festival 1992 (Shaw Festival production program, 1992). Includes "Director's Notes" by Christopher Newton and "A View from the Dust Cart" by John Sparkes, formerly a garbageman. He surveys the dramatis personae of *Pygmalion*, finding all but Higgins to be good company. Born in 1955, Sparkes "shall look forward with great anticipation to the next play George Bernard Shaw cares to write."

Rabey, David Ian. "Power, Culture, and the Politics of Absolute Play: *Heartbreak House* and *Too True to Be Good* as Existential Expressionism." *SHAW: The Annual of Bernard Shaw Studies*, Volume Twelve. University Park: Penn State University Press, 1992.

Review of *SHAW 9, Shaw Offstage: The Nondramatic Writings*. In *The Year's Work in English Studies* 70 (1989): 565–66.

Reviews of many books and articles on Shaw, including the *SHAW Annual*. *The Year's Work in English Studies* 69 (1988; published in 1991): 467–68, 538–39.

Riddle, Carol L. "Mrs. Dudgeon: More Sinned Against Than Sinning?" *SHAW: The Annual of Bernard Shaw Studies*, Volume Twelve. University Park: Penn State University Press, 1992.

Robinson, Forrest G. *Love's Story Told: A Life of Henry A. Murray*. Cambridge: Harvard University Press, 1992. One reference to G.B.S. in this biography of one of the more important American psychologists. Murray wrote for the 1925 Tenth Annual Harvard Class Report, "The most potent external stimulants besides Bordeaux wines have come from Ecclesiastes, Shakespeare, Goethe, Wagner, Nietzsche, Shaw, Anatole France, Henry Adams, Emerson, and William James."

Rogers, Kevin E. "The Machiavellian Tendencies of Adolphus Cusins." *SHAW: The Annual of Bernard Shaw Studies*, Volume Twelve. University Park: Penn State University Press, 1992.

Russ, Joanna. "An Interview with Joanna Russ." In *Across the Wounded Galaxies: Interviews with Contemporary American Science Fiction Writers*, conducted and edited by Larry McCaffrey. Urbana and Chicago: University of Illinois Press, 1990; pp. 176–210. Russ often mentions G.B.S. with respect. Here there are three references. A sample: "Shaw makes a distinction between real authority and conventional authority, which must always be *enforced* because it's not rational, not real, not based on any substantive source of power. When I say I'm not anti-authority, I'm referring to that real authority whose source is the real world, the sunlight, the trees, the nitty-gritty, . . . the authentic."

Russell, Bertrand. *The Selected Letters of Bertrand Russell: Volume I, The Private Years, 1884–1914*. Edited by Nicholas Griffin. Boston, New York, London: Houghton Mifflin Company, 1991. References to Shaw are in two letters, one to Lucy Donnelly (28 October 1911): He reports being at a party hosted by Wildon Carr, seated next to Henri Bergson, next to Carr, with G.B.S. on Carr's left. "Shaw made an amusing speech explaining how glad he was that Bergson had adopted his (Shaw's) views, and expounding how Bergson thought we came to have eyes. B. said it wasn't quite that way, but Shaw set him right, and said B. evidently didn't understand his own philosophy. . . . When people laughed during Shaw's speech he said 'I don't mean to make a comic speech, and I don't know why you laugh, unless because religion is such an essentially laughable subject.' They seemed to me like naughty children when they think (mistakenly) that the governess is away—boasting of their power over matter, when matter might kill them at any moment."

Sackville-West, Vita, and Harold Nicolson. *Vita and Harold: The Letters of Vita Sackville-West and Harold Nicolson*. Edited by Nigel Nicolson. New York: G. P. Putnam's Sons, 1992. One reference to G.B.S.: From Harold's letter to Vita (12 December 1950): "Went to Shaw's house yesterday. . . . But, darling, it was thrilling. Shaw was there, in the gar-

den. Still in the shape of ashes. It was difficult and indeed impossible to tell which was
Shaw and which was Mrs. Shaw as their ashes had been mixed. But there on the rose
bed and garden paths were these white ashes— . . . I could easily have picked some up
and taken it home in an envelope. But I do not admire Shaw all that much."

Seymour-Jones, Carole. *Beatrice Webb, Woman of Conflict.* London: Allison & Busby, 1992.
Contains numerous substantial references to G.B.S., including the proposition that
Shaw was the most potent influence on Webb in her embrace of Soviet communism.
There is as well an analysis of Shaw's participation in the "evisceration" of the Fabian
movement's political effect. His elegant diction pronounced influential claims of Fabian sucesses that were in fact not the achievements of the Fabians, but in spite of
them. The index does not list all G.B.S. references.

Spoto, Donald. *Laurence Olivier, A Biography.* New York: Harper Collins, 1992. Olivier did
not have a large repertoire of Shaw roles. This account associates him in one way or
another with *Methuselah, Doctor's Dilemma, Arms, Caesar,* and *Devil's Disciple.* Olivier
reports that in 1944, co-starring in *Arms* as Sergius, he found the role "inordinately
unsympathetic and unappealing." Guthrie bolstered him, " 'If you can't love him,
you'll never be any good.' " Olivier: "I began to love Sergius, and my whole performance seemed to get better and better. For the rest of my life, I would apply this
[principle]."

Stephen, Martin. *English Literature: A Student Guide.* White Plains, N.Y.: Longman Publishing, 1991. Not seen. Longman's catalogue indicates that a section of the book is "Victorian Drama: Ibsen, Chekhov, Shaw and Wilde."

Stowell, Sheila. *A Stage of Their Own: Feminist Playwrights of the Sufferage Era.* Ann Arbor:
University of Michigan Press, 1992. Stowell knows Shaw well and refers to him often,
including references to *Doctor's Dilemma, Don Juan in Hell, Fanny's First Play, Getting
Married, Intelligent Woman's Guide, Major Barbara, Superman, Misalliance, Mrs Warren, Our
Theatres in the Nineties, Press Cuttings, Pygmalion, The Quintessence of Ibsenism,* and *Widow-
ers' Houses.*

Suskin, Steven. *Opening Night on Broadway: A Critical Quotebook of the Golden Era of the Musical
Theatre, Oklahoma! (1943) to Fiddler on the Roof (1964).* New York: Macmillan, 1990.
Includes three and a half pages of review excerpts on *My Fair Lady* by Brooks Atkin-
son, John Chapman, Robert Coleman, William Hawkins, and Walter Kerr.

Tarnas, Richard. *The Passion of the Western Mind: Understanding the Ideas That Have Shaped
Our World View.* New York: Harmony Books, 1991. Mentions Shaw and *Man and Superman* in its twenty-one page "Chronology."

Tyson, Brian. "Shaw's Early Journalism in the *Pall Mall Gazette.*" *SHAW: The Annual of
Bernard Shaw Studies,* Volume Twelve. University Park: Penn State University Press,
1992.

Wardle, Irving. *Theatre Criticism.* London and New York: Routledge, 1992. An explanation
of what theater criticism might or should be, with Shaw a frequent touchstone (12
references).

Wearing, J. P. *The London Stage 1940–1949: A Calendar of Plays and Players.* Two volumes.
Metuchen, N.J., and London: Scarecrow Press, 1991. Entries give dates of run, place,
number of performances, cast, producer, director, and number of places reviewed.
Several Shaw plays are listed.

Webb, Sidney and Beatrice. *The Webbs in Asia: The 1911–12 Travel Diary.* New York: Macmillan, 1992. Not seen.

Weintraub, Stanley. *Bernard Shaw: A Guide to Research.* University Park: Penn State University Press, 1992. Reviewed in this volume of *SHAW.*

——. "Shaw by His Contemporaries." Review of A. M. Gibbs, *Shaw: Interviews and Recollec-*

tions. SHAW: The Annual of Bernard Shaw Studies, Volume Twelve. University Park: Penn State University Press, 1992.

Wheeler, Margaret. See Letters to Margaret Wheeler, in Works by Shaw, above.

White, Anna MacBride. See Gonne, above.

White, Patrick. "*Candida*: Bernard Shaw's Chaucerian Drama." *SHAW: The Annual of Bernard Shaw Studies,* Volume Twelve. University Park: Penn State University Press, 1992.

Widowers' Houses: Shaw Festival 1992 (Shaw Festival production program, 1992). Includes "Getting Started: 1892" by Dan H. Laurence, explaining the genesis, production, critical reception, importance in Shaw's canon, and significance to the history of drama of *Widowers' Houses;* and "Director's Notes" by Jim Mezon.

Wilson, Colin. See Pfeiffer, above.

Worthen, John. *D. H. Lawrence: The Early Years 1895–1917.* Cambridge: Cambridge University Press, 1991. In the week of 18–23 March 1912, the beginning of their courtship, Lawrence and Frieda saw *Man and Superman* together.

Xun, Lu. "Six Essays in Defense of Bernard Shaw," trans. Florence Chien. *SHAW: The Annual of Bernard Shaw Studies,* Volume Twelve. University Park: Penn State University Press, 1992.

Yeats, William Butler. See Gonne, above.

III. Periodicals

Abbott, Sean. "The Critics, the Superwoman, and the Collapse of Civilization: Shaw's *Misalliance*." *American Repertory Theatre News* 12 (January 1992): 1, 4–5. Surveys the accumulating interpretations of *Misalliance* by modern critics which find its themes and strategy profound and sophisticated—in contrast to the low esteem in which the play was held by its earliest reviewers. This essay responds to the occasion of the A.R.T. production of the play for the 1992 season, noticing that the set designed by Derek McLane adopts the "dream play/'Ionesco' " mood proposed by Rodelle Weintraub in her 1987 essay, "Johnny's Dream" (*SHAW* 7).

Amalric, Jean-Claude. Review of J. L. Wisenthal, *Shaw's Sense of History. Etudes Anglaises* 44 (April–June 1991): 229–30.

———. "*Shaw's Man and Superman* and the Myth of Don Juan: Intertextuality and Irony." *Cahiers Victoriens et Edouardiens: Revue du Centre d'Etudes et de Recherches Victoriennes et Edouardiennes de l'Université Paul Valéry,* Montpellier (April 1991). Not seen. Don Juan and Don Giovanni allusions are shown as slyly foreshadowing the dream interlude in the frame play.

American Repertory Theatre News 12 (January 1992). Includes articles by Sean Abbott (see above), Martin Meisel (see below), and Carol Verburg (see below); also "Crashing into the Crystal Palace" (see below), plus a number of photos and sketches relating to G.B.S. and *Misalliance,* of which each of these articles presents an account.

Badolato, Francesco. "Una Carriera conclusa prima che fosse iniziata: Il romanziere George B. Shaw." *Il Corriere de Roma* 30 (October 1991): 6, 8. A review of an Italian translation by Francesco Marroni of Shaw's novel *An Unsocial Socialist* (Lucarini). Not seen.

Baldwin, Jessica. "Writer Finishes up Biography of Shaw." *Morning Sun* (Mt. Pleasant, Mich.) (27 December 1991), p. 7B. An interview with Holroyd that promotes his biography of Shaw.

Bennett, Susan. Review of Richard F. Dietrich, *British Drama, 1890 to 1950: A Critical History* (1989). *Theatre Journal* 43 (May 1991): 269–71.

Berst, Charles A. "G.B.S., Act III." Review of Michael Holroyd's *Bernard Shaw: Vol. 3. English Literature in Transition* 35, no. 3 (1992): 325–29.

Bertolini, John A. "Shaw's Book Reviews." Review of Brian Tyson's edition *Bernard Shaw's Book Reviews*. *English Literature in Transition* 35, no. 4 (1992): 493–97.

"Best of Summer: Theatre: Some of London's Most Interesting and Entertaining Events." *Illustrated London News*. (Summer 1992), p. 81. Includes the Olivier National Theatre production of *Pygmalion*.

Bloomfield, Zachary. "America's Response to George Bernard Shaw: A Study of Professional Productions, 1894–1905." *Theatre Studies* 36 (1991): 5–17. "Attention focuses on commentary regarding dramatic structure, theme, and entertainment value in the New York premieres of *Arms and the Man, The Devil's Disciple, Candida,* and *Man and Superman*. In discussing these and related works, commonalities in critical reaction are identified, as is a pattern of growing popular support for Shaw's work."

"Book Choice: A Selection of Current Titles Which Are, Or Deserve To Be, on the Bestseller List." *Illustrated London News*. (Summer 1992): 90. Includes Michael Holroyd, *Bernard Shaw*, Vol. 4, *1950–1991: The Last Laugh*.

"Book Choice: Short Notes on Current Titles for Autumn Reading." *Illustrated London News* 279 (Autumn 1991): 90. Includes Holroyd's *Bernard Shaw*, vol. 3.

"Book Choice: Short Notes on Some Suggested Books for Winter Reading." *Illustrated London News* 279 (Winter 1991): 98. Includes Holroyd's *Bernard Shaw*, vol. 2.

Brenton, Howard. "Freeing Spirits in Covent Garden." Review of the Olivier National Theatre production of *Pygmalion. TLS* (24 April 1992), p. 17.

Brown, David. "Shaw's Genesis." *Explicator* 50 (Fall 1991): 31–32. Part I of *Methuselah* "can neither by the letter of the law nor by the spirit . . . be said to closely follow the biblical account"—there being several points of contradiction.

Bruckner, D.J.R. "Theater in Review . . . When Hitler Could be Laughed At." Review of the Bouwerie Lane Theater production of *Geneva. New York Times* (23 October 1991), p. C19.

Buchan, James. "Back to Methuselah." Review of Michael Holroyd, *Bernard Shaw:* Vol. 3. *Spectator* (31 August 1991), pp. 21–22.

Cameron, Rebecca. See Carpenter, Charles A., below.

Carey, John. "Crushed by the Life Force." Review of Michael Holroyd, *Bernard Shaw:* Vol. 3. *Sunday Times* (London) (8 September 1991), section 6, pp. 1–2.

Carpenter, Charles A. "Shaw (G. B.)," in "Modern Drama Studies: An Annual Bibliography." *Modern Drama* 34 (June 1991): 212–13. About forty entries, many of which have not been noted in the *SHAW* Checklist. Carpenter is a former bibliographer of the *Shaw Review*. His annual bibliographical report on G.B.S. is indispensable.

Carpenter, Charles A., and Linda Corman, with the assistance of Rebecca Cameron. "Shaw" in "Modern Drama Studies: An Annual Bibliography." *Modern Drama* 35, no. 2 (June 1992): 233–34. About twenty items, a few of which have not appeared in *SHAW* Checklists.

Christy, Marian. "Holroyd Looks at Shaw's Childhood and Sees His Own." *Boston Globe* (31 October 1991), p. 86. An interview with Holroyd that promotes his biography of Shaw.

Cohen, Edward H. "Shaw," in "Victorian Bibliography for 1990, VI." *Victorian Studies* 34 (Summer 1991): 650–51. For Shaw, twenty-six items, dating from 1986 to 1990, "bearing only on the Victorian period," all of which have been included previously in this Checklist.

Corman, Linda. See Carpenter, Charles A., above.

Coyne, Pat. "Under the Hammer." *New Statesman and Society* (29 November 1991), p. 17. Not seen. Abstract from *Infotrac:* "The files of *The New Statesman and Society* [founded by Bernard Shaw] will be auctioned off. . . . There are papers from almost every figure from the left and center in British politics."

"Crashing into the Crystal Palace." *American Repertory Theatre News* 12 (January 1992): 5. A

teaser note on how the airplane and the crash are accomplished visibly for the audience in some significant way in the A.R.T. 1992 production of *Misalliance*.

Davies, Robertson. "The Playwright of the Western World." Review of Michael Holroyd,
Bernard Shaw: Vol. 3. *Washington Post Book World* (6 October 1991), pp. 1–2.

Deane, Seamus. "In the Republic of Letters: A Dialogue between W. B. Yeats and James
Joyce on the Occasion of their Reincarnation on the Expiry of Copyright, Recorded by
Seamus Deane." *TLS* (17 January 1992), p. 12. The ghost of G.B.S. rises in this séance.
Yeats: "But Shaw, I regret to say, has been sighted. Remarkably, though, not heard, as
yet." Joyce: "GBS, short for Gobshite. . . ." The piece ends with the epilogic "(They
turn away as the sound of Shaw, talking, gets louder.)"

Dukore, Bernard F. In "Notes and Queries." *Theatre Notebook* 45 (1991): 143–44. Includes
eight queries for an edition of Shaw's drama and theater criticism.

———. "Plays and Playing: Conversations at Leeds." *Theatre Topics* 1 (September 1991):
99–116. Dukore, interviewing Peter Barnes, the playwright, elicits this comment:
"One of the compensations and one of the glories of writing a play as opposed to a
novel is the fact that it can experience a great sea change—not in terms of changing
the text, it must stick absolutely closely to the word, yet when it's on it is another
experience from reading it. I believe Shaw is like that too. . . . Shaw is like that.
Reading the text you get a lot of intellectual pleasure out of it."

Einsohn, H. I. Review of Michael Holroyd, *Bernard Shaw:* Vol. 3. *Choice* (February 1992), p.
894.

Eldred, Janet Carey. "Reading Literacy Narratives." *College English* 54, no. 5 (September
1992): 512–39. "What we call literacy narratives are those stories, like Bernard Shaw's
Pygmalion, that foreground issues of language acquisition and literacy." The essay
employs an analysis of *Pygmalion* relentlessly to illustrate its theses.

Fanning, David. "Book Survey: Ireland: Land and People." *British Book News* (January
1991), pp. 16–19. Mentions Holroyd's biography of G.B.S. among thirty-five items
dating back to the mid-1970s.

Friedman, Arthur. "Shaw's Wit Flows at Lyric Stage." Review of Lyric Stage (Boston)
production of *You Never Can Tell*. *Boston Herald* (27 February 1992), p. 52.

Gainor, J. Ellen. Review of John A. Bertolini's *Playwrighting Self of Bernard Shaw*. *Theatre
Research International* 17, no. 2 (Summer 1992): 165–66.

"George Bernard Shaw." In "1988 Annual Review . . . Individual Writers." *JML* 16 (Fall/
Winter 1988–1989 [1991]): 411. Five entries, each listed previously in the *SHAW*
Checklist.

Gillespie, Elgy. "Michael Holroyd: On Sex and the New Biographer." *San Francisco Review
of Books* 16 (1991): 50–51. Very little on the writing of the G.B.S. biography or "sex" in
biography, except that Holroyd is credited with first introducing the sex lives of the
famous into biography—which he thoughtfully says is not so. Holroyd comments that
modern biography takes the place of novels for many readers.

Gordon, Grace M. "Oh Pshaw!" Edited by Eugene T. Maleska. *New York Times Magazine* (18
October 1992), p. 76. Crossword puzzle with G.B.S. as its theme.

Grossberg, Michael. "OSU Makes Good with Popular *Candida*." Review of the Ohio State
University Theatre production. *Columbus Dispatch* (13 February 1992), p. 6F.

Hederman, Mark Patrick. "Shaw: Behind the Public Mask." Review of Michael Holroyd,
Bernard Shaw: Vol. 3. *Commonweal* 119 (14 February 1992): 23–24.

Himmelfarb, Gertrude. "Where Have All the Footnotes Gone?" *New York Times Book Review*
(16 June 1991), pp. 1, 24. A sprightly essay that reviews the enterprise of the venerable
Miss Turabian and concludes, "God, it has been said, resides in the detail. I hope it is
not sacrilegious to suggest that scholarship too resides in the detail. It is fashionable
today, among one school of historians, to deride 'facticity' and exalt 'invention.' This is

the bottom of the slippery slope that started when footnotes were replaced by endnotes and endnotes by no notes," after which, among others, she instances Michael Holroyd's *Bernard Shaw*: "The references have been promised at the close of the third volume [now, actually, to be in a fifth volume], at which time, presumably, the readers of the first two volumes, published some years earlier, may be expected to go back and consult those notes."

Holroyd, Michael. "Shaw Shot." *Independent Magazine* (4 April 1992), pp. 48–51. The *Magazine* is a newspaper supplement to *The Independent* (London). Apparently a promotional piece for the National Portrait Gallery (London) exhibition which includes a number of the least-known pictures of G.B.S. This article presents six of them. The text remembers Shaw's great interest in photography, its hardware, and its really good early practitioners. Shaw himself owned and used many cameras, but was not very good with them according to this report.

Jones, Emrys. "A Nation Awakes." Review of the Theatre Royal, Haymarket, production of *Heartbreak House*. *TLS* (10 April 1992), p. 18.

Kauffmann, Stanley. "The Late Beginner: Bernard Shaw Becoming a Dramatist." *South Atlantic Quarterly* 91 (Spring 1992): 289–301. Kauffman sets out to answer two questions not fully addressed by any of Shaw's biographers: "Why did Shaw, the greatest English-language dramatist after Shakespeare, take so long to begin his theatrical career? Why did he begin it when he did?" The answers:

Three forces in Shaw's life emerge as answers to these questions. First is the strong influence on him of Ibsen. Second is the different but pervasive influence of Wagner. Third is the invitation in 1892 to provide a play for the Independent Theatre, an invitation that confirmed in him the influences of Ibsen and Wagner, that gave him entry into the theater, and that was in itself the result of giant currents in nineteenth-century art.

Kelly, Kevin. "Theater: George Bernard Shaw Was a Man of (Many) Letters." *Boston Sunday Globe* (6 November 1988), pp. B6–7. An interview with Michael Holroyd is the heart of this article as he discusses the dispersal of the materials for a Shaw biography and the similarity of his early life to Shaw's.

Kermode, Frank. "Molly's Methuselah." Review of Michael Holroyd, *Bernard Shaw:* Vol. 3. *London Review of Books* (26 September 1991), pp. 14–15.

Leary, Daniel. "Freudian Reductionism and Lack of Sympathy." Review of Michael Holroyd, *Bernard Shaw:* Vol. 2. *American Book Review* 12 (November–December 1990): 13.

Lindop, Grevel. "Survival of the Fittest." Review of the Royal Exchange Theatre, Manchester, production of *The Doctor's Dilemma*. *TLS* (31 May 1991), p. 18.

"Literary Lives: Stalin's Black Moustaches." Review of Michael Holroyd's *Bernard Shaw:* Vol. 3. *The Economist* 321 (26 October 1991): 113–14.

Maurer, A. E. Wallace. Review of A. M. Gibbs's edition, *Shaw: Interviews and Recollections*. *Modern Drama* 35, no. 3 (September 1992): 478–80.

McAleer, John. "A Shavian Tapestry: Michael Holroyd's Monumental Life of GBS Reaches Its Conclusion." Review of *Bernard Shaw:* Vol. 3. *Chicago Tribune, Books* (27 October 1991), section 14, pp. 1–4.

McDowell, Frederick P. W. "Shaw the Dramatic Artist." Review of John A. Bertolini's *Play-wrighting Self of Bernard Shaw*. *English Literature in Transition* 35, no. 3 (1992): 347–50.

Meisel, Martin. "Everything That Came into Shaw's Head." *American Repertory Theatre News* 12 (January 1992): 9, 12. This title quotes a comment by Max Beerbohm on the meaning of *Misalliance*. Meisel continues, "The fact is that Shaw was wary of a play that resolved in a stateable 'point' (rather than in a musical or theatrical cadence); or one whose argument progressed with Euclidean linearity. . . . In the miscellaneousness and mingling that struck Beerbohm and is part of the method and character of the play, there is charged material in abundance from Shaw's own personal experience, from the news of the day, and from the world of the theatre."

Morris, Jerry. "Globe-trotting: Shaw Festival Presents Unique Programs." Preview of the Summer 1991 season at Niagara-on-the-Lake. *Boston Sunday Globe* (21 April 1991), p. A2.

Mortensen, Peter. See Eldred, Janet Carey, above.

Mortimer, Molly. "Bernard Shaw—Photographer." *Contemporary Review* 258 (April 1991): 211–12. The special interest of this short piece is in the following: Shaw's writing on photography

> was mainly confined to thirteen articles in the *Amateur Photographer*, edited for many years by my father, F. J. Mortimer, the seascape supremo. In opposition to the conservatism of the Royal Photographic Society, he opened his pages to Shaw's pen. . . . F. J. also gave publicity for Shaw's lectures to the London Camera Club which provided a captive and distinguished audience. In 1911 there is a full report of an Evening of Wit and Music with Shaw; Evans and the Pianola (which they both regarded as the camera of music). In 1917 there was the not unamusing spectacle of Shaw trying to explain to a bemused audience the significance of Alvin Coburn's "Vorticism."

There is more.

Parini, Jay. "A Fittingly Prodigious Shaw Biography." Review of Michael Holroyd, *Bernard Shaw:* Vol. 3. *USA Today* (20 December 1991), p. 7D.

Potter, Roseanne G. "From Literary Output to Literary Criticism: Discovering Shaw's Rhetoric." *Computers and the Humanities* 23 (1987): 333–40. Not seen. "Computational stylistics tends to generate vast quantities of data. Controlling that data is of primary importance in using it [*sic*] in any study. The first rule is to go to the data only for answers to specific questions. Eleven other rules combine literacy and scientific assumptions to lead to more productive work by humanists using computers."

Rawson, Claude. "International Books of the Year." *TLS* (6 December 1991), p. 12. Rawson, one of twenty-three writers making selections, chose, with three other titles, Michael Holroyd's *Bernard Shaw:* Vol. 3.

———. "Playwright Pleasant and Unpleasant." Review of Michael Holroyd, *Bernard Shaw:* Vol. 3. *New York Times Book Review* (20 October 1991), pp. 3, 22.

Richards, David. "Picturesque May Be Pleasant, But Is It Drama?" Review of Shaw Festival productions of *Overruled, Pygmalion,* and *Widowers' Houses. New York Times* (26 July 1992), pp. H5, 21.

Richards, Shaun. " 'Useless, Dangerous, and Ought to Be Abolished': The Intellectual in the Plays of G. B. Shaw and Trevor Griffiths." *Literature and History* 2 (Spring 1991): 60–77.

> While Shaw was provoked into writing by the desire to avoid bloody class-conflict on the streets of England, Griffiths' dramatic engagement was, conversely, with the absence of revolutionary activity and a sense of frustration as English radicals participated in the society of the spectacle, voyeuristically, even impotently, watching revolution unfold nightly on their TV screens. It is, then, around the desire for, the nature of, and centrally, the agents of social change, that the dramas of Shaw and Griffiths can be most fruitfully discussed: as revelations of the profound disillusion which has entered the theatrical expression of British political life as the intellectual is seen increasingly as part of the problem, rather than as the source of the solution. It is then with "the intellectual" and the rational discourse which in the Shavian play is associated with that figure, that this essay is concerned.

The study takes much of its evidence from Griffiths's *Party* and *Comedians,* and Shaw's *Major Barbara* and *Heartbreak House.* It notes that G.B.S. wavered between favoring Fabian "permeation" and violent revolution.

Saslav, Isidor. "Shaw's Progress: How He Laid Siege to New Zealand from 15 March to 15 April 1934." *Stout Centre Review* (Wellington, N.Z.) 2, no. 3 (May 1992): 7–13. Dr. Saslav, who has been collecting Shaviana for some 35 years, describes Shaw's visit to New Zealand and copiously illustrates his article with photographs, political cartoons, and other material from his Shaw collection, including a questionnaire from the editor of the *Wanganui Herald* with Shaw's responses.

Scammell, William. "A Fortune's Buffets and Rewards." Review of Michael Holroyd, *Bernard Shaw:* Vol. 4. *Spectator* (9 May 1992), p. 27.

"Shaw, Bernard." *Infotrac* (1989–April 1992). Lists eighteen items for 1991, mostly reviews of books and play productions.

"Shaw, George Bernard." In "IASAIL Bibliography Bulletin for 1990." *Irish University Review* 21 (Autumn/Winter 1991): 354–56. About sixty entries, from 1987 to 1990, several of which have not appeared in the *SHAW* Checklist.

"Shaw, George Bernard (1856–1950)." In "Irish Literature/1900–1999." *1990 MLA International Bibliography of Books and Articles on the Modern Languages and Literatures.* New York: Modern Language Association, 1991; p. 135. Twenty-two entries, a few of which have not appeared in the *SHAW* Checklist.

Shen, Huihui. "*Babala shaoxiao* yu Xiaowong lixiang" [*Major Barbara* and the Ideals of Shaw]. *Guangming ribao* [*Guangming Daily*] 15 June 1991, p. 3. Shen's second review of *Major Barbara* gives the sponsoring groups, the cast, the translator, and, lastly but no less significantly, the ideals of Shaw. Entry provided and translated by Florence Chien.

———. "Zhenhan renxin de *Babala shaoxiao*" [*Major Barbara*, a Stimulating Play]. *Beijing wanbao* [*Beijing Evening News*] 13 June 1991, p. 14. This is the first of two reviews by Shen, a senior editor of *Shijie wenxue* [*World Literature*], a bimonthly magazine introducing world literary works, written after the performance of *Major Barbara* in Beijing, which was the first public staging of a Shaw play in its entirety in China. The Chinese stage script, translated by the director Ying Roucheng, loses none of the verve and nuance of the original. It was well received. Entry provided and translated by Florence Chien.

"Stage-struck." *The Economist* 324 (12 September 1992): 98. This anonymous two-thirds page thought-piece on how much London theater play programs should tell playgoers (usually much more than they do), includes a cartoon of G.B.S. backdropped with comic playbills that conflate Shaw and Shakespeare play titles for the National Theatre. Example: "*Othello or How He Lied to Her Husband.*" The cartoon caption: "The RSC programmes Shaw to mock Shakespeare."

Styan, J. L. Review of Christopher Innes, *Modern British Drama, 1890–1990. Comparative Drama* 26, no. 3 (Fall 1992): 276–79.

Teachout, Terry. "Man of the Century." Review of Michael Holroyd, *Bernard Shaw:* Vol. 3. *Commentary* 93 (February 1992): 56–58.

Thomson, J. M. "Editorial." *Stout Centre Review* (Wellington, N.Z.) 2, no. 3 (May 1992): 2. Thomson comments on Shaw's 1934 visit to New Zealand described in the issue's illustrated article by Dr. Isidor Saslav (see above).

Trotter, David. "Losing Heart." Review of the Hampstead Theatre production of *The Philanderer. TLS* (29 November 1991), p. 20.

Turco, Alfred, Jr. Review of *Bernard Shaw on the London Art Scene: 1885–1950*, ed. Stanley Weintraub. *English Literature in Transition* 35 (1992): 231–34.

Turner, E. S. "Answering the Call: Alexander Graham Bell's Legacy and Its Far-Flung Connections." *TLS* (6 December 1991), pp. 3–4. This review of three books on the impact of the telephone on civilization and culture remarks in passing, "Bernard Shaw, as many will know by now, once worked for the Edison company, his task being to negotiate permission to disfigure the townscape with poles and wires; he was not very good at it."

————. "Shaw's Legacy Defied or Defended." Review of Michael Holroyd, *Bernard Shaw:* Vol. 4. *TLS* (8 May 1992), p. 32.

Turner, June. "T. E. Lawrence." *American Imago* 48 (Fall 1991): 395–411. This essay on Lawrence's masochism is principally indebted for evidence to Lawrence's letters to Charlotte Shaw.

Verburg, Carol. "G.B.S. and His 'Poor Miss Alliance.'" *American Repertory Theatre News* 12 (January 1992): 6–7. This slightly misleadingly titled article interweaves a review of Shaw's life with the content and developing reputation of *Misalliance*. The title is an allusion to the actress Lena Ashwell, who had played Lina in the play's first production—closed for bad reviews after eleven performances—and thus was called "poor Miss Alliance" by G.B.S.

Weales, Gerald. "George Bernard Shaw: The Twilight Years." Review of Michael Holroyd, *Bernard Shaw:* Vol. 3. *Boston Sunday Globe* (20 October 1991), p. A16.

Wearing, J. P. "Victorian Drama." Review of Anthony Jenkins's *Making of Victorian Drama*. *English Literature in Transition* 35, no. 4 (1992): 497–99.

Weintraub, Stanley. "Bernard Shaw." In "Letters to the Editor." *TLS* (27 September 1991), p. 19. A correction to the reviewer (6 September 1991) of Holroyd's third volume of *Bernard Shaw*: the septuagenarian affair is not a new revelation.

————. "Bernard Shaw and the American Theatre." *UNISA English Studies* 29 (September 1991): 36–42. A detailed overview of the Shavian influence and presence in the United States, including references to David Belasco, Bret Harte, T. Edgar Pemberton, Eugene O'Neill, Clyde Fitch, Langdon Mitchell, Edward Sheldon, Jo Swerling, Abe Burrows, Rachel Crothers, Henry James, Philip Barry, S. N. Behrman, Garson Kanin, Clifford Odets, Samuel Taylor, Thornton Wilder, Tennessee Williams, Gore Vidal, A. R. Gurney, Richard Nelson, and Alan Jay Lerner and Frederick Loewe. See also the chapter, "Influence and Reputation," in Weintraub's *Bernard Shaw: A Guide to Research*, in Books and Pamphlets, above.

Ying, Roucheng. "Wo de suyuan—xie zai *Babala shaoxiao* shangyan zhishi" [My Old Wish Comes True—Written Before the Opening Night of *Major Barbara*]. *Renyi zhi you bao* [*Friend of People's Art Monthly*] June 1991, p. 2. An accomplished actor, director, and translator, Ying has played major roles in the films *The Last Emperor* and *Marco Polo*, directed Arthur Miller's *Death of a Salesman* and now *Major Barbara*, and interpreted for Bob Hope in a show in China during the early thaw in U.S.–China relations. His desire to present a Shaw play dates back some forty years. Due in large part to Ying's efforts, Chinese theatrical art has been infused with Western works. Entry provided and translated by Florence Chien.

The Independent Shavian 29, nos. 2/3 (1991). Journal of the Bernard Shaw Society. Includes "Not Men, Only Soldiers" by Bernard Shaw, "Amos 'n' Andy 'n' Bernie," "Shaw and Impressionism" by Michael Weimer, "Shavian Indignation," "Shaw and Catholic Universities," "Robertson Davies on Shaw," "La Sincérité est Dangereuse," "Letter from England" by T. F. Evans, "On Being Didactic," "H. L. Mencken on G. B. Shaw" by George Levinson, "Quote Unquote," "'Bishop' Bernard Shaw's Search for God," "*Getting Married:* Uncharacteristic Shaw," "A T. E. Lawrence Newsletter," "G.B.S. and K.G.B." by Richard Nickson, "Shaw as Viewed Sixty Years Ago," "Setback for *Back to Methuselah*," "Rebecca West on 'Uncle Shaw',"" "Ingrid Bergman Remembers Flirtatious Shaw," "A Mid-Summer Theater Party: *Arms and the Man*," "News About Our Members," "Society Activities," and "Our Cover."

The Independent Shavian 30, nos. 1/2 (1992). Journal of the Bernard Shaw Society. Includes "Beneath and Above the Belt: Shaw, Anonymous, and William Carlos Williams" by Samuel A. Weiss, "The Centennial of Opus One," "The Pugilist in Fiction" by P. G.

Wodehouse, "G.B.S.: Spoilsport," "From Private Drama to Political Drama: Shaw and Transcendence through Socialism" by Sally Peters, "Mad Dogs—Bad Men: Both Should be Killed without Compunction" by Bernard Shaw, "Shaw Materials: A Library Acquisition," "Book Notes by the Editor" by Richard Nickson, "American Irish Society," "Letter from England" by T. F. Evans, "Wild about Wilde," "Why Dublin Honors Shaw," "The Bernard Shaw Society Acknowledges . . . ," "Book Review" by John Koontz, "First Performer of Shaw's First Woman," "Rocky Mountain Shaw Festival," "Mrs. Ada M. Morgan," "Society Activities," "News About Our Members," and "Our Cover."

The Shavian 7, no. 3 (Summer 1992). The Journal of the Shaw Society. Includes "Editorial," "Obituary," "The First Play," "The Intelligent Person's Guide to Shaw's Comic Art" by Simon Tresize, "Shaw's Fabian Tracts and His Political Plays" by Judith Evans, "Our Theatres in the Nineteen-Nineties," book reviews by Colin Wilson, John Levitt, and Frances Glendenning, "Literary Survey," and "Notes of Meetings."

IV. Dissertations

Berger-Prössdorf, Tamara. "Die Funktion der Heilsarmeegeistlichen in den Dramen Brechts" [German text]. Rutgers University, 1991. *DAI* 52 (September 1991), 931-A. "This dissertation examines the paradigmatic function of the Salvation Army figures in Brecht's plays." The three Brecht pieces mentioned in this abstract are *Brotladen, Die heilige Johanna der Schlachthöfe,* and *Im Dickicht der Stadte.* Shaw is not mentioned, but the interest of this study to his *Major Barbara,* at least, is obvious.

Carter, Patricia Murphy. "The Gospel of the Biologist Shaw: 'Back to Methuselah'." George Washington University, 1992. *DAI* 53 (July 1992), 156-A. "The gospel of the new religion, Creative Evolution, is apparently," according to a review of the critical reception from 1922 to 1988, "too biological to be received as religion."

Miller, Janice Catherine. "Broken Hearts, Broken Heads: The Critical Response to Bernard Shaw's 'Heartbreak House,' 1919–1921." University of Nebraska, 1990. *DAI* 52 (September 1991), 912-A. Discusses literary and dramatic reviews from a wide variety of newspapers and magazines, providing as much background as relevant to Shaw's work. Chapter 1 describes Shaw's prewar popularity. Chapter 2 analyzes reviews by such critics as A. B. Walkley, John Middleton Murry, William Archer, and anonymous ones in the *Times, Spectator,* and *Saturday Review.* Chapter 3 discusses the British and American receptions of the play. Chapter 4 provides brief histories of Shaw's reputation in America and of the New York Theatre Guild. Chapter 5 places *Heartbreak* against the record of Shaw's great success at the Royal Court Theatre from 1904 to 1907, and chapter 6 follows the reception of *Heartbreak* to the end of the 1920s.

Tahir, Laura. "The Development of a Point of View in Young George Bernard Shaw." Rutgers University, 1989. *DAI* 50 (May 1990), 5350-B. Based on theories of cognitive development proposed by Piaget and Gruber, "This cognitive case study traces the development of Bernard Shaw's unique point of view between the ages of 21 and 27. Shaw's particular aptitude was his ability to use English language to develop questions and arguments and to express them clearly. Shaw's postformal thought is seen in the context of an evolving system that regulates creative activity, which in turn regulates the system. Shaw's network of enterprises is examined. His organization of knowledge is characterized by a process of constructive opposition . . . ," typified in *My Dear Dorothea, Passion Play, Immaturity,* and *An Unsocial Socialist.*

V. Recordings

Cukor, George, director. *My Fair Lady*. Widescreen edition. Los Angeles: Warner Brothers, 1964. Laser Videodisc recording. Los Angeles: CBS/Fox Video, 1991. Not seen.

Foster, Jodie, director. *Little Man Tate*. Orion Pictures, 1991. This story of a child genius has secondary character, Damon, quoting G.B.S.: "The reasonable man adapts himself to the world around him. The unreasonable man expects the world around him to adapt to him. All progress is made by unreasonable men."

Shaw, Bernard. *Caesar and Cleopatra* (1945 film, starring Vivien Leigh, Claude Rains, Stewart Granger), CLVID007028, $29.98. Critics' Choice Video, P.O. Box 549, Elk Grove Village, IL 60009-0549. Phone: 1-800-367-7765. Lists also *My Fair Lady* (1964 film, starring Rex Harrison and Audrey Hepburn), CLFOX007038, $29.98.

———. *Caesar and Cleopatra* (1945 film, starring Vivien Leigh, Claude Rains, Stewart Granger), 4342L, $39.95. Filmic Archives 1992–93, The Cinema Center, Botsford Connecticut 06404. Phone: (203) 261-1920. Lists also *Pygmalion* (1938 film, starring Leslie Howard, Wendy Hiller), 4073F, $29.95; *Androcles* (1952 film, with Jean Simmons, Victor Mature, and Maurice Evans), 5007L, $24.95; *Saint Joan* (1957 film, starring Jean Seberg and John Gielgud), 5008L, $19.95; *My Fair Lady* (1964 film, starring Rex Harrison and Audrey Hepburn), 5009L, $29.95. The 1991–92 Filmic Archives catalogue listed *Heartbreak House* (1986 film, starring Rex Harrison and Amy Irving), 4467F, $69.95. All on videocassette.

———. Excerpt from an unnamed work. *What is Satire?* 30 minutes/#LG281, $129.00. Literature and Writing, On Video. Insight Media, 121 85th Street, New York, New York. Phone: (212) 721-6316. Not seen.

———. *An Unsocial Socialist*. Washington, D.C.: Audio Book Contractors, 1991. Six audio cassettes. Not seen.

Walton, William. *Film Music*, Vol. 4. London: St. Jude on the Hill, recorded in November 1980. Includes *Major Barbara*, A Shavian Sequence for Orchestra. Chandos Compact Disc 8841. Academy of Saint Martin in the Fields, Sir Neville Marriner, "Conducting," 1991. Not seen.

NOTICES

Request for Manuscripts: *SHAW* 17

SHAW 17, guest edited by Milton T. Wolf, will have as its theme "Shaw and Speculative Fiction." The volume will include articles on various aspects of Shaw's relationship to, influence by, and influence on traditions of utopian literature, fantasy, science fiction, and other genres with an eye to the future, both generally and in terms of individual writers. Contributors should submit manuscripts in three copies by December 1995 to Fred D. Crawford, *SHAW* Editor, 1034 Hickory Street, Lansing, MI 48912-1711. Contributors should follow the *MLA Style Sheet* format (referring to recent *SHAW* volumes is advisable), double-space throughout (including block-indented quotations and notes), and include SASE for return of material.

Milwaukee Chamber Theatre Shaw Festival
21 May–13 June 1993

The Milwaukee Chamber Theatre's eleventh annual Shaw Festival (Artistic Director, Montgomery Davis) will feature performances of *The Millionairess* and of Shakespeare's *Timon of Athens*. During the Shaw Festival assorted lectures and seminars will be conducted by members of the MCT Artistic Advisory Panel. For ticket information, please call (414) 276-8842 or write to Milwaukee Chamber Theatre, 152 W. Wisconsin, Suite 731, Milwaukee, WI 53203.

32nd Anniversary Season, Shaw Festival
Niagara-on-the-Lake

The 1993 playbill of the Shaw Festival (Artistic Director, Christopher Newton) will include nine plays, three by Shaw: *Saint Joan* (opening in

May), *Candida* (opening in July), and *The Man of Destiny* (opening in July). Other productions include *The Silver King* by Henry Arthur Jones and Henry Herman, *Blithe Spirit* by Noël Coward, *The Unmentionables* by Carl Sternheim, *The Marrying of Ann Leete* by Harley Granville Barker, *And Then There Were None* by Agatha Christie, and the musical *Gentlemen Prefer Blondes*.

For further information, write to Shaw Festival, P.O. Box 774, Niagara-on-the-Lake, Ontario, Canada L0S 1J0, or telephone (416) 468-2172 (direct from Toronto, call 361-1544). Toll free from the United States, call (800) 724-2934. Toll free from Canada, call (800) 267-4759.

CONTRIBUTORS

John A. Bertolini, guest editor of this volume, is professor of English at Middlebury College and author of *The Playwrighting Self of Bernard Shaw.*

Fred D. Crawford, general editor of *SHAW,* is the author of *British Poets of the Great War.* He has completed a study of Richard Aldington and Lawrence of Arabia and is researching a biography of the American journalist Lowell Thomas.

Richard F. Dietrich, a member of the *SHAW* editorial board, is professor of English at the University of South Florida, director of the Office of Scholarly Publications, and member of the University Press of Florida editorial board. He is the author of *Portrait of the Artist as a Young Superman, British Drama 1890–1950,* and *The Art of Fiction,* as well as many articles on Shaw, Ibsen, and other modern writers.

T. F. Evans was deputy director of the Department of Extra-Mural Studies, University of London. He is editor of the *Shavian* and has edited *Shaw: The Critical Heritage* and *SHAW 11: Shaw and Politics.*

A. M. Gibbs, professor of English at Macquarie University, Sydney, has written and edited four books on Bernard Shaw, including *Shaw: Interviews and Recollections.* He has recently completed a book-length study of *Heartbreak House* and is carrying out research for a new biography of Shaw.

Leon H. Hugo, a member of the *SHAW* editorial board, is emeritus professor of English at the University of South Africa. He is the author of *Bernard Shaw: Playwright and Preacher.*

Dan H. Laurence has served as the literary and dramatic adviser to the Shaw Estate and as literary adviser to the Shaw Festival (Niagara-on-the-Lake). He has completed many editions of Shaw's writing, including four volumes of *Collected Letters,* and is the author of *Bernard Shaw: A Bibliography.* He and Daniel Leary are preparing an edition of Shaw's *Complete Prefaces* in three volumes, the first of which will appear in 1993.

Christopher Newton has been Artistic Director of the Shaw Festival, the second largest theater company in North America, for thirteen years. He is a Canadian who was born in Britain and educated there and in the United States.

Sally Peters, a member of the *SHAW* editorial board, is visiting lecturer in English in Liberal Studies at Wesleyan University. She has published articles on Shaw's plays, on Shavian biography, and on dance. She is completing an interpretive study entitled *Bernard Shaw: Fantastic Sojourner.*

John R. Pfeiffer, *SHAW* bibliographer, is professor of English at Central Michigan University. His most recent articles are on Günter Grass, John Stuart Mill, and nineteenth-century science fiction.

Evert Sprinchorn, professor of drama at Vassar College, has written about Joyce, Ibsen, and Shakespeare, edited Ibsen's letters and Wagner's writings on theater, and translated several volumes of Strindberg's plays and autobiographical writings. Most recently he has written on the Elizabethan Stage in *Theatre Notebook*.

Stanley Weintraub, Evan Pugh Professor of Arts and Humanities at Penn State, is former editor of *SHAW* and a member of the *SHAW* editorial board. He has written and edited more than fifty books on Shaw and his times.